Daughters

of DISTANCE

VANESSA RUNS

For my sisters to know they can do anything

TABLE OF CONTENTS

Foreword

I am running in a foreign country, through a remote area little inhabited by humans and even littler visited by them. I think I am alone, as I have been for quite some time. A teenager—well, he looks like a boy on the cusp of teenage-hood—appears out of the bushes. He is a local, and must be from some unseen-to-me homestead. He wears a navy-blue knitted sweater that hangs on his thin frame, tattered jeans, and brown leather sandals. With a huge grin that exposes teeth already stained by plaque, a result of the poor dental care that is rampant among people living in poverty, he picks up his pace to a run, very close beside me. His dark eyes sparkle and seem welcoming, but his immediate invasion of my personal space sets off my personal-safety alarm.

Before my brain acknowledges what is happening, his hand is inside the front waistband of my running shorts. I feel his fingers grope downward, his fingernails scratching my skin. Instinct kicks in before even the first rational thought occurs and I shove him to the ground. I hear and see his little body bounce, in that weird slow-motion version of reality that your brain lives in when life becomes suddenly traumatic. He is up and running again, just like that, clearly not affected by my push. Next to me he runs, and I can feel the big stitches of his sweater brush against my arm. I don't know what I say but I must scream some version of bloody murder, enough that he peels off to the side, stops, and watches me run on.

I look over my shoulder and see him standing there, his hand to his forehead to block the sun and that same friendly expression still on his face. This image is burned into my memory. I will have nightmares about this for a long time, and this is how my subconscious mind will choose to represent this young man. I have hours left to run to my destination, to relative safety. I spend a lot of it crying, screaming, raging, or just letting tears silently fall down my cheeks.

This experience has changed the way I perceive men — all men. I pass judgment on almost every man and teenager I see: my brain gives them each a rating of their potential to do me harm. I am far less friendly to male strangers than female. It has modified the way I behave when I run, walk down the street, take groceries to my car, everything, everywhere.

Many women have lived through situations involving deeper trauma at the hands of men. I am fortunate that mine was not worse. It is incredibly unfortunate that this sort of thing happens at all. Women all over the world are made the victims of sexual assault thousands of times a day. And the mistreatment of women by societal norms, tradition, and men is even more frequent. Fact: women live in a world that is, in almost every way possible, unequal to the world in which men live. This reality extends to distance running.

Daughters of Distance is an acknowledgement of the unfortunate places that women's athletics has been, a celebration of who we now are, and a dream about what we could become. Author Vanessa Runs has written *Daughters of Distance* to address the different playing field for women in endurance running. She also wrote this book to incite conversation about what all members of the distance-running community — men and women alike — can do to change our

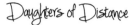

future.

To be honest, this book is a rough read at times, but this is because the truth of our history and the way inequality still pervades women's distance running is sometimes brutal. Should you become discouraged, I encourage you to read on. The only reason we should be ashamed of our past is if we allow it to live into our future. We are who we are because of where we've been. I often think that the strength I see in women—you know, that kind of power that emanates from so deep within us that it just explodes into the world—is in part a result of the challenges through which we live.

Change is happening. Every day I see it, feel it. Sometimes I am shaken by it, of how our culture's inclusion of women is evolving, the positivity of progress. The same is true in our sport as well. *Daughters of Distance* is one of those pieces to our story that moves me, and that moves our gender forward. If you are a daughter of distance or you love a woman who is, dive headfirst into this book and ride the beautiful wave of progress it generates.

Meghan M. Hicks
Senior Editor, iRunFar.com

Vanessa Runs

Introduction

My mom died the same year I got my period: I was nine years old. Suddenly trapped in a new body, I was a woman before I had figured out how to be a girl. I didn't understand my new body, full of awkward lumps and fluids, so I tried to ignore it. Unfortunately, others noticed.

At school, boys would come up behind me to snatch my back bra strap, pulling it hard then letting it go so it would snap against my back until I howled in pain. I was the first girl in my grade to wear a bra, and the sole target for forty sadistic little boys. For the next two years (until the other girls starting wearing bras), I would end each school day with raised red welts across my back. On a good day, I could outrun them or climb higher than they could on the monkey bars, safely out of their reach.

I never said a word to get those boys in trouble. On the contrary, I felt instinctively that *I* had been the one to do something wrong: I had grown breasts.

Five years later, I still didn't feel at home in my new body. I was fourteen when my family went to a summer cottage in Dorset, Ontario—a sleepy little spot on Lake Kushog. In the mornings, the larks would play along the water's edge and I'd resolve to spend most of the day in the water or lying in the sun on the dock.

One happy summer afternoon, the unthinkable happened—I got my period.

Irritated, I ran inside, grabbed a pad, stuck it in between

my legs right onto my bathing suit, and hopped back into the water. Within seconds, I realized my mistake.

The pad between my legs started swelling to a size that no pad should ever swell. It sucked in water like a dehydrated camel and the more water it held, the more trouble I had keeping it submerged. I rode it like a pool noodle, desperately using the full force of my teenaged thighs to keep it out of sight.

When I was certain nobody was around, I leaped out of the water in a state of near-panic and buried my swollen pad deep into the bottom of the garbage. It was the size of a Nerf football.

It took me about twenty-five years to make peace with my body. I tiptoed through womanhood like a reluctant explorer, poking and prodding with great caution.

But this book isn't about pads and periods.

Fast forward thirteen years later and I'm racing down into Noble Canyon in Southern California at my first ultramarathon. Picking my way through the rocky terrain I am competing—for the first time since my prepubescent school days—against males, and I'm holding my own. My pulsing thighs are carrying me—breasts and all—through the twisting switchbacks. I am back on those monkey bars, climbing higher than the boys. I am back on Lake Kushog, floating on my back without a care in the world.

*

My friend and fellow ultrarunner Jimmy Dean Freeman left the following comment on one of my race reports:

Only 28 percent of all ultra finishers in the USA last

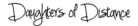

year were women. Why? I have a ton of theories. I also have a myriad of reasons why women are better suited to long distance running than men. Has anyone covered the 'girls only' aspects, or compiled a book highlighting the female perspective? Though there are books out there by individual female ultrarunners — there is nothing covering ultrarunning for females.

Two years, more than 100 studies, and 100-plus interviews later, I put together this book. Although the focus is primarily running, I spoke with a variety of female endurance athletes from thru-hikers to triathletes. We discussed everything from the deeply intimate to the unexceptionally mundane.

When I asked endurance runner and editor Meghan Hicks why she thought more women don't compete in ultras, she said she didn't have an opinion. "Our numbers are increasing at near-exponential numbers and races are growing more competitive for women each year, so I'd probably prefer that we as women focus on what is rather than what isn't."

So this is a book about what is, and what could be.

Initially I planned to write a series of profiles of female ultrarunners. I thought I would ask them all the same questions and publish their answers back-to-back. But I soon realized that there were gems in those interviews that demanded further research and analysis. The stories of these women called me to consider something more profound.

From start to finish, this project consumed my time and thoughts, with two questions recurring in my head: How is

endurance sport unique to females? How does our womanhood play a role in endurance?

From there, other questions presented themselves:

- What is unique about the way women approach competition in endurance racing?
- What types of sexism or discrimination still exist for women in endurance sports?
- How do female athletes define femininity, and what role does femininity play in training and performance?

Along the way, I learned that some of my own questions were full of biases. My preconceived notions of womanhood were shaped by my culture and experience. The women I spoke with challenged my questions instead of only answering them, opening my mind to a labyrinth of feminine complexity.

*

A few weeks ago I listened with great interest to a CBC Radio podcast called *The Current*. The topic was Women Against Feminism. Several women on the podcast engaged in a heated debate of what it means to be a feminist and whether or not feminism is still relevant in this day and age.

The anti-feminist camp argued that "chip-on-the-shoulder" feminism is no longer relevant in our modern society where women are free to play and work as men do. They felt that equality had already been achieved and balked at being associated with a man-hating feminism, or a feminism that frowned upon stay-at-home moms.

The pro-feminist camp insisted that feminism was neither man-hating nor anti-stay-at-home moms. They argued that the

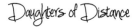

idea that women had already achieved equality was misinformed at best and ignorant at worst. It was nowhere near true.

In listening to this debate, my mind turned to sport. Now that women are "allowed" to participate in most major sports, does that mean we have arrived? Have we achieved equality in athletics?

Certainly we have made some great strides and advances over the past few years. When the first Olympic Games took place in 1896, women in sports were nearly unheard of. By 1900, eleven women stood at the Olympic opening ceremonies in Paris (although they were only allowed to compete in tennis and golf). By 2004, a new world record had been set: more than 40 percent of Olympic participants at the Olympic Games in Athens were female.

Standing in a friend's kitchen in Leadville, Colorado, I discussed this topic with accomplished endurance athlete Patrick Sweeney. He insisted that inequality in sports was often skewed in women's favor. He pointed out some facts I had been unaware of and was surprised to discover:

- The circumference of the women's ball in American professional basketball is one inch smaller than the men's ball. The women's three-point line is also slightly closer to the basket than the men's;

- In men's American college basketball, the ball must cross the half-court line in ten seconds. This rule is not enforced for women;

- In tennis, women use a lighter and faster tennis ball. Men play the best of five sets while women play best of three;

- In golf, the women's tee is closer to the hole;
- Women's volleyball uses a lower net than men's.

There are other, less female-favorable differences. According to the Women's Sports Foundation, male athletes get $179 million more in athletic scholarships each year than female athletes do. In 2004, the media coverage ratio between male and female professional sports was 9:1 in US television and 20:1 in print media.

But in most endurance races, women line up alongside men, sometimes winning outright. Doesn't that prove equality? We run the same course, climb the same hills, and are just as likely to finish as men are.

So what, if anything, is different about women in endurance? What unique challenges do women face? Have we achieved equality in endurance sports? This book explores all those questions.

The topics that follow have not previously been examined or written about. Most are non-issues in the endurance memoirs of elite men, and are only hinted at in the memoirs of elite women.

Nothing has been written before about the experiences of female mid-packers or back-of-the-packers. Little or nothing has been said about women's experiences with sexual harassment, eating disorders associated with endurance training, or the guilt women associate with training when they are wives and mothers. There are countless female experiences like these that need a voice.

What does it mean to race like a girl?

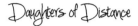

The first few months of researching this book I struggled with why I should address this topic at all. There are so many other more pressing female issues to tackle. There are still so many countries where women are denied basic rights. We are victims of sex trade, rape, slavery, abuse and other horrors. We are denied basic education, held up to impossibly high moral standards, and degraded by society. Is it frivolous to write a book about sport?

Within weeks, I began to formulate an answer. An abused woman is a terrible thing, but a woman who is happy, fulfilled and inspired always transforms her family, her community and her world.

When a man finds success at running ultras, he may inspire several people around him. He may write a book or become an elite runner. Often, his wife will just roll her eyes as he heads out for yet another long run.

However, there's something about the scent of a woman's athletic success that soaks through her entire universe. She will keep her kids active. She will invite her friends out to the trails. She will invest time and effort into sharing her experiences within her community. An empowered woman will benefit every single relationship she touches. Instead of compartmentalizing her sport, she will allow it to infiltrate every aspect of her life. She will live better.

I love these words from Isabel Allende's 2007 TED Talk: "I have worked with women and for women all my life…Women are 51 percent of humankind. Empowering them will change everything—more than technology and design and entertainment. I can promise you that."

Feminist playwright Eve Ensler pointed out that women are a primary resource on this planet: "We're talking about the place where we come from, we're talking about parenting…if we could figure out how to make women safe and honor women, it would be parallel or equal to honoring life itself."

In discussing this book project with my Canadian friend and coach Michael Kurup, he said: "Bringing those topics out of the backwoods and into the public forum can benefit not just the sport of extreme distance running, but sports in general and broader society as well." That is my hope.

The goal of this book is to:

- Open a conversation about female-specific issues in sport
- Empower, honor, and inform female endurance athletes
- Connect female athletes to each other and let them know they're not alone
- Enlighten men on how to best support females in sport

I believe that the best thing that can happen to women's sports is the emergence and coverage of more female role models. I would love to see more women step up as wellness leaders, and that includes athletes, coaches, trainers and journalists. My goal for this book is to tell the stories of these female role models. Not just the voices of the elites, but those who trail behind them as well.

Within these pages you will discover female awesomeness that transcends athletics. I had to smile at one woman's answer to my question, "What type of person were you before you ran your first ultra?" Her honest reply: "I was me."

So perhaps this is not a book about female athletes after all, but rather a book about strong and spectacular women...who just happen to endure.

Who are these Daughters of Distance? Put simply, they are women who have come to understand that they have no limits. They claim their rightful place on the podium of life and sport. These are their stories.

Vanessa Runs

1: Is My Mascara Running? (Femininity)

"If a woman wants to push herself beyond sanity and reality, isn't that the Olympic tradition?...Why is it that women have to cross the finish line with their hair neatly combed and their makeup fresh? Why can't they gasp and sweat and stagger, just like the guys do? Amid all the pixies and sweethearts comes a Swiss marathoner who stumbles and staggers and somehow finishes. If she were a man, they would salute her courage. But she is a woman and the TV people wonder why the officials don't grab this poor girl and help her."

– Scott Ostler, *Los Angeles Times*, 1984

Colleen Zato rushes up to me with her camera and her most common request: "Let's get a photo!" I am at the starting line of the San Diego 100-Mile Endurance Run, my first and possibly only 100 attempt this year. I am starting to get nervous.

Colleen is a bundle of anything but nerves. She flutters through the crowd, chatting and snapping photos. Only two weeks ago, she ran a hundred miles at Nanny Goat 100, where I paced her to a strong finish, but now she's back for more. Dipping into her Nathan hydration vest, she accidently drops her pack and out rolls a stick of bright pink lipstick. It was right in the front pocket where it's most easily accessible. I know she's planning on carrying it for the next 32 hours of running.

Colleen is a chatty and busty blonde with beautiful swirling hair and piercing blue eyes. Her Marilyn Monroe

21

curves and short skirts offer casual viewers all the assets by which they might judge a young Vegas girl like her.

Except they'd be wrong.

Colleen's world is both night-on-the-town and unspoiled wilderness. Every trail in her world is runnable and every pose is a legendary Colleen-pose: hands on hips, one leg extended in front and bent at the knee, slight side angle to the camera, hip accentuated.

The juxtaposition of Colleen's porcelain skin and nature's harshest terrain is intriguing. In one of her Facebook photos, she poses with a wild Californian long-nosed snake tangled in her arms at Zion National Park. In another, her bright pink lips are about to kiss a banana slug under a towering Redwood. In a third, what would at first appear to be the pretty face of a free-spirited blonde smiling up at you pans out to reveal Colleen in winter gear, jamming an ice pick deep into a slab of ice at Mummy Springs in Nevada.

My favorite photo is one in which Colleen has extended herself across a boulder at Yosemite National Park with Mount Dana in the background. She wears a short, pink, sleeveless summer dress with light blue trim. However, if you look closely, you'll notice that her heels are taped up and her feet are a mess: the aftermath of her first 100-mile foot race.

If Lara Croft from *Tomb Raider* and Bubbles from *The Powerpuff Girls* and Carrie Bradshaw from *Sex and the City* mixed their genes in a big pot, Colleen would bounce out of there with her hiking poles, a smile and a flower in her hair.

"I'm going to try to keep up with you for the first 30 miles," I tell Colleen, "but don't wait for me." I know she'll set a consistent and reasonable pace, but I also know better than to underestimate her. Colleen will end up dropping me at mile 24, bouncing uphill and kicking ass in style.

Although I'm not weighed down by extra lipstick, I eventually get pulled at mile 56 for failing to meet a time cutoff. Colleen runs on to finish the course, complete with an epic one-leg-out photo finish and fresh pink lipstick.

Years ago, I used to write off "girly girls" like Colleen, letting my eyes roll when I saw them toe the line at a race. I was naïve enough to think that I had to choose between being feminine and being an athlete. It never occurred to me until meeting Colleen and others like her that I could be both.

Defining Femininity
Not all women define femininity in shades of pink. For the most part, we have long abandoned the gender roles of our mothers and grandmothers. Ask a hundred women today what femininity means to them, and you'll get a hundred different responses. What does it mean to be feminine?

I posted this question on Facebook and got a variety of replies:

- Being confident enough in one's own skin where you can do anything in the world, even when they say it's impossible (Tracey Palmer)
- Nurturing beauty (Gregory J. Sihler)
- Being badass (Neda Iranpour)
- To do everything you love and still be desirable in a dress and heels (Koko Rikou)
- Being kind towards others, without taking anyone's

shit (Brad Niess)

- Happily enjoying some "girly" things like chocolate, pretty dresses and cookery, while also being happy that I like certain traditionally masculine things like stomping around the countryside getting covered in mud or working on building my muscle strength (Anne Vasey)
- The yang to masculinity's yin—or vice versa (Judi Diamond Walthour)
- Bringing your inner beauty out (Anne McClain)
- Being able to pull off the running outfit or the formal attire with inner and outer grace, and not making excuses for rocking them both (Tracyn Thayer)
- Don't engage in rugged work, very proper in act, dress and look (Joe Bos)
- Confidence and the ability to seek out my passions (Amber Fifield)
- Getting muddy and sweaty on a long run and then pounding a few beers (Sally Heath)
- Strength and softness all at once (Chelsea French)
- Mother Nature, the sacred feminine (John Schneider)
- Being confident in one's own place in this world and in one's own convictions that you are strong enough to treat others with respect and kindness (Lisa Vezzetti O'Grady)
- Loving and appreciating; "the rag" (Rachael Osteen)
- A woman expressing herself (Johnny Lippeatt)
- Softness, grace, and a kick-ass inner strength (Dede Godwin Owens)

- Caring and loving and appreciating others (Lisa Stranc Bliss)
- Maintaining the essence of female: a little softer physically and emotionally and showing it: speaking a little softer, acting more gentle, walking lighter, approaching things with heart versus brain (Cindy Chiperzak)
- Spending a lot of my young life embracing society's assumptions and restrictions and now in my later years periodically waking myself up and realizing that it's all still BS (Lani Anacan)
- Being comfortable in my own skin…goes hand in hand with confidence (Catherine Thompson)
- Being independent…being able to rise above the stereotypes and live how I want to live (Jennifer Liang)

I also examined various studies about femininity. In my research, I stumbled on something called the Conformity to Feminine Norms Inventory - 45. The purpose of this inventory is to "assess women's conformity to various feminine norms that are widely endorsed in dominant American culture." I found the nine subscales of this 45-item self-reporting scale shocking:

- Thinness (e.g. "I am terrified of gaining weight")
- Domestic (e.g. "I clean my home on a regular basis")
- Invest in Appearance (e.g., "I spend more than 30 minutes a day doing my hair and makeup")
- Modesty (e.g. "I hate telling people about my accomplishments")
- Relational (e.g. "I believe that my friendships should

25

be maintained at all costs")
- Involvement With Children (e.g. "Taking care of children is extremely fulfilling")
- Sexual Fidelity (e.g. "I would feel guilty if I had a one-night stand")
- Romantic Relationship (e.g. "Having a romantic relationship is essential in life")
- Sweet and Nice (e.g. "I would be ashamed if someone thought I was mean").

For the record, there's also a male version called the Conformity to Masculine Norms Inventory - 46. Its subscales are: Winning (e.g. "In general, I will do anything to win"); Emotional Control (e.g. "I tend to keep my feelings to myself"); Risk-Taking (e.g. "I enjoy taking risks"); Violence (e.g. "Sometimes violent action is necessary"); Power Over Women (e.g. "In general, I control the women in my life"); Playboy (e.g. "If I could, I would frequently change sexual partners"); Self-Reliance (e.g. "It bothers me when I have to ask for help"); Primacy of Work (e.g. "My work is the most important part of my life"); and, Heterosexual Self-Presentation (e.g. "I would be furious if someone thought I was gay").

Can you imagine what a completely feminine woman (or a masculine male) would look like based on those subscales?

While some argue that feminine females and masculine males are necessary for a balanced society to function, others believe that stereotypical feminine traits were imposed to maintain a patriarchal social system. Still others reject the concept of gender altogether, believing the distinction to be irrelevant or dangerous.

An example of this can be seen in Fayetteville-Manlius, an innovative upstate New York school that won seven straight Nike Cross Nationals. Their coach, Bill Aris, trains his runners to regard both male and females as athletic equals. In a *Runner's World* article, Mark Bloom quoted a student competitor from the school: "Our belief is, we're not boys or girls. We're athletes."

The concept of femininity gets tricky when it varies drastically between cultures. When I was in my early 20s, I spent two months living in Spain and I felt like an ugly duckling the entire time. Women there would dress for the runway just to walk to the store—full makeup, salon-styled hair. Their look was straight off a beauty magazine cover. It was a far cry from the grungy-cute, take-me-camping look I tended to rock.

Feminine traits are also fluid over time. In the early 1900s, pink was actually considered to be a male color, while blue was associated with females. In 16th century France, high heels defined a masculine shoe, and in Ancient Egypt both men and women used cosmetics, perfume and jewelry.

The good news is that if femininity is ultimately a social construct, irrelevant outside of our specific time and geographic location, then we can choose for ourselves the type of women we want to be.

So what does femininity in endurance look like? It may be as simple as being ourselves: women on our own terms and of our own making. The key is to embrace our freedom to choose, and to allow other women to do the same. There is no "right way" to be a female athlete.

In the book *Run Like a Girl*, Mina Samuels writes:

> We run like girls when we run for ourselves and inside ourselves. We run like girls when we tune out the negativity that might come our way—from men, from women, from any of myriad sources, including ourselves. We run like girls when we own our power, when we celebrate what we are capable of, when we take joy from our vulgar strength.

My vision of femininity is defined by spirited strength, oozing sexuality, rugged beauty and a deep intimacy with nature. It means approaching everything with an engorged heart that engulfs everything it touches. The feminine woman can't help but face life and sport head-on, full throttle, with no regrets. She is all heart, all the time. She holds back for no one, dares to be naïve, and believes in the impossible. She believes in second chances—and third ones. No matter how many times her heart is broken, she loves again. In everything, she endures.

Too Pretty for Sports?

Whether we measure femininity in muscle mass or bright colors, problems arise when we start judging other women who don't share our concept of femininity. One woman told me, "I sometimes struggle when I toe the starting line and see some runners in their exceptionally well-planned out matching outfit, hair perfectly arranged, and makeup applied ever-so-slightly. I often feel sympathy for them as they haven't truly discovered how powerful and beautiful they are."

Her comments reminded me of Shirley Matson from Shanti Sosienski's book, *Women Who Run*. When Shirley competes, she wears full makeup: lipstick, mascara, and even hair spray. After a race, people ask her whether she even ran — she looks *that* put together. However, to feel sympathy for Shirley would be a grave error.

At age 65, she has been awarded Runner of the Year for Long Distance Running for women in her age group not once or twice...but a whopping thirteen times. She was named USATF Masters Track Runner of the Year three times, Age Group Runner of the Year for *Running Times* magazine seventeen times, and was inducted in the Senior Athletes Hall of Fame in 1993, then the Masters Hall of Fame in 1998.

"On the start line, it's a psychological ploy," says Shirley. "I like the dichotomy that you can be really aggressive and athletic and flirty and sporty, and still be feminine. Why shouldn't you be able to do all of that at the same time?"

Like Shirley, Hoka-sponsored ultrarunner Jennifer Benna is a serious athlete...while wearing makeup. "I love being a girl," says Jennifer. "I seek out cute running outfits and will probably put waterproof mascara on before I hit the start line. I don't care if being more girly makes me seem less competitive. In fact, it's kind of fun to be underestimated — and then to fly by." Jennifer has flown her way to the front of the pack at nearly every race she's run. She is the 2013 Bandera 50K champion as well as the 2013 Zion 100-mile champion and course record holder, among other successes too long to list.

Jennifer is not alone. Accomplished elite runner and

multiple world record holder, Mimi Anderson is the queen of pink, and arguably the most grossly underestimated athlete because of it.

In her interview on *Ultra Talk* podcast, Mimi talks about the skeptical questions she sometimes receives at a race start line such as: "Do you have the right race? Are you sure you're not signed up to crew?" Mimi's doubters tend to eat her dust.

Sometimes our misguided judgments are based on the assumption that women are "dressing up" for the spectator or to meet a societal standard. In reality, many women say they do it for themselves.

When Neva "Chipmunk" Warren set out to become the youngest female to thru-hike the Appalachian Trail solo at 15 years of age, she dressed her best every single day, even when her chances of her seeing another human being on the trail were slim to none. "I noticed I was less depressed and felt better hiking when I was wearing cute hiking clothes instead of ugly rain gear," Neva explained to me. "I felt better when my nails were painted, and my hair didn't feel greasy. I did my hair and makeup when I went into town. I don't know why exactly all this helped on my hike, but it certainly did. I enjoy doing hair, makeup and nails, and in fact, I'm considering pursuing cosmetology in my future."

When Neva shared her passion for cosmetology on the trail, people often laughed at her, or they looked sad. They said things like, "Well, you're smart, you could be something like a teacher or a writer." We tell our little girls that they can grow up to be anything they want, so why is Neva's choice still shunned and her abilities questioned? Neva told me that other hikers would eye her curled hair or painted nails and visibly scoff, dismissing her as a lesser hiker.

"Neither hiking nor cosmetology changes who I am as a person," insists Neva. "Femininity is important to me because I enjoy being feminine, and I also enjoy being adventurous. It's sad that most people think those two things are mutually exclusive." Have we shifted our discrimination from "You can't be on the trail: you're a woman" to "You can't be on the trail: you're too pretty?"

Judgments like these can sometimes be a sign of our own insecurities. Rebecca Schaefer described this concept on runnerwithanappetite.com in an entry titled *Being a Female Runner*. She writes:

> When I was in high school and early on in college, I cared more about looking like a real runner and didn't particularly dress in a feminine manner. I feared dressing in a feminine way would make me look weaker or less like a tried and true tough runner. I do understand how sexist it is for me to think looking like a girl could make me look weak, but that's how I felt...
>
> I'd avoid pink tank tops and choose to wear a t-shirt instead. When running skirts first became popular, I scoffed at the idea of running in a skirt. Who is that high maintenance that they must wear a skirt and be super-girly at all times? I hated the shirts I saw girls wear that said, "I don't sweat, I glisten." No, you sweat. Everyone does.
>
> Things have changed, though. I don't know if it was me being insecure before and gaining confidence or what,

but I actually have started to really enjoy dressing feminine while running. I look for cute clothes to run in that make me feel feminine and show off that I'm a lady... Hell, I've run a marathon in a tutu and one in a dress... I've shown up to races, hair in pigtail braids...When it's over and I've beaten a lot of people, I smile all the way home.

I will never glisten! I'm a girl and I sweat, proudly...I can be strong AND feminine any day of the week.

Ultrarunner Alison Cleary told me that she used to shy away from nail polish and skirts because that image wasn't part of "tough Alison." She felt she had something to prove on the trail and wanted to be taken seriously. However, after finishing her second 50K, her perspective changed. "I wore crazy colored nail polish if I wanted, and dressed up cute when I felt like it because no one could accuse me of not being tough—I'd proved it." She had gained confidence through endurance and with that followed the freedom to wear whatever she wanted.

When we associate taking our sport seriously as a masculine expression, we are implying that our femaleness is inherently shallow, weak and frivolous. Passing judgment on the clothes and makeup of other women only reveals our own internal sexism.

In weighing my own beliefs regarding womanhood and femininity, I learned a new-to-me phrase that seemed to support my feelings on this topic. The concept was "lipstick feminism" or "third-wave feminism."

Lipstick feminism is known for embracing the sexual power of women. It fights against the "anti-sex" or "ugly feminist" stereotype, embracing physical beauty and potent sexuality. It brings back makeup, stilettos and suggestive clothing as items of empowerment. Although as a concept it has its own share of fair criticisms, I am drawn to the idea of a woman in sport who is both sexy and powerful.

I love this quote from *I Am an Emotional Creature* by Eve Ensler: "My short skirt is my defiance. I will not let you make me afraid. My short skirt is not showing off — this is who I am before you made me cover it or tone it down. Get used to it."

The truth is, we can perform in short skirts, long pants, expensive jerseys or barely-there bikinis, and we'd still be the strong, athletic women we trained to be. Femininity isn't something we wear. It's who we are.

The Power of Femininity

What mental strategies do elite athletes turn to when they are digging deep — I mean really deep — for inspiration during a race? This is a question that has intrigued me for years and over time I have collected a series of tips and tricks from various women, filed away in my brain for those dark miles.

Of all these tactics, none have struck me as profoundly as elite runner Molly Sheridan's strategy. When the going gets tough, her mantras on the trail are the names of her five sisters, two daughters and other powerful women she knows personally.

"Kathy, Karen, Eileen, Colleen, Bridget, Bailey, Taylor, Jane…." she chants to herself. The power of their names and

33

Vanessa Runs

the essence of their womanhood fuel her like caffeine at mile 80.

"There is power in the feminine," Molly tells me. "I learned that through my sisters and tapped into it in the temples of India. I have a tanka of the Green Tara from India on my wall, and my sister Karen gave me a book on the Hindu goddesses...Femininity is the outward essence of the female power."

In *Run Like a Girl*, author Mina Samuels tells the story of how this she-power surprised her unexpectedly in St. Petersburg, Florida, during the Women's Running Magazine Half Marathon.

Mina had stopped by the Running Skirts booth with Kathrine Switzer and had reluctantly tried on a skirt. It fit her, but she raised an internal eyebrow: it didn't seem like her style. When the Running Skirts owners insisted she take it for free, Mina halfheartedly told them she'd wear it on the race the next day. When she did, to her surprise, the skirt seemed to unlock a secret feminine power she had never before tapped into. "I felt kind of cute, in a speedy way," Mina writes. "I felt fleet and sleek, like I had a secret power, like I had hidden retro-rockets under my skirt. In other words, I felt like a strong woman."

In *Run Like a Mother*, author Dimitry McDowell confesses a similar conclusion. "I care about what I look like," she writes. "I'm confident there's some yet unproven scientific connection between clothes that look good and fast, and feeling good and fast."

What surprised me the most about these women—these

badass, hardcore, get-down-in-the-mud-and-dirt women—
was the fierceness with which they defended and preserved
their own femininity. This was true even for those I had
pegged to be unfeminine, indifferent or too successful to care.

"Oh, it's *extremely* important!" exclaimed Lisa Tamati
when I asked her whether femininity played a role in her
everyday life and training, and Lisa is about as hardcore as it
gets: she's run across almost every major desert in the world,
including the entire length of New Zealand in 38 days.

"We can be hardcore when it's time to be hardcore, and
we can be girls and ladies when we want to be," Tamati
explains, although it took her a long time to meld the two
seemingly polar opposites. Her first boyfriend didn't like
anything that was "girly." This meant no makeup and no
dresses. "It took me a long time to get over that
tomboyishness," Tamati confesses, but now insists she doesn't
find the combination to be a contradiction. On her daily runs,
Tamati finds small ways to preserve her femininity. For
example, she wears sport skirts instead of shorts because she
likes the look.

A 2011 study published in *Psychology of Men & Masculinity*
about conformity to gender roles among student athletes
suggests that young women in sport do not actually perceive
themselves as any less feminine than their non-athletic peers,
nor do they feel they are forfeiting their femininity in some
way by participating in sports. However, some women did
report "engaging in compensatory behaviors" like wearing
makeup, ribbons and dresses both within their sports and
outside of it to reinforce their femininity.

The Dark Side of Femininity

Although we'd like to believe that every woman is free to express or subdue her own femininity, those choices come with consequences. Masculine female athletes can be seen as social deviants while feminine competitors reap social rewards. One study in *Sex Roles* explains:

> It is evident that the privilege, and concomitant power, afforded sportswomen who adhere to the social expectations for women (i.e., perform hegemonic femininity) eludes masculine-perceived female athletes. As female athletes who perform femininity correctly accrue power and privilege, female athletes perceived as masculine are labeled as social deviants (Blinde & Taub, 1992), and they experience discrimination (Crawley, 1998; Krane, 1997). Feminine women in sport reap benefits such as positive media attention, fan adoration, and sponsorship (Kolnes, 1995; Krane, 2001a; Pirinen, 1997). As these feminine athletes gain acclaim, they become spokespeople for their sport (e.g., Mia Hamm for professional soccer, Lisa Leslie for the Women's Professional Basketball League). They also garner respect for their ability to be successful athletes while remaining true to their gender. As these feminine female athletes are highlighted by the media and receive financial and political clout, they reinforce the socially constructed expectations for feminine behavior and appearance of sportswomen.

That same study shares a story of a team of female cricketers who resisted proposals to change their uniforms from skirts to trousers. Although the trousers were more practical and performance-friendly, the skirt was viewed as the only symbol of their femaleness on the playing field and the women fought hard to keep it.

Another study by Molly George at the University of California in Santa Barbara tells the story of a tall girl with short hair and a flat chest sitting on a bench during a sophomore athletic event. One of her peers ran by and commented in a loud voice, "My God, she's ugly. Is that a man?" Her teammates laughed. While we may not be as openly vicious, athletic women who are perceived as being unfeminine are still seen as committing a major social violation.

In an *Ideas* podcast on CBC Radio, Paul Kennedy pays tribute to endurance racing. Near the end of the show, Kathrine Switzer (the first woman to officially finish the Boston Marathon) describes her passion for bringing the possibility of endurance sport to women. Her first order of business after completing the 1967 Boston Marathon was to promote the acceptance of all females in this obscure sport. She accomplished this by deliberately cultivating femininity. "I always ran well within myself because I didn't want to look unfeminine or get diarrhea or throw up," she recalls. "I didn't want people to say 'Ew, women! That's icky!' I wanted us to look fabulous."

It wasn't until 1972 after the Boston Marathon officially opened its registration to women that Kathrine felt she could

focus on her training and test her limits. She went from a 4:20 marathon finish time to a 2:51 — at the time the sixth fastest performance in the world. It strikes me that it wasn't until society had accepted a slower, feminized version of the female athlete that Kathrine felt she could let loose and show what she was capable of.

Are we wearing pink because we like the color and it makes us perform better — or are we afraid of the social stigma that results from female athletes looking too masculine? When one of two choices handicaps the female athlete so severely — with our own female teammates and competitors acting as the most ruthless critics — is there really any choice at all?

Pacific Crest Trail speed demon Heather Anderson is still adamantly certain about her choice. Heather went from weighing 200 pounds in high school to breaking the speed record on the PCT by averaging 44 miles a day for 60 days straight. "I love pink because it's pretty, not because I'm trying to act like a woman," she insists. "I run and hike in skirts because I find them functional, not because I am trying to remind myself I am a woman in a man's sport. I am who I am."

Mother Nature is a Woman

My epiphany came in the mountains of Colorado, right in the heart of the White River and San Isabel National Forests. I was halfway through a six-day stage race called TransRockies that would run us from Buena Vista, Colorado to Beaver Creek: 120 miles and 20,000 feet of elevation gain in six days. That week I climbed a vertical personal record, reaching altitudes of more than 12,500 feet. I felt amazing.

I was standing at the top of a long climb waiting for my husband Shacky to catch up when I realized: I was getting stronger (not weaker) as the days progressed. The elevation, the terrain, and the climbs were no longer obstacles that I had to overcome, but a jungle gym I was lucky to play through. I was no less an extension of the wilderness than a weathered Douglas fir or a soaring red-tailed hawk. The memories of my office cubicle were a past life, a pre-existence before my actual trail-birth that day.

Essentially, I took up ultrarunning as an excuse to be in the wilderness. Fewer people question your sanity when you say you're "training" for hours on end instead of admitting what you're actually doing: frolicking like a child ignoring her dinner call.

In nature, I feel more alive. Whether surrounded by friends or alone, I am most at peace with myself in the mountains. Although the same has historically been true for males, the wild woman archetype is a concept worth exploring.

Parallels between woman and nature are everywhere. Both are traditionally associated with purity, simplicity, beauty and grace. A female's seasons and cycles can be linked to the earth's own recurring seasons and lunar cycles. Both nature and women have the power to grow life.

In researching this chapter, I learned about eco-feminism. This concept supports a historical connection between women and nature, and compares the exploitation of women with that of the environment. Further connections are drawn between

cycles like menstruation and the moon, childbirth and creation.

Eco-feminism has been criticized for being too mythical and not practical enough to be of help to women, or for ignoring the fact that nature consists of both masculine and feminine qualities. Others say it does nothing to improve women's pay equity or power. Still, the wild woman is a concept that howls truth to me.

In her book, *Women Who Run With Wolves*, Dr. Clarissa Pinkola draws further parallels between women and nature. Both share:

- Keen sensing
- Playful spirits
- A heightened capacity for devotion
- Relational tendencies
- Inquiring spirits
- Great endurance and strength
- Territorial awareness
- Inventive ideas
- Loyalty

Is it a coincidence that so many natural geographical features are personified as female? We feminize mountains, lakes, streams, rivers, trees and forests. Mother Nature herself is considered female, ruling with power and maternal care.

The linking of female deities to the outdoors is also pervasive between cultures and faiths. Kuhu, Sinivali, Anumati and Raka are lunar divinities symbolizing the waxing and waning of the lunar cycle. Persephone is associated with spring and vegetation. Vanadevis is the forest goddess and Usas is the mistress of dawn. The list goes on.

The goddess Artemis particularly intrigued me. Ruler of wilderness and wild animals, as well as protector of young girls, Artemis was herself chaste after asking her father Zeus to grant her the gift of eternal virginity at the age of three. Artemis was athletic and adventurous. She preferred solitude and concerned herself with environmental protection. However, that didn't stop gods and men from taking notice of her. Artemis was known for her swift revenge on anyone who would try to dishonor her.

One story claims that Artemis killed Orion after he tried to rape her, turning him into the constellation he is today. It is said she didn't need a man to complete her, but would enjoy a companion with whom she could share a "deep, intuitive connection with minimal chatter."

The busier and more modern we become, the stronger our pull to the wilderness. In 1998, the National Wild Turkey Federation (NWTF) started an outreach program called Women in the Outdoors, with the goal of helping women "learn more about interactive outdoor activities through hands-on education and expert-driven instruction." The NWTF expected some interest, but nothing close to what it received. In the first year, 3,000 women signed on. By the second year, more than 10,000 women were lining up to get outside. The call of the wild is a hard one to ignore.

Even when the conversation topic has nothing to do with nature, we instinctively link womanhood to the earth. "Is femininity important to you?" I ask ultrarunner Sarah Johnson in an email. A short time later, I receive her reply: "That's like

41

asking if the sun is important to the earth."

Nahoko Iwata is a shy Japanese ultrarunner who draws her inspiration directly from nature. "Sorry, I don't have good answers," she apologizes sheepishly when I question her about being a woman. Nahoko doesn't debate about gender roles or expectations. Her femininity is a simple kind of grace, rooted directly to the earth. "I want to be beautiful and strong like butterflies and flowers in the wild nature," she tells me.

Her simple answer humbles me and I can't help but wonder: why all this debate about feminine versus masculine, girly versus tomboy? Why can't we just be who we are and accept that there may not be a category for us? Or that maybe the real categories are not male or female, but rather ocean or mountain, soil or sand.

Dr. Clarissa Pinkola writes of La Loba (The She-Wolf), a woman deeply in tune with her innate, wild nature. La Loba is "circumspect, often hairy, always fat, and especially wishes to evade most company. She is both a crower and a cackler, generally having more animal sounds than human ones."

La Loba lives among the rotten granite slopes in Tarahumara Indian territory and her job is to collect bones. Over mountains and along dry riverbeds she searches and searches, until she has pieced together a full wolf skeleton. She then sits by the fire and thinks about what song to sing. When she is certain she has the right song, she stands over the dry bones and raises her voice.

The bones begin to flesh out and grow fur. La Loba sings some more and the creature begins to breathe. Finally, she sings so deeply that the desert floor shakes and the wild animal leaps up and runs down the canyon.

As Clarissa tells it, "somewhere in its running, whether by the speed of its running or by splashing its way into a river, or by way of a ray of sunlight or moonlight hitting it right in the side, the wolf is suddenly transformed into a laughing woman who runs free toward the horizon."

All women begin as a bundle of bones lost somewhere in the desert. A few of us—the lucky ones—will live to howl the songs of our souls from the depths of our wild, wild hearts.

What does any of this have to do with endurance? Here I will draw on the wise words of the late and legendary endurance runner Caballo Blanco (Micah True): "When you run on the earth and with the earth, you can run forever."

Vanessa Runs

2: "There's No Crying In Baseball!" (Emotion)

"Don't tell me not to cry, to calm it down, not to be so extreme, to be reasonable. I am an emotional creature. It's how the earth got made, how the wind continues to pollinate. You don't tell the Atlantic Ocean to behave. I am an emotional creature. Why would you want to shut me down or turn me off?...I love that I can feel the feelings inside you, even if they stop my life, even if they break my heart, even if they take me off track..."
– Eve Ensler

When I was growing up, my grandmother had four movies in her VHS collection: *Groundhog Day*, *Curly Sue*, *Silence of the Lambs*, and *A League of Their Own*. Since I didn't have a TV at home, I often plopped down on her couch with my little sister. We watched each of these movies at least two million times.

Groundhog Day bored me; *Curly Sue* was my favorite; *Silence of the Lambs* gave me an early taste for horror; and *A League of Their Own* taught me what kind of woman I could become.

A League of Their Own is set during World War II. Women were taking over traditional male jobs while men were fighting the war. The first women's professional baseball league was organized and two sisters were recruited from a small farm in Oregon. The story is one of sport, struggle and rivalry.

As close as I could figure, the choices for me were:

- Slutty girl (Madonna)
- Fat and funny girl (Rosie O'Donnell)
- Pretty and talented girl who gets everything handed to her but doesn't appreciate it (Geena Davis)
- Average girl who has to work hard for everything she has (Lori Petty)
- Extremely talented but ugly girl who can't catch a break because of her off-putting looks (Megan Cavanagh)

I saw traits from all those women in myself, and I wasn't quite sure which one I would become. One thing I understood for sure: there is no crying in baseball. There is no crying in sport.

I knew this from one scene in the movie where the baseball coach Jimmy Dugan (Tom Hanks) is yelling at a female player for throwing to home during a two-run lead and letting the tying run get on second base. She starts to cry, and he starts screaming, "There is no crying in baseball! There is no crying in baseball!" The female player continues to sob and is ultimately defended by the referee and comforted by her teammates.

I figured that in order to play sports I would have to harden myself against tears or the showing of emotion. I needed to look tough and invincible. To be strong meant not to feel.

When I first got into endurance sport, and especially ultrarunning, I was surprised at the free-flowing emotion from so many competitors, both men and women. Not many seemed concerned with looking tough. On the contrary, these athletes freely admitted to crying, embraced race day feelings and used them to fuel their performance.

I had believed that as a woman I had to choose between heart and brain. I could be smart and calculating but primarily unfeeling—or I could allow myself to be carried away by emotion and sacrifice any illusion of intelligence. My sport taught me that I didn't need to choose after all. I could have both a heart and a brain.

In Defense of Teen Girls

As a teen, I was obsessed with baseball, the Toronto Blue Jays and more particularly second baseman Roberto Alomar. It was the glory days for the Blue Jays back then. Alomar played from 1991 to 1995 and my team won the World Series in 1992 and 1993. Alomar was a central player in Game 6 of the 1992 World Series where he scored a series-winning run in the 11th inning. In 1993, Alomar produced 17 home runs, 93 RBI and 55 stolen bases. He was batting at .326. I was a huge fan.

For my birthday one year, my stepmom bought me my first tickets to a Blue Jays game. They were nosebleed seats but that didn't matter—I was close to Robbie Alomar.

We didn't have a television then, so I used to listen to the games on a tiny radio. After bedtime I would stick the radio under my pillow and play the games into one ear as I lay my head on the broadcast, pretending to be asleep.

On the outside, I presented as a bookish nerd, having chosen brain over heart. I wanted to display high intellect and low emotion. But on the inside, I was crazy about athletics and passionate about my home team. I loved sports.

My teenaged girlfriends were just as passionate about their own obsessions: music, horses, books and art. Whatever they loved, they loved hard and they didn't bother to hide it.

Young girls haven't changed much. These days, they throw themselves passionately into whatever catches their interest and they worry very little about balance or moderation. They are filled with emotion. Often, the world tries to tone these girls down, seeing their passion in a negative light. I was told growing up that teen girls were unbalanced and obsessive, but now I know better. Teen girls remind us what it means to care deeply and love fully. It doesn't matter what the focus of affection is—they choose unrestrained passion over indifference every single day.

As a young girl at my church, I picked up on insinuations that the passions of young women could easily turn into dangerous or unhealthy addictions, so repression was important. However, when I reached out to real women in endurance, they remembered having their own crazy passions as teens:

Susan Schrader: "I was passionate about horses. I didn't have one or know anyone with a horse, but there was a horse about four miles from my house. I'd walk there and back, and pick grass to feed it through the fence: my first solo long-distance outings. I had lots of horse toys and notebooks of horse pictures I had cut out of magazines too."

Kathryn Richardson Schjei: "I used to spend entire days clearing brush and fallen trees from streams and trails. Mostly, I was just fascinated with watching the streams carve out the landscape and it used to make me sad when they would get dammed up from debris resulting from nasty northwest rainstorms. Also, I just loved being alone in the woods. I still do."

Alena Kupchella Gourley: "I was obsessed with being different, so I wore gold sneakers, Spam t-shirts (I've never eaten the stuff!), dyed my hair bright red, painted my nails dark colors, and convinced my grandma to get me a black bra. Now it's barefoot and huarache running. The awesome thing is that all of these were enjoyable and taught good life lessons."

Martine Kinkade: "Reading and writing. My love for words was my first great passion, the longest enduring affair of my life. Although, now that I recall, it started when I was six years old and wrote my first book: STARNOSE THE COLT. Starnose had a tendency to get into a lot of snake, mountain lion and human-related troubles. Much like I did at his age."

Adele Garcia: "Marine Biology! I was obsessed with all things ocean and marine life. I would fish in the summer and read anything marine-biology related. Pretty sure I was voted most likely to live in a bubble on the ocean floor my senior year."

Leah Eddy: "The environment. I spent a ton of time in the woods and it always upset me greatly when I would find piles of garbage. I picked up garbage and cans when I found them. One time I spray-painted NO DUMPING on an old shed I found in the woods that was a favorite spot for people looking to get rid of garbage. It actually worked."

Michele Granger: "I wanted desperately to run the mile at

track meets...The longest race for girls was 800 meters, and even then I had to race girls older than me because the longest race was 200 meters until you turned thirteen."

Tiffany Henness: "I would do absolutely nothing until I finished a book, neglecting eating and sleeping. Then I'd start another one. I spent way too much time in AOL chat rooms. I learned to type fast because of that and was proud of myself for being able to carry on 10 conversations at once. I thought connecting with other people in other parts of the world was fascinating!"

Deana Davis: "I loved skateboarding and thought I could do this for a job if only I could get paid for it. I do think skateboarding set me up for running; it gave me physical fitness."

Our culture has launched a war against young girls. To be a girl is to be a joke, an embarrassment or a weak link. Feminist playwright Eve Ensler once said:

> I think the whole world has essentially been brought up not to be a girl. How do we bring up boys? What does it mean to be a boy? To be a boy really means not to be a girl. To be a man means not to be a girl. To be a woman means not to be a girl. To be strong means not to be a girl. To be a leader means not to be a girl. I actually think that being a girl is so powerful that we've had to train everyone not to be that.

In silencing what Eve calls our "girl cells" we also mute important parts of our compassion, kindness and warmth. Somewhere along the way, most of us tone it down, but the best of us never do. Some women are still ravenous for new challenges and make no apologies for their passions. To those outside looking in, this intensity can be scary. It is unpredictable and unrestrained. It seems dangerous and immature. These women either fall hard or win big, and that's a risk. It's also the most valuable part of being a girl or woman.

Endurance racing helps me tune into my girl cells. It strips me down to raw stubbornness and irrational persistence. It makes me push on when it doesn't make sense to, and that emotion-based quality has been the core of my success in endurance.

The Science of Tears

To say that Michele Granger was undertrained going into Ironman Austria would be an understatement. Although she had signed up early and started training well in advance of the event, a nasty workplace fall left her with bruising at the top of her femur and a knock to the head. Post-recovery, she only had four months left to train, virtually from scratch. It was a race, however, she wasn't about to miss.

Michele's father passed away in 2000 and ever since she had considered him to be her Iron Angel. She would visualize him perched on her shoulder during training and racing, refusing to let her quit. This year Lesley, the mother of a friend, had passed away after a long illness. That was weighing on Michele's heart. Ready or not, she would race for them both.

Race day came all too soon and Michele found herself on

the shore of Lake Wörthersee, ready to complete the swim portion of her race. The gun went off and Michele plunged into the water. She managed to keep a strong, steady stroke throughout the entire swim portion. She got out of the water in good spirits only to discover that someone had misplaced her glasses. She spent an hour looking for them before she decided to just leave. Half-blind, she set out to ride the bike course.

Another hour later, one of her crew found her glasses at the Lost and Found and returned them to her. Michele shoved them on her face and set out for her second bike loop. About the same time, her left quad started to hurt. Michele had no choice but to push through the pain as best as she could. Quitting was not an option.

Michele missed the cutoff by a few minutes at the end of the bike portion, but through a race error she was allowed to continue. She reached up and touched a heart she had pinned on her jersey, over her own heart with the names "Dad" and "Lesley" inked above and below. They were watching out for her.

Michele slogged through the marathon, running when she could and walking the rest of the time. She was surviving on water and the odd banana with orange slices. With only one marked kilometer to go, she learned that the last kilometer was actually 1500 meters and she was dangerously close to the cutoff.

With every ounce of strength she could muster, Michele picked up her tired legs and ran through fatigue that was like none she had ever felt before. In the distance, she heard music and a voice over a microphone. It was approaching midnight and she expected to see only a small handful of loyal spectators.

As she turned the final corner, Michele was shocked to witness thousands of people waiting for her to finish: the last official finisher. She gritted her teeth and bit her lip, determined not to cry. The announcer bellowed "Michele Granger, you are an Ironman!" just as she crossed the finish line.

Michele high-fived hundreds of people, hugged her friends, and received her medal from the women's winner, Erika Csomor. She was asked to give interviews for local media where she had the opportunity to thank her dad and Lesley for spurring her on. If they could endure years of pain and suffering, surely she could suffer for 17 hours to get across that finish line.

At the stroke of midnight, fireworks went off and the race director told Michele to turn around and look out on the lake. He hugged her and said, "Michele, those fireworks are for your dad." That was when Michele lost it.

All the tears she had been holding back flowed freely in one cathartic explosion. The frustration and pain she had been holding on to fell away with her tears. She describes this as the best day of racing in her life, "worth every pain, tear and step in an awesome journey."

Tears may seem pretty inconvenient in an endurance context. It's hard to breathe between sobs, and snot running down your face can be embarrassing. However, crying in the right context can also provide a release that helps us let go, refocus on the goal ahead and persevere.

In the archives of *The New York Times*, I dug up an eye-opening article from 1982 by Jane E. Brody about the biological role of emotional tears. Brody interviewed Dr. William H. Frey who explained that crying is an exocrine process. Other exocrine processes include exhaling, urinating, defecating and sweating, all processes concerned with releasing toxic substances from the body. Dr. Frey believed there was no reason to think that crying wouldn't do the same. When we cry, we may be releasing the chemicals the body produces in response to stress.

Understanding our tears is important, Dr. Frey stressed, especially in a society that frowns on freely crying. By suppressing tears, we may be increasing our susceptibility to stress and possibly stress-related disorders. Dr. Frey believed that we should comfort people without telling them to stop crying. He notes that "children with a rare inherited disease called familial dysautonomia show two characteristics that may be related: they cry without tears and they have a highly exaggerated reaction to mild stress." Ultimately, people feel better after crying.

One misconception is that tears in endurance represent the pain of regret. If we're crying, we shouldn't be doing whatever it is that is making us cry. In an iRunFar article about Heather Anderson setting the fastest known time crossing the Pacific Crest Trail, she was called out in the comments section for crying. Hank writes:

> I was reading that she cried every day for the second half of the hike. I couldn't help but ask: is that the way I

would want most days of a two-month journey to feel like? Forcing myself to do something to meet an arbitrary time goal? I think we are becoming slightly disillusioned that Heather's way deserves to be placed on some pedestal over another persons who took two to three times longer, when in fact it's probably a terrible way to experience the PCT…If the hike isn't about experiencing the PCT and what it has to offer, what is the point? It's clearly highly ego-driven and social media is really fanning the flames.

Editor Meghan Hicks replied to Hank and pointed out that she herself has cried in the middle of doing very hard things that she has no regret doing. "People cry for many reasons," she counters. "Some people rarely cry. Crying is a fascinating physiological response."

For ultrarunner Brittany Brickweg, emotion is an important aspect of endurance. She describes herself as someone who loves "feeling and expressing" without reserve, and points out that we don't often get to do that in life. Endurance sport is a great outlet for feeling.

Ultramarathon race director and nutrition coach, Keira Henninger, believes tears and emotion are all part of digging deep and doing your best. "I get very emotional at races," she confesses. "I give 100 percent of myself most of the time, and that takes a lot out of me mentally." When you give your all at an event, you don't hold anything back. That includes your emotions.

Vanessa Runs

Endurance: The Emotional Equalizer

Paul Hassett is trotting down the Main Divide Truck Trail in the mountains of Cleveland National Forest, almost 40 kilometers into one of the most brutal 50K races he has ever attempted: the Los Pinos 50K in Southern California. This course was so tough and the carnage so significant that after this day race director Keira Henninger would permanently cancel the event for fear of the safety of the runners. (Two new race directors would pick it up again a couple of years later.)

Paul's face is paper-white. His eyes are sunken into his skull. He is tortured by the heat and exposure of the trail, but he is grateful to be going downhill for a change. Paul just finished the Los Pinos climb: a brutal 8.5-mile stretch with no cover, no aid, and seemingly no end. The climb is dotted with false summits to crush the soul, each one leading to a harder and hotter incline. Paul's mind has nearly shut down, but he's on the home stretch.

Out of the corner of his eye, Paul spots his teenaged son Errin and can no longer contain his emotion. Errin has hiked out to meet him and falls into step jogging behind his dad. Paul is a weeping mess. He can't believe that after all these years, after everything he's been through, he's actually running with his son.

Paul has a rough history marked by a sick mother, an abusive brother and a battle with depression. At his worst, he weighed more than 300 pounds and was ready to give up on life. He felt he had let his family down so many times and now all he wanted was to finish this race so they could be proud of him.

56

Endurance running pulled Paul out of his depression with renewed purpose and resolve. He dropped his excess weight, took up ultrarunning, and published a memoir called *My Battle Within*. He dreams of someday running across America, but at this moment he's just trying not to choke on his own tears.

Finally, Paul sees the finish line and he can't hold it together anymore. He bursts into uncontrollable crying as the race director places a medal around his neck. Through sheer mental fortitude, Paul has managed to finish. He still isn't sure how.

Crying at a race is not unusual for Paul. He wears his emotions on his bib and he finds the tears to be restorative. He's often wet with gratitude and a deep appreciation for the man he has become—no longer out of control, frightened or victimized. He can choose his battles and fight them with a newfound strength.

In many scenarios, men are socially forbidden from expressing certain emotions. It is more socially acceptable for a man to be hardened and hurtful than to present as flamboyant and expressive. Hippocrates, the ancient father of medicine, believed that the uterus was in fact the source of emotions, triggering a condition called hysteria in women, a diagnosis that lasted for centuries. In endurance, however, social norms are dismissed. Both men and woman can (and do) reveal a wide range of emotions. Many men in endurance are comfortable with their emotions as a normal part of the sport experience.

When Tegyn Angel ran the Northburn 100 through the

mountains of New Zealand, he learned firsthand how to connect to his deepest emotional source. It took Tegyn 34 hours to complete the race, and although he reported feeling physically fine, he was emotionally desolate. "It's exhausting work exploring the depths of our darkest emotions," he later reported on wildplans.com. "When they're freshest, thoughts smash around our skulls...We feel like there's a broken record playing up there, our thoughts playing some sick game of psychosomatic hide-and-seek with our clenched and twisted guts. Coming out of an ultra, it's safe to say we're fatigued. The exhaustion lingering from the event washes away our defenses and this conscious scraping-back of the soul further erodes our reserves allowing unbidden thoughts and feelings to threaten the already threadbare fabric of our sanity."

Gail Martin was a female pacer during the last 25K of a 24-hour event. She witnessed the emotional rebirth of her runner, Michael St. Hilaire, in the final miles of the course. She describes his experience as "a smorgasbord of emotions, from fear and doubt, to the meltdown of realization that he is not all that." She told me proudly, "I watched him find the love in his heart, for his wife, his kids, his family and himself. After that meltdown came acceptance, self-belief, success, and joy in all that he had accomplished. It truly was not all about the miles at the finish. He was a changed and grown man."

When I opened up the floor to other men in endurance, many came forward to report frequent and unapologetic emotion. The verdict was unanimous: big boys and big girls do cry. Here is what the men said:

Shawn Wood: "I got a little snivelly about 80 miles into my first 100 when I realized I was actually going to finish; I got tearful when my girlfriend was at about the same point in the same race a year later and I knew that she was going to finish. I lay on the ground and cried a little 70ish miles into the Zion 100 because I felt broken and defeated, but I got up and finished. I think ultrarunners are a different breed of people, maybe more sincere than normal guys. Also, 20 to 30 hours of continuous exertion are enough to strip away all the bullshit we might have about acting a certain way. During a hundred you don't really have the energy to act tough."

Ritchie Trinos Amansec: "I always cry and I'm not ashamed of it. I started to run for my mom at the same time her sickness started to worsen about four years ago. I saw her slowly trapped in her own body. It was very painful to see and to not be able to stop it. I ran and told her about it every time: how I felt, what I thought about, how training went, just to make her feel what I felt. She lost her battle. For almost four years I had someone to run to and share what I felt and now she is no longer in her chair waiting for me to come home. She lost her life to ALS (Lou Gehrig's Disease), so yes, I cry when I run. It's painful, but it's the only way I can feel connected to her. I will never let it go."

François Flint Bourdeau: "Such outbursts of emotion are one of the reasons ultrarunning is so much of an experience, as the physical and mental exertion drag you ever closer to the essence of yourself, where no facade is possible."

Keith Flint: "We often push ourselves to extraordinary levels of exhaustion in this sport—physically, mentally and emotionally. It is not surprising that passionate people express themselves so openly. I love it, and I'm proud of it...In 1994, shortly after my youngest son was born, I ran the Pikes Peak Ascent. As usual, I wore an old singlet from Ohio University, my alma mater. As I neared the summit at over 14,000 feet, a girl sitting on a rock wearing an OU hoodie called out, 'Go Bobcats!' I immediately burst into tears."

Edward Layland: "I'd signed up to do a marathon in aid of victims of famine in Somalia. There was about a thousand dollars riding on my finish. All my preparations had gone well and I was in shape to do it. The week before the race, organizers postponed it from September to January (high summer in Rio), but since there was money at stake I decided to do 14 laps of a local 3K circuit. Cutting a long story short, running a marathon alone with no support is a bit more intense than your average marathon, especially when you suffer chronic diarrhea at 28K. So on my final lap when my wife drove slowly past with my two-year-old banging on the car window, smiling and shouting 'Daddy,' I couldn't help but shed a tear...or ten."

Ultrarunner Victoria Anne Rochat sums it up best: "If you can show me someone who has not cried during a race then I will show you someone who has not actually run an ultra."

It appears that, unlike baseball, there *is* crying in endurance.

3: Race Like A Girl (Discrimination & Inequality)

"Sport has the power to change the world. It has the power to unite in a way that little else does. It speaks to youth in a language they understand. Sport can create hope where once there was only despair. It is more powerful than governments in breaking down racial barriers. It laughs in the face of all types of discrimination."
- Nelson Mandela

In 1967 Kathrine Switzer was almost chased off the Boston Marathon race course for being a woman. Every seasoned endurance athlete knows the story. We tell it to describe how bad things used to be and to pat ourselves on the back about how far we've advanced. Women can run marathons now! What an achievement!

Yes, we have come a long way. Yes, we have improved. Yes, we have male supporters. We aren't threatened or chased off race courses, but we often neglect to pause to question the areas in which we haven't advanced. What hasn't changed for women in sports since 1967?

Did you know that women are still banned from some endurance events and receive unequal prize money at many races? I didn't. In endurance, the genders are still far from equal. Some subtle discrimination can be hard to pick up on, but the transgressions are just as great as what happened to Kathrine Switzer in 1967.

We can compare ourselves to the past and believe we are

doing well, or we can look to the future and continue to fight for equality. We need to do better because we're not there yet. We're so, so far from there.

The Right to Be Outdoors

Andrea Lankford is a park ranger and an author. In her book, *Ranger Confidential,* she tells the story of four male rock climbers stranded on the wall of Yosemite National Park's El Cap. A storm had moved in and they were soaked to the bone. Their situation was urgent: they would not have survived another night.

A rescue mission was launched and a law enforcement ranger named Mary was lowered via helicopter down to the granite shelf where the shivering men were squatting, praying for help. When the first climber saw her, his expression was not one of relief. Instead, he exclaimed: "Oh no, it's a chick!"

On his climbing helmet was a cartoon of a pair of women's legs spread wide. The woman's vagina was a mountain and her clitoris was the peak: a summit to be conquered and checked off his list.

Mary started explaining how the rescue was going to happen, but the vagina-headed douchebag interrupted with his opinion about what should be done. Had she thought about this option? Maybe there was a better way that hadn't occurred to her?

A second climber eventually shut Vagina Helmet up and they were all lifted off the mountain safely, according to plan. This attitude is not uncommon for women who live and work in the outdoors.

When Andrea Lankford first came to work at Yosemite
Valley, she was warned by the assistant superintendent that
whenever a woman worked in the Valley at night, things went
sour. He informed her that she had only been hired as a "test
case" at his insistence, and that she would have to prove that
women could handle working at Yosemite Valley. Few
women lasted more than one season. Several years before, one
female ranger had come to work to find a severed cat head on
her desk.

Andrea's male coworkers all seemed to be apprised of her
"test case" status. They would say things to her like, "You
were hired because you have breasts," and "Don't get your
panties in a bunch, honey."

The uniformed park ranger is still predominantly a white
male and it wasn't until 1978 that women were allowed to
wear the same uniform as male rangers and assume equal
responsibilities. Today, only about a third of park rangers are
women.

Sometimes discrimination against women in the outdoors
is mean-spirited, but mostly it comes from well-intentioned
men who feel they are doing their duty to protect the weaker
sex. This chivalrous attitude often causes more harm to
women than outright sexism.

One male tourist strolls by a woman doing trail
maintenance, down on her hands and knees in the dirt and
comments: "Guys must be gettin' awful lazy, lettin' the pretty
girls do all the work!" He thinks he's being kind.

Men are not exclusively to blame. How many of us as
women have played the damsel-in-distress card? How many

times have we benefited from chivalrous intentions? I know I have—directly and indirectly—for most of my life. It's so easy to hand over that pickle jar, but what are we really handing off?

Many times the wording we use is non-inclusive and in small, unintentional ways, it chips away at our right to be outside. When Jennifer Pharr Davis set out to break the speed record on the Appalachian Trail she had a male friend advise her: "If you fall behind before the half-way point, it will be oppressive knowing that you will have to average over fifty miles a day to break the men's record."

Jennifer corrected him: "You mean the overall record."

In her memoir *Called Again: A Story of Love and Triumph*, Jennifer notes that wording was crucial to her success. Breaking the "male record" made her the outsider and the underdog. She was not there to beat the boys. She was there to do her best, and her best was good enough for the overall record.

Personal autonomy draws me to endurance sports. The sheer difficulty is such that there is little opportunity for hand-holding. Both men and women, in the toughest stages of a race, are so beaten down, so exhausted, so sleep-deprived, so mentally drained, that the last thing on their minds is how to ease the burden of the nearest female.

At that point, there are no genders. There is only humanity. If we see someone struggling, we stop to assist him or her regardless of gender because the dangers of being alone in the wilderness are the same regardless of what we sport between our legs. This is the best of humanity: protecting each other regardless of gender and because we are human, racing as one unit to a common end.

Chicked: Empowering or Sexist?

One of my early working titles for this book was *Chicked*, but I ultimately rejected it because of its negative connotations. The word "chicked" refers to a situation where a woman outperforms a man: the man gets "chicked."

There are essentially two camps of opinions on this word. On one side, it is considered empowering and inspirational, representing a woman's full athletic potential. She may be a chick but she is able, competitive and not to be underestimated.

Several clothing lines have printed shirts and other merchandise with the word "Chicked." Entire businesses have been built around the concept. For sixty-five dollars you can go to chicked.com and purchase a sweat-wicking Dri-FIT Nike Airborne tank top with a reflective stripe on the back that reads: "YOU JUST GOT CHICKED." Or make it a t-shirt. Or headbands. Or capris. Or…you get the idea.

At TransRockies, a 120-mile stage race in Colorado, endurance runner Michelle Barton hands out small business cards to everyone who crosses the finish line after her. They read: "You've been chicked."

To others, "chicked" is a sexist and offensive phrase. The counter-argument is that the more you use the word to describe an amazing performance, the more you reinforce the stereotype that athletic talent is unusual in a woman—so unusual that it requires special terminology. The underlying message downplays a woman's place in endurance sport, reinforcing the belief that women don't belong there and therefore don't officially count as competition. At one ultramarathon, a man who came in third place overall was heard to describe his position as: "second man in and got chicked."

For a third category of athletes, the word chicked is nothing more than a lighthearted tease, hardly worth debating. It is used in their vocabulary alongside other distinctions such as "I got wifed" or "I got geezered," to poke fun at the competitors they most love and care about.

Ultrarunner Adam Chase reports using the phrase to help pro runner Nikki Kimball find her competitive fire during the Leadville 100 in 2005. He tells the story in *Women's Adventure Magazine*:

> I concocted a scheme that capitalized on her competitive nature, and what she'd perceive as a macho-man attitude of a military friend of mine a few minutes ahead of her. Casually, while I paced her between miles 75 and 80, I mentioned that my pal would be the butt of the joke with his jarhead Special Forces friends if she beat him in the race. Sure enough, she told me later that the thought of chicking him helped drive her past him during the last tough miles of that race. In fact, my Special Forces friend cheered for Nikki as she passed him, proving that the act of chicking can be more about driving a woman's competitive self than about crushing anyone's ego.

Endurance runner Tiffany Henness told me a story of a

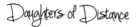

distance relay she ran where she passed a male competitor several times. He kept trying to get ahead of her and although Tiffany "won" in the end, she didn't gain any pleasure from it: he was only trying to beat her as a woman, not a respected athletic competitor. She then overheard other males making fun of each other because they had been "chicked," some expressing how upset they were.

Later in that same race, she found herself leapfrogging with another woman, but the vibe was different. Tiffany felt comfortable introducing herself and high-fiving her competitor. "Knowing that some men are very unhappy about being chicked makes me treat guys differently," confessed Tiffany. "I suppose it shouldn't. But it does."

Runner Trisha Berube remembers the first time she ever "chicked" a boy as a young child on a family vacation. A boy couldn't pass her on his bike, so he grabbed her handlebars and pushed her over, screaming: "Noo! I can't get beaten by a girl!" When such reactions happen these days, even though they are on a slightly less dramatic scale, it still feels shallow and childish to Trisha. "I don't like the idea of even acknowledging the whole gender-based competitiveness," Trisha says. "It's totally sexist and needlessly aggressive. Why add to it?"

Here are some other opinions that made me think:

Jennifer Liang: "Chicked? What does that mean anyway? I am not a chick (last I checked I have no feathers or a beak). I am a woman. Saying that I chicked someone is just a slimy way of degrading me at the same time as fluffing me up. No thank you."

Michael Duer: "I have heard [the term "chicked"] used purely in a playful way by fellow male runners who fully respect women who can and do beat them in races. I can understand it being perceived as sexist or degrading, but I don't think most men in the ultra world mean it that way. There are way too many good female runners out there for most men (although I'm sure there are still some) to get uptight, or try to bring down women who beat them."

Shelley Bishop Koenig: "Generally, [being chicked] is a term used when a woman outperforms someone else in an athletic endeavor, usually a man. It is presumed that the idea of being beaten by a woman should somehow be emasculating, which I guess is supposed to make the woman feel good. Personally, I am out there to achieve my own goals, not to put someone else down on their own journey. I'd rather cheer them on and encourage them to do their personal best then to criticize or belittle their achievements."

Denny Krahe: "I've always viewed getting chicked as more of a term of endearment for the woman that is blowing by me, almost in the same vein as 'girl power.' I have no problem getting chicked. It has happened to me many times before, and it will continue to happen to me in the future."

Kattee Proberto: "Your question reminded me of this brilliant TED talk by Tony Porter who says that men should step out of the 'man box' and not be frightened about being equal to or bettered by women. He tells a story about a little boy being sent off the football pitch. The little boy tells him that he's upset the coach said he wasn't good enough, but the worst insult of all would be if he got called out for playing like a girl. Tony Porter reflects on this, and concludes, 'If this is the worst insult a little boy can get, then what are we as grown-ups, teaching our young boys about girls?'"

Chantal Cravens: "I love the word chicked. I've spent a lot of my running career running with guys. I love them. They will never let me pass them without a fight and they always make me a tougher and better runner…I also have some fellow runners that will drop a kidney before they let me pass them up. Makes it sweeter when I do. There are no freebies."

Rachael Osteen: "I'm pretty fucking offended by [the term "chicked"]. I work hard, train hard and run hard. I like it hard. So if and when I pass you, don't degrade my hard-found passion by pointing out that my mere vagina hurts your pride."

Laura Bailiff: "I think anyone who is bothered by chicked is just being sensitive or way overboard with women's lib. It's just an expression, and I personally still love being called that even at 62. Chick was my Dad's nickname for me and I am certainly not offended. It's not degrading….I think some women need to stop thinking everyone is out to insult them. Those are confidence issues in my opinion."

Tiffany Guerra: "I recently hiked up San Jacinto and as I reached the top, I heard some guys up there waiting to give a guy behind me a hard time as 'you let a girl beat you'…They also called me a 'nice little carrot' for him to follow. They did not speak to me at all, just said it in front of me, laughing. They were filming the whole thing and told me to smile and wave at their camera. I could have laughed the whole thing off but it's just flat out rude. I had felt totally equal to them before that, but their actions made me feel like I was less than. Some would say this reflects on my own issues—that may be, but there is no debating the meaning of their words (that he should be mocked for being behind a girl). Hearing this stuff once is easy to shrug off. Hearing it consistently is more irritating. It's a stupid term."

Cailin Constantine: "More than a couple of times I've been racing with my husband, only to hear random guys yell 'don't let her chick you' at him. Am I supposed to find that to be a compliment? I don't, just as I don't find it a compliment when someone says, 'You're not like most women.'"

Female-Only Races: Inspiring Women or Regressing Them?

It's hard to argue with the success and popularity of women's-only events. The Nike Women's Marathon in San Francisco, California boasts 30,000 registered runners, and a similar trend can be found worldwide. The Budapest Women's Run sees around 40,000 female runners each year, while the Austrian Women's Run in Vienna brings in 30,000. Leeds, England; Albany, New York; and Billings, Montana also host immense female-only runs. We can expect this trend to continue.

A woman named Erin left a comment on a saltyrunning.com article that described a little girl's race benefiting the women's mental health program in her town. At the beginning of the event, the race director announced, "As girls, we are all in it for the bling bling," referring to the finisher medals. There was no mention that running could be

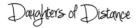

fun, empowering or even healthy. Running was something little girls endured in order to get jewelry. "I'm a girly girl at heart," wrote Erin, "but I'd never claim that I was in it for the bling. No matter what the swag is, no matter who the run is aimed at, I'm there to run, I'm there to push myself, and I'm there to enjoy the sport."

Stories like these were common when women recalled female-only races they had participated in. Do female-only events have a value in our sport or do they further a harmful stereotype?

The majority of endurance athletes I spoke to reported disliking these races for a wide variety of reasons, though some pointed out a few redeeming qualities. Here's a summary of the feedback I collected:

What we love about female-only races:

1. The camaraderie

There's a "girl power" vibe at many of these races that gets the adrenaline pumping. You feel like you belong. You're part of a tribe. You're strong, determined and beautiful, and you're in great company. There is also the benefit of running alongside other women who train at your level.

One woman commented that in co-ed races, she would often find herself running alongside men. While she is front-of-the-pack for women, the men she runs with are mid-packers in their gender. She doesn't often get to see other women who train with the same intensity and dedication. At female-only races, she does. She feels more connected to the women surrounding her and she may pick up a few new training buddies.

2. The view at the front of the pack

If you're on the faster side, you get a chance to experience what it's like to run at the true front-of-the-pack—a rare experience for women. The fastest women in co-ed races usually still see men in front of them.

One woman said she had always believed she was not a very good runner while racing co-ed events. When she ran a female-only race she found herself at the front of the pack and it changed her perspective on who she was as an athlete. She was capable and competitive—she just didn't know it.

3. The easy-going vibe

Female-only races feel less intimidating. It's okay to slow down and run for fun. There is no pressure to push yourself or to impress anyone. Many reported taking advantage of creative aid station stops that offered treats like chocolate or "girly" drinks. It's a fun run.

4. The attention to top contenders

In a co-ed race, the top female finishers tend to be overlooked in favor of the top males. In a female-only race, they are more celebrated. They are recognized and acknowledged in a way that's hard to find in co-ed racing.

What we dislike about women-only events:

1. The sales and marketing

One woman described female races as "captive opportunities to sell stuff." The marketing can be atrocious: BLING! And PINK! And DIAMONDS! And TUTUS! And COOKIES! It can range from nauseatingly stereotypical to downright insulting and highly annoying. The assumption is that women want an easy medal and lots of pampering.

One female runner suggested that if these races really

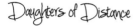

cared about the needs of females, they would offer stroller-friendly courses and childcare instead of tutus and tiaras. Another woman described the marketing as: "Less 'you're a runner!' and more 'you're super pretty and also running!'"

2. The condescension of a non-competitive approach

Many of these races seem to imply that no woman is ever interested in competing. In fact, they appear to believe that the less effort we have to put into actually racing, the better. One woman mentioned a race that had a "freshening up" station so runners could stop just before crossing the finish line to fix their hair and makeup—because a sexy finish-line photo is way more important than actually finishing in a decent time. Another told a story of a triathlon that allowed women to complete the swim portion using a pool noodle.

3. The principle

Many women were uncomfortable with the entire principle of a female-only race. Why can't we just race with men? After all these years of fighting for equality, why are we regressing to segregated events? Some women felt that these types of races reinforced negative gender roles and stalled the advancement of women in sport.

4. The lack of males

Many women want to run with men. They want to run with their friends, husbands, boyfriends, brothers and fathers. Often, they have trained with males and feel uncomfortable leaving them out on race day.

5. The wrong focus on female health

Men are touched and affected by every single "female issue" these races are put on for, whether it is breast cancer or domestic violence. If they have not been victims themselves, they often have daughters, wives, mothers or sisters who have been affected. Why exclude these men from a solution?

6. The wrong focus on female safety

If a woman feels unsafe or uncomfortable racing with men, running with a bunch of other women may make her feel better, but it isn't going to help her. Some suggested co-ed training groups where women could ease into running with men, while others were more black-and-white: either get over it or choose a different sport.

Runner Lori Lyons believes this is actually an experience issue disguised as a gender issue. For beginners who may feel intimidated, why not train together in a "beginners" group based on skill level, not gender. She told me: "When you start a new job, do you ask to sit only with women or people who are also new? No. You surround yourself with men and women who know what they are doing, so that you learn quickly. That's my life motto: surround yourself with people who are better than you."

While there is nothing wrong with approaching a race as a fun, non-competitive day full of tutus and tiaras, more women are asking for different options.

Male-only Races

A few women pointed out that they were against female-only races because male-only races would raise an outcry. However, there are a few male-themed events around the world. Below are three examples:

1. Wife-Carrying Races

This is a sport with sanctioned events all over the world.

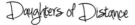

The goal is for a man to carry a woman (who doesn't have to be legally married to him) across a 278-yard obstacle course featuring log hurdles, sand traps and water hazards. The most popular wife-carrying technique is the "Estonian carry" where the female holds the male around the waist and wraps her legs around his neck. She essentially forms an upside down human backpack, with her face up against the male's bottom. This frees his hands and arms to take on the obstacles. The winner takes home his wife's weight in beer, and five times her weight in cash.

2. Big Man Run

The streets of Somerville, Massachusetts are home to a race that originated when two men decided — over many pints of beer one late Thursday evening — that there weren't enough races that included beer and hotdogs. The Big Man Run stops at pre-selected saloons where participants eat a hotdog and drink a beer. They also include bikini contests (worn by women; the men are the judges). One year they caught wind of the fact that a woman from New Hampshire was planning on sneaking into the race "a la Katherine Switzer." Instead of ambushing her on the course, they had a special trophy made up for her...but she didn't show.

3. Walk a Mile in Her Shoes

This last one is more of a fundraiser than a competitive race. Male participants are challenged to complete one mile in high heels (not much running going on here) to raise awareness for violence against women. The message is that violence against females is not exclusively a women's issue, but something that affects men as well. By "walking a mile in

her shoes" they are expressing solidarity for female victims of violence. Funds are given to local rape crisis centers, domestic violence shelters and other sexualized violence education, prevention and remediation programs.

Like female races, men's events have a lighthearted, fun-loving vibe. The focus is generally camaraderie over competition. Women aren't banned from these races and there is no outcry about their existence. This makes me wonder whether we are making too much of the debate over female-themed races? Maybe the key for both genders is to simply relax and enjoy the day.

There was one male-only race that did ban women: the Man on the Run 5K in Canterbury, UK that aims to raise awareness for male cancers. Ironically, a woman first conceived the idea for the race. It was organized in response to a female-only race, the Race for Life, which focuses on female cancers and bans men from participating. This means that a single father whose wife had died from breast cancer cannot participate in raising money or awareness for this event because breast cancer is a woman's cancer. This is a puzzling approach. Since when does cancer make gender distinctions as far as whose life it forever changes?

Sexism with a Side of Endurance

I was sitting at a small, rustic pizza joint at a pre-race gathering with some runners registered for Across the Years, a 24-hour to six-day race in Arizona. My friend Shawna Wentland and I were waiting for our pizzas to arrive. The atmosphere was dingy and the service was painfully slow, but we were content with the company and pretty much willing to eat anything. Tomorrow I knew I'd be burning all sorts of calories at the 72-hour event around a looped, one-mile course in Phoenix; Shawna was registered for the 48-hour option.

Across from us sat another registered runner I'd never met before. A tad on the heavy side, he talked non-stop about his last 50-miler, the longest distance he had ever run. He was full of tips and advice for Shawna, and she listened patiently to his bragging. Shawna herself had completed several 100-mile races and would go on to place first female in her 48-hour event, but he had mistaken her for a novice runner.

The Trail Sherpa blog was where I first heard the term *mansplainer*: a male who assumes he is superior in knowledge and experience when conversing with a woman. Most women in endurance have met this guy. They know what it feels like to be underestimated, overlooked or written off.

Sometimes comments are well-meaning and come in the form of compliments. "Oh my, look how strong you are!" when you've accomplished something basic at only a fraction of your potential. Others will say you are strong or smart or athletic...for a woman.

Words can be brushed off or ignored, but every once in a while a sexist male becomes abusive on the trails. I listened to a small handful of these stories, including Aletta Kennedy's account of racing in Whistler and trying to pass an older man on a single track among sensitive terrain. (In many locations, stepping off-trail can cause damage to the local flora and fauna.) This man would move aside for males, but refused to let Aletta by. He didn't want a woman in front of him, even

though they were 100 spots back of the lead and in no way running competitively.

After several failed attempts, Aletta finally cut across a boulder garden and slipped past the man. The man immediately began pelting her with verbal abuse, infuriated with her. His words were enough to bring Aletta to tears and he continued his abuse for as long as she was within earshot.

Many will say that stories like these are rare and while that is certainly true, that fact can also be used as an excuse for inaction. A woman who is broken down by an experience like this often feels shame. Not one single story of abuse that I heard had been officially reported to racing staff or volunteers. It's more comfortable to write it off as a rare exception.

Perhaps it's time to turn up the volume on these experiences. Offending men should be subject to immediate disqualification and banned from future races. Women should know this and report abusive behavior.

Opportunity Inequalities

When Marie Marvingt applied to ride the 1908 Tour de France cycling race, she was far from an amateur athlete. At the age of five she swam 4000m in a day. At 15, she had canoed more than 400 kilometers. In 1907 she had won an international military shooting competition and was a strong competitor in football, hockey, tennis, golf and mountaineering.

Marie was refused entry to the Tour de France because she was a woman. Undaunted, she showed up anyway and proceeded to complete the entire course, starting each stage

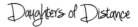

fifteen minutes after the men had taken off. Only thirty-six men finished the race that year out of 110. Marie also finished the race, proving that women could handle the distance. Unfortunately, her brave actions didn't do much to advance women in cycling.

Today, Emma Pooley is an English professional cyclist and Olympic silver medalist. Emma has the exact same athletic dream that Marie had in 1908: to race on the same day and on the same course as the men. Women still cannot race the Tour de France and there is no female equivalent event.

In professional cycling, women race shorter distances than men, over fewer stages, despite years of pleading for equality. The standard Tour de France covers 4,448 kilometers over 14 stages. The closest a female can get is the Route de France Feminine which takes place in August and consists of only seven stages.

Today, the only women you'll see on the podium of the Tour are called "podium girls," who are there for the sole purpose of looking pretty, kissing cheeks and smiling for photos. One podium girl made the news in 2013 when Slovakian cyclist Peter Sagan felt entitled to grope her buttocks. Women are accessories to the athletes, but not athletes themselves.

Why is this the case? Sadly, the reasons given are shockingly similar to what Marie was told back in 1908: women are frail and should not compete for their own good.

Brian Cookson, the current president of the cycling union, said in an interview that women could not physically complete a three-week Tour. "You couldn't do it over the same distances," he said.

The frailty argument is becoming harder to buy. Alisha Welsh, USA Primal Pro Cyclist and Arizona State Champion, once entered a local bike race and decided to hop into the men's field because there was only one other woman who had registered and she "needed a good workout that day." She ended up winning the race—outright. In the Philadelphia Classic 2009, the women's field overtook the men's field.

Unlike some endurance sports like ultrarunning where events spring up and fold every year under different race directors based on demand, women's cycling events are organized through the governing body of the International Cycling Union. The Union manages both the creation and classification of races. Even if a majority of women want equal participation, it doesn't mean they will get it. The decision ultimately lies with the organization and if the president believes that women cannot compete over the same distances, then they cannot.

Pay and Prize Money Inequalities

In most circles, it is accepted that women deserve equal pay for equal work. In endurance cycling however, this topic is still debated. Not only are women paid less, but we can't quite decide whether they should be paid equally.

All male cyclists who reach the Union Cycliste Internationale (UCI) Pro Continental level are allocated a minimum-wage annual base salary. In 2011, UCI President Pat McQuaid was asked whether female professional cyclists also deserved a minimum base salary. He replied, "I am not so sure. Women's cycling has not yet developed enough."

A 2013 survey by the Women's Cycling Association showed that 50 percent of female pro cyclists are paid $3,000 or less per year. Because women in cycling cannot earn a living wage, many resort to working fulltime on top of their busy training schedules and personal lives. Women's cycling suffers a high dropout rate due to financial pressure and a shortage of women's teams. 2011 National Road Champion Robin Farina works more than 40 hours a week, while training fulltime as a pro cyclist.

Consider the following examples from Kathryn Bertine's *Half the Road: The Passion, Pitfalls & Power of Women's Professional Cycling*:

- The 2013 UCI calendar had 370 races for the men and only 77 for women.
- As of 1998, the "Tour de France" would not allow its name to be used for a women's event.
- There are 23 UCI events worldwide for junior boys. There are only seven for junior girls.

As Kathryn points out in an ESPN column, the sport of pigeon racing is more lucrative than professional women's cycling. A pigeon owner with a fast bird can take home 10,000 euros (about $11,000 US). A winning women's cycling team usually makes $1,000 or less, to be split up between team members. Each athlete may walk away with a couple hundred dollars. In comparison, the top male winner at Paris-Roubaix, a famous cycling race, takes home about $40,000 US. Women are not allowed to race the Paris-Roubaix, and there is no female equivalent.

Here are a few of the arguments behind why women should not be paid equally. Keep in mind: these are not comments from the early 1900s. These are arguments that are made *today* about female cycling.

1. Women don't work as hard.

Because the races are shorter and the stages are fewer, professional female cyclists don't put in the same amount of training hours that men do. Since there is no equal work, there should be no equal pay.

The counter argument to this is that riders insist they do indeed train as hard, but that they lack equal opportunities to prove themselves alongside men.

2. Women aren't as popular.

There is a lack of market appeal in women's cycling, and ultimately the market determines how much an athlete should get paid. Spectators don't want to pay to watch females race.

The counter-argument: The perceived lack of market appeal exists because the media doesn't cover female racing equally. Cyclist Emma Pooley says, "I've heard a lot of people say that the best race they've ever seen was the women's race at the Olympics. A lot of our races are like that, but you don't get to see it." Besides, cycling is a sport, not a popularity contest.

3. Women don't get enough sponsors.

Sponsors help pay salaries and women don't get enough. Companies aren't interested in female athletes because they don't have as much exposure. It's not sexist; it's just a business decision.

But, if women have trouble getting sponsors, it's because

they face handicaps in media and race opportunities. It is not true that female sports are a bad business decision. Colavita, an olive oil and fine foods company, is one of the biggest sponsors in women's pro cycling. They originally sponsored both a male and female team, but found the women's team delivered the greatest value for their brand.

4. Women aren't big enough, fast enough, strong enough.

Biologically, men are built better suited for sport. You can't overlook the fact that men are simply stronger. They ride harder and faster than women.

The counter-argument observes that smaller athletes use different tactics and techniques than larger ones, but that doesn't make them any less athletic, gifted or entertaining. Bigger is not always better, especially in endurance. Also, male cycling is notorious for the use of illegal performance-enhancing drugs. To compare a clean female cyclist to a doping male is ridiculous.

5. Women don't get enough media coverage.

Female cycling isn't news. The public just isn't interested. Since 50 percent of the public isn't interested in women's sports, they shouldn't get half the coverage.

Countering this, it can be argued that it's impossible to measure interest when there is little coverage, and few opportunities to see women play. In 2013, 10,000 people signed an online petition over two days asking women to be allowed to race the Tour. Three weeks later, nearly 100,000 people had signed. So much for no interest.

6. Women have less competition.

Because fewer women are racing, the competition is soft.

A woman who gets first female because she's the only female does not deserve the same prize money as the first male who had to best hundreds of his competitors.

But, female athletes should not be penalized because other women choose not to race. Especially at the elite level, both genders have put in comparable time and training. Female participation is growing. Remember that women have only been allowed to participate for a short amount of time.

What can we do to improve these glaring inequalities? Here are some ideas courtesy of The Women's Sports Foundation:

- Attend women's sporting events;
- Support companies that advocate for women's athletics;
- Encourage television stations and newspapers to cover women's sports;
- Sign up to coach a girls' sports team, whether at the recreational or high school level;
- Encourage young women to participate in sports; and,
- Become an advocate: if you are or know a female athlete who is being discriminated against, advocate for her rights.

These are not women's issues. These are societal issue of deep concern to both men and women. We don't just need women fighting this battle—inequality lowers the quality of sport for us all, not to mention diluting the spirit of camaraderie and competition. We need to change this together.

In her book, *As Good as Gold*, Kathryn Bertine says that

many devoted ESPN readers have promised to print out her columns and give them to their daughters to read. Kathryn thanks them, but suggests they also share her words with their sons. She writes:

> I believe the beauty of athletics knows no gender boundaries, as stories of loss, triumph, underdogs, and superstars all ring true to male and female athletes alike. Giving boys articles on female athletes will have an incredible if subtle impact on gender equality. Straight from the womb, many girls, like boys, have innate athletic drive and ambition. Imagine what strides could be made — what female athletes of all ages and abilities could achieve — if women's sports were given equal coverage and attention to men's.

In the interest of space and focus, I only included endurance sports in this chapter, but many team sports like tennis and volleyball have their own extreme examples of gender disparity. To learn more about the plight of females in non-endurance sports, I recommend watching the short film by ESPN Women called *Title IX*. In the end, we are all fighting the same battle and a win for one sport is a win for active women everywhere.

Media Inequality

Women in endurance bust ass, but still fly under the radar. Fewer people know their names, and women who don't know about them can't look to them as role models and inspiration.

Media studies have shown that coverage of the Olympics is far more likely to focus on male athletes over females. One study focused on the 2010 Vancouver Winter Olympic telecast on NBC. They analyzed 64 hours of prime time telecast and found that when excluding mixed-gender pair competitions, men received more than three-fifths of the remaining airtime. It was also calculated that 75 percent of the most-mentioned athletes were men.

Two months after the 2012 Olympics, the Women's Sport and Fitness Foundation reported that females received only 5 percent of media coverage and 0.5 percent of commercial sponsorship. Barbara Slater, Director of Sport at the BBC, estimates that of the 9,000 hours of sport broadcast yearly, as few as 320 hours may be used to televise women's sport.

Instead of simply calling for new females, we need to promote the ones we already have. We need to give them platforms and allow their stories to inspire other women. Make them household names in endurance. Hold them up as mentors in the sport. Show the newer generations of runners that we highly value and respect our female athletes.

As far as endurance media goes, we could do better in profiling deserving women. How many top women in our sport can we actually name? What about the men? Women tend not to be as self-promoting. Their stories are slipping through the cracks.

I asked my Facebook community to name women who had achieved great athletic feats at an elite or near-elite level, but were still primarily unknown. I was looking for women who, based on talent alone, were vastly underrepresented or

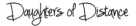

ignored by sport media despite having accomplished feats similar to or greater than their male counterparts who have enjoyed greater publicity. The list we came up with represents some of the strongest women in endurance today. This is by no means an exhaustive list and in no particular order.

How many names do you recognize?

Abby McQueeney Penamonte

Alyson Venti

Amy Lane Rusiecki

Amy Palmiero Winters

Amy Sproston

Andrea McLarty

Angela Shartel

Anne McClain

Ashley Moyer (now Lister)

Becky Wheeler

Beth Cardelli

Beth McCurdy

Beverley Anderson-Abbs

Cath Todd

Charlotte Vasarhelyi

Debbie Livingston

Fiona Oakes

Honey Albrecht

Jane Larkindale

Jennifer Moos

Jennifer Vogel

Jess Baker

Joelle Vaught

Joy Moats
Kaci Lickteig
Katalin Nagy
Kaye Anne Pappas Starosciak
Keira Henninger
Kelly Bruno
Keri Nelson
Kerrie Bruxvoort
Kristina Marie Folcik-Welts
Krystle Martinez
Larisa Dannis
Laura Perry (now Paquette)
Lisa Buohler
Lisa Hughley
Lisa Polizzi
Lisa Smith-Batchen
Lisa Tamati
Liz Bauer
Liza Howard
Lucy Bartholomew
Maggie Guteri
Margaret Nelsen
Mari Chandler
Maria Lemus
Melanie Fryar
Melissa Gillette
Meredith Dolhare
Michelle Barton
Morgan Arritola

Nicole Studer
Paulette Stevenson
Peri Gray
Sabrina Little (Sabrina Moran)
Sally Edwards
Sally McRae
Shaheen Sattar
Shannon Farar-Griefer
Shelby Hayden-Clifton
Shelley Bishop Koenig
Shelley Cook
Silke Koester
Stacey Costa-Zweifel
Sue Lucas
Tera Woolridge Dube
Tina Kefalas
Tracy Hoeg
Vanessa Kline

For many women, promoting themselves can be scary. Will it come across as attention-seeking? Cocky? Self-obsessed?

Badwater winner Pam Reed is one woman who has faced all these accusations. The media slammed her for craving fame after she complained that, when Dean Karnazes won Badwater in 2004, his picture was on the cover of *Runner's World* magazine. But Pam feels her point was misunderstood. She explains in her memoir, *The Extra Mile*:

It is expected that Badwater will be won by a man —

until my 2002 win, it had never been won by a woman —
the media should have treated the first female victory as a
bigger deal. Then, for a woman to defend that win,
winning two years in a row — you'd think that someone
might have found that worthy of more than a passing
comment. There were articles about it, but the coverage
was not spectacular. The following year, it was back to
business as usual: a man won. Now this was big news.
Picture-on-the-cover news. I think it sent a general
message to women that we are not newsworthy, no
matter how laudable our accomplishments. I perceive an
obvious double standard. The outdoors magazine article
about Dean and I did include a comment that I made
about women needing their due recognition. The article's
overall tone of ridicule — of both me and Dean —
overshadowed anything positive they said about the sport
or anything serious they said about women.

Pam knows that, even when women do accomplish
something great, often their achievements are put under a
microscope of doubt instead of immediately being celebrated
the way they are for males. When Pam won Badwater outright
in 2002, many people saw it as a fluke. They wondered if she
had doped and one person suggested they do chromosome
testing on her.

For a woman who has worked hard to train for a goal and
has accomplished it, such criticism can be overwhelmingly
disheartening. She is essentially being told that she doesn't
deserve her win, that she didn't get there on her own merit.

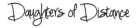

That's why Pam felt she had to return the following year to win again—to secure her legitimacy as a distance runner. Would a man have felt that same pressure to prove himself again? It's unlikely.

Similarly, elite ultrarunner Connie Gardner commented to me that she experiences pre-race discrimination when local media publishes the bios of the men they expect will be the frontrunners. Although several of the men listed have never beaten Connie, she is not mentioned as a contender, despite holding the American record in the 24-hour run with a whopping 149.3 miles in one day.

When women are covered in the media, sometimes their athletic accomplishments aren't enough to lead the story. They may be asked less about training and more about how they manage to spend time with their families. Or worse—they can be profiled with a sensationalist angle as outliers, not athletes, with the implication being that she may be insane or mentally unbalanced.

Women are often referred to as "girls" instead of women, athletes or competitors. Other times, sport commentators may remark on a female's physical appearance or choice of apparel rather than her performance.

After one British paper pledged to "make sure our pages highlight the best of women's sports," a closer look at their subsequent coverage revealed that according to them, the best of women's sports consisted of Victoria Pendleton's progress on Celebrity Bake Off and photos of multiple cycling gold medalists in evening dress.

Inevitably, when the topic of the lack of female coverage

in the media comes up, there is also finger-pointing and blame. Who is responsible for setting the agenda? The writers blame their editors for not assigning or accepting more balanced stories. The editors blame the publishers for not being open to a different angle. Publishers blame the readers for not being interested enough in female sports. Readers claim they can't dislike what they never see.

One 2003 study of sport editors from 285 newspapers in the southeastern United States found that 25 percent of editors still believe women are naturally less athletic than men. Ninety percent were confident that the gender balance in their publications reflected reader interests. Forty-five percent said that women had little or no interest in sports.

What saddens me most is not that women face this type of discrimination, but the fact that the world is missing out on thousands of strong female voices telling spectacular stories.

Are Women the Weaker Sport Consumers?

When I first started reading endurance coverage on iRunFar.com, I didn't get it. I didn't know the races. I didn't know the frontrunners or what their times meant. If it took a trail runner 20 hours to finish a rugged 100-mile course, I had no idea whether that was a fast time or a slow time (it's pretty good, actually). I wasn't even sure what "rugged" meant (mountainous, rocky, steep).

Over time I began learning about the races. I learned the difference between Rocky Raccoon 100 and Hardrock 100 (Hardrock is an extremely challenging course you must qualify for and Rocky Raccoon is suited for first-timers). I met and learned about the runners. I heard their stories.

As context began to form, I started to care. I actually wanted to know who had won Western States 100 and who had set which course record under what circumstances. The stats began to mean something.

Traditionally, men can achieve a sport connection from an early age through their male role models. Their fathers, grandfathers, uncles, or stepfathers have encouraged and fostered an interest and an understanding of sport. A young child doesn't love sport because of the stats. They learn to love the stats because of the male bonds that are formed around the games.

For women, this may not happen right away, or ever. Several women told me that they had difficulty connecting with elites but instead sought inspiration from "regular" men and women who played sport.

Sport spectatorship is still a man's world. However, that doesn't mean that women are not interested in consuming sports. We just need to build that context and connection.

One 2013 study in the *North American Journal of Psychology* studied sport fandom in women. It found that although sport news programs with statistics and game analysis weren't as appealing to women, sport documentaries were equally interesting to both genders. The documentaries focused on life stories beyond the sport stats themselves. In short, they provided context. The women studied were not relating to numbers; they were relating to stories.

That study was an epiphany for me. I realized that women need a better understanding of the stories, context and

spirit behind the competition. I realized that women like myself already involved in sports could do a better job of passing down a sense of community and love of sport, much like a father would at his boy's first baseball game.

4: Putting On The Big Girl Panties (Confidence)

"Move as fast as you do as long as it's your speed. Ask yourself these questions: Why am I whispering when I have something to say? Why am I adding a question mark at the end of all my sentences? Why am I apologizing every time I express my needs? Why am I hunching over? Starving myself when I love food? Pretending it doesn't mean that much to me? Hurting myself when I mean to scream? Why am I waiting, whining, pining, fitting in?"
– Eve Ensler

When you think about confidence, what images come to mind? Maybe you imagine star-studded celebrities or beefed up muscle guys.

Not me. I think about my cat.

Our resident RV cat first came to us when we still owned a house in San Diego. I found her huddled on our front porch during a rainstorm. She refused to come in, but politely ate all the food I could find for her.

She started showing up more often until she had our schedule down. After work, I would find her waiting on our front porch for dinner. We lured her inside, trained our dog to not eat her, then got her vet-approved and micro-chipped. When we were ready to hit the road, she made herself at home in the RV and the rest is history.

Everything my kitty does, she does with all her heart. Every time she falls, she is genuinely surprised she has failed at something. She always thinks she can and expects she will. That's confidence.

All cats are like this. Every kitty YouTube video, every stupid photo of a feline in a predicament all originated with a cat that believed that it could.

In life and sport, you actually *do* want to be a pussy.

I Could Go On

It can be hard for women to believe in themselves. Even when we do, it can be difficult to vocalize that confidence. A few times, I have lined up at an endurance run absolutely certain of myself. I know I'm going to do well. I've trained, I feel strong, and I've had a good night's sleep. However, if you ask me to predict my success at the start line, I'll downplay my abilities.

I'll say I "just want to finish" or "just want to enjoy the day." I'll tell you about how I'm not sure about my shoe choice, or my breakfast choice, or the weather that day. I will especially do this if I'm talking to a woman. It's our code.

I won't say to you that I feel like a badass and I'm going to rock it. Even now, as I write this, my instinct is to give an example about a time I showed a lack of confidence, not a time when I portrayed it. I want to show you that I'm no threat. I want you to like me.

In she-land, we weren't raised to "act like a man" or "grow a pair." We may have been coddled, protected, or just not enlightened as to our potential for athletic success. Unlike guys, we don't do pissing contests or compare vaginas to see who has the biggest. Being a woman is an entirely different experience with a whole different set of norms and rules. Although we can still be competitive and aggressive, we present those traits in different ways. Most women have a hard time talking about their own successes.

When I was researching this book, I posted a Facebook query asking my friends to name the women who inspired them. Hundreds of names were posted. The next day, a man shared my query on Facebook, except he worded it differently. Instead of asking people to call out their favorite women in endurance, he addressed female athletes directly by asking them to "stand up and be counted."

He got zero replies.

How did I know to phrase my request the way I did? It didn't occur to me to ask women to list their own accomplishments. I just knew they wouldn't, but the man who shared my query lives in a world where guys are falling over themselves to list their records and flash their medals.

To further hypothesize, what would I have thought if a woman *had* replied to that male query? Would I have reached out to her in admiration? Or would I have rolled my eyes and muttered under my breath, "Who does she think she is?" As much as I want to think that I would have received her well, I'm just not sure.

Confidence is an important topic for any athlete regardless of gender, but this chapter specifically tells the story of what it means to have confidence (or a lack thereof) as a female.

*

In the land of female endurance athletes, Jen Vogel is a

confidence pioneer. In an article on Ultra Chix Unite, Jen complains, "I absolutely hate when a female athlete says 'Oh, I just had a good day!' Good days don't happen without a ton of hard work. Don't be afraid to work hard, and when the hard work pays off, don't be afraid to admit that you worked hard and deserve it!"

But we are afraid—and according to Sheryl Sandberg's research, rightfully so. Sheryl is the Chief Operating Officer of Facebook as well as an activist and an author. Although Sheryl approaches this topic from a business angle, the similarities for sport are strikingly similar. Here's how Sheryl explains the handicap of a confident woman:

There's a famous Harvard Business School study on a woman named Heidi Roizen. And she's an operator in a company in Silicon Valley, and she uses her contacts to become a very successful venture capitalist. In 2002—not so long ago—a professor who was then at Columbia University took that case and made it Howard Roizen. And he gave the case out, both of them, to two groups of students. He changed exactly one word: "Heidi" to "Howard." But that one word made a really big difference.

He then surveyed the students, and the good news was that the students, both men and women, thought Heidi and Howard were equally competent, and that's good. The bad news was that everyone liked Howard. He's a great guy. You want to work for him. You want to spend the day fishing with him. But Heidi? Not so sure. She's a little out for herself. She's a little political. You're not sure you'd want to work for her.

This is the complication. We have to tell our daughters and our colleagues, we have to tell ourselves to believe we got the A, to reach for the promotion, to sit at the table, and we have to do it in a world where, for them, there are sacrifices they will make for that, even though for their brothers, there are not.

For the most part, the endurance community can agree that women are capable of holding their own in a co-ed field. But, do we *like* them? Do we feel like we would enjoy going on a run with them or going out for coffee, as much as we would with an Anton Krupicka or a Kilian Jornet? This is a question that hasn't been raised.

I have heard many successful male ultrarunners described as down-to-earth and approachable, but I have to rack my brain to remember a time a winning female runner was described the same way.

As a back-of-the-packer (or middle-packer on a good day), I'm used to seeing the male elite winners waiting at the finish line to cheer on the stragglers. Is it my imagination, or are the elite women missing from this scene? Do they seem to disappear a little sooner? Are they just slightly out of reach, just a little less approachable?

The University of Western Ontario conducted a study on exercise stereotypes during pregnancy. They concluded that:

> the excessive exerciser had the lowest ratings on interpersonal characteristics and attributes associated with personal satisfaction. Specifically, this target was

perceived to be the meanest, to have the fewest friends, to be the saddest, least self-confident, and least friendly. Taken together, these results indicate that our participants perceived the excessive exercise target to be more driven and determined, but at the same time personally unhappy and socially inept.

David Brooks, an op-ed columnist at *The New York Times*, wrote about a study in the journal *Emotion* by Jessica Tracy and Alex Beall. The study showed that men were rated as more attractive when they showed pride, whereas women were rated as less attractive when they displayed that same emotion. However, when women expressed shame, they were rated as attractive. "There is a reason men tend to be much more overconfident than women," reported Brooks. "Overconfidence (pride) wins mates. For women, it doesn't."

In her book *Lean In*, Sheryl Sandberg quotes author Ken Auletta's observations from a *New Yorker* article. He says that for women, "self-doubt becomes a form of self-defense. In order to protect ourselves from being disliked, we question our abilities and downplay our achievements, especially in the presence of others. We put ourselves down before others can."

But can we really say that women are less confident than men? A study in the *Journal of Sport Scientists* titled *The Role of Confidence in World Class Performance* suggests that female athletes may just be more honest and open in their self-reporting of anxiety and confidence. They don't feel pressured to present that hard exterior and they are more comfortable revealing emotions that may be perceived as weak or undesirable in men.

If that's the case, could a higher level of self-criticism actually be an undervalued talent? According to David Brooks, "There is no easy correlation between self-esteem and actual performance...Maybe the self-observation talents that lead to bad feelings because we are imperfect also lead to better decision-making and better behavior for those capable of being acutely aware of their imperfections."

In endurance, a dash of self-doubt may actually be a strong advantage. It's called "respecting the distance." Although men are more likely to enter a 100-mile foot-race in the United States, women boast a higher finisher rate. The women who do choose to start generally finish. Women don't register for an endurance race because of raging egos, on a dare, or out of reliance on their self-love. They respect the distance. They train for it. They pace themselves. They get it done.

Still, some women display a lack of confidence under the guise of humility. They don't want to come across as self-centered, so they highlight their faults. This is a misunderstanding of what humility means. "I can't" or "I'm not good enough" are not examples of humility. Neither are criticizing and belittling oneself.

Humility is defined as "a modest or low view of one's own importance," but I view it as a positive trait that is closely linked to vulnerability. After all, confident people don't need to brag or constantly seek praise for themselves. It's insecure people who do that, trying to convince others (and themselves) of their own importance. A confident person can

show humility because s/he is not defined by failure, success or the opinions of others. True humility (and confidence) can be seen in our willingness to expose a soft underbelly.

Confidence Meets Vulnerability

One of the most rarely seen underbellies in the world belongs to the wolverine. Researchers spend years—sometimes their entire careers—tracking wolverines, only to catch a far-away glimpse of these elusive animals—if they're lucky.

The wolverine is one of the least studied carnivores on the planet. It has a reputation for strength out of proportion to its size, with a documented ability to kill full-grown moose and towering grizzlies. That's like a small housecat taking down a deer.

Although wolverines are descendants of the weasel family, they more closely resemble bears with their small eyes, rounded ears and rounded head. And if you thought bears were tough, consider this: bears find a quiet place to hibernate for the winter while the wolverine seeks out the most rugged and wild land. They manage to travel at approximately four miles per hour, regardless of terrain, in obscenely cold temperatures. They fly over snow, ice, mountain ranges, and glaciers, patrolling territories of 500 square miles. They do all this while weighing about 30 pounds, stretching only three feet long, and hovering mere inches off the ground. Also known as the Demon of the North, wolverines have a ton of attitude, and they fear nothing.

Steve Kroschel has spent more than 25 years of his life

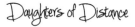

living with wolverines on his 60-acre property in the tiny town of Haines in southeast Alaska. Steve is the proud papa of two of the only tame wolverines in the world — Jasper and Banff — he raised as orphans.

I had the honor of meeting Steve in California while he was filming his most recent documentary, then visiting him in Alaska in 2012. I watched as Steve play-tussled with one of his wolverines, and then stretched the animal out to expose a soft and one-of-a-kind underbelly. The patterns on a wolverine's belly are as unique as human fingerprints. That powerful image — a ferocious animal surrendering his belly to Steve's touch — stayed with me for a long time.

In my chosen sport of ultrarunning, it is a compliment when someone says a woman is "tough as nails," but I decided in Alaska that I would rather be soft as a wolverine's belly. I want to know that I have the potential to bare my teeth and take down my grizzlies when necessary, yet most of the time I want to show my unique and vulnerable side. Not all acts of confidence need to be loud and aggressive. The best ones are quiet actions, barely noticeable choices in our daily lives.

I started this section with an anecdote about a situation where I lacked confidence. Let me tell you about a time when I displayed it.

Just a few miles shy of the 50K mark during the San Diego 100 Endurance Run, I had a moment. Normally on a race of this distance I start slowly, but ease into the mileage and get to a point where I feel I can trot on forever. I generally hit my groove around the time most people hit their first wall, around

30 miles. Sure enough, I had just passed Shacky and that's how my dilemma started. Here is the way I described it in my race report:

The next stretch was lovely and effortless. We ran into Sunrise 1 and I was surprised to find Shacky sitting in a chair looking rather miserable. He was holding a bottle with a powder mix. A wet powder blob was stuck in his beard. "I don't think I can do this," he told me.

"Sure you can!" I practically yelled. "Just grab your stuff and we'll walk the next section." It was seven miles to the 50K mark and we had plenty of time to make the cutoff, even if it was a slog.

It was getting warm, but I figured it was just my lack of heat training (I later learned it had actually hit more than 120F in some sections). David Lopez helped me soak my head in ice water, we posed for another picture with my friend Colleen, and then we were off.

I tried to keep up with Colleen, but she was faster than Shacky so I decided to lag behind a bit. I walked a lot and kept looking behind me to see if Shacky was following. At first he was…until he wasn't. I walked slower…no Shacky. I stopped for a few minutes and let people pass me. Two gentlemen I had been leapfrogging slipped by, then a few minutes later my friends Corina and Jeff. Still no Shacky.

I knew I still had time to make the cutoff…should I go back for him? I started taking a few steps back, and immediately stopped. What was I doing?? I'm going backwards? Never go backwards. I lingered for another minute or so, and still no sign of Shacky.

"What should I do?" I wondered.

I'm sure this sounds like a stupid dilemma, but for me it was a big deal. Everything in my couple-nature wanted to go back for my dude, but every part of the runner in me thought that was absolutely ridiculous. I had already lost time. Whose race was I running, anyway? *My* race. I wasn't a pacer. I knew that Shacky would hate for me to wait for him, but that didn't matter. I felt— somehow — that it was my job to go back.

My internal dilemma only lasted for a few seconds, but it felt like an eternity. My mind wandered to the last song I played on my ukulele: Jesse Ruben's *We Can*.

Do not hesitate when people bring you down
Do not settle, Do not wait
Do not ever turn around
You're almost there…
I swear, I swear it's yours

I started running and didn't stop until I got to Pioneer Mail 1, the 50K mark. It was now 94F.

At Pioneer Mail, I soaked my head and stuck a bandage on a hot spot on my foot. I was feeling strong and got out of there in under two minutes. It was four miles to Penny Pines 1, and I ran it in. I was well ahead of cut-offs.

There won't always be a parade for us when we choose to display confidence. Often, we'll be alone on a trail in the middle of the woods with no one around to applaud. Our confidence lies not at the finish line, but in the middle of the hardest, longest, darkest, steepest stretch when we whisper to ourselves: "I could go on."

Miles in the Mirror

It's no secret that so many of our insecurities as women stem from our self-perceived physical imperfections, real or imagined. We don't see ourselves the way the world does. We note every stray hair and take stock of every spot. We imagine other people notice too.

These insecurities are magnified to some extent when we rely on our bodies for performance in sport. Our bodies are no longer just vessels but also tools. They don't just have to look good, but also perform well.

For the past few years I have watched with interest the growing number of body acceptance movements and their accompanying critics. There are the Dove campaigns, fat acceptance movements and body love efforts. You only need to Google a few key words to find a wide variety of both supporters and critics centered on these campaigns. It would take too long for me to summarize each of these movements, but I did want to mention two tips I found valuable as a female endurance athlete:

1. Getting in the Picture

I learned about this movement through Allison Tate. Allison is a writer and a mother of four who realized that although she took tons of photos of her kids, she didn't have many photos of herself with her kids. She would avoid the

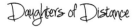

camera because of her baby weight or disheveled appearance. She realized her children were growing up without any photos of her. She writes:

> Our sons need to see how young and beautiful and human their mamas were. Our daughters need to see us vulnerable and open and just being ourselves — women, mamas, people living lives. Avoiding the camera because we don't like to see our own pictures? How can that be okay?...I am not perfect to look at and I am not perfect to love, but I am perfectly their mother.
>
> When I look at pictures of my own mother, I don't look at cellulite or hair debacles. I just see her — her kind eyes, her open-mouthed, joyful smile, her familiar clothes. That's the mother I remember. My mother's body is the vessel that carries all the memories of my childhood. I always loved that her stomach was soft, her skin freckled, her fingers long. I didn't care that she didn't look like a model. She was my mama.

Although I don't carry extra baby weight to shame me away from a camera, I do still shy away from running photos. I'll take scenery shots all day long or shoot my friends running, but I have fewer photos of myself in action. How do I look after 20 miles on a dusty trail? Am I skinny enough? Do I look sweaty and shiny? Do I look gross?

Kristin Armstrong makes another good argument for getting in the picture in her book *Mile Markers*. She writes:

> Have you ever noticed the way people, particularly women, look back at old photographs of themselves and

are wistful? "Oh, I looked so young then!" "Look at my skin!" (Sigh.) "Good grief, I was so skinny! And here I thought I was heavy at the time!" "Awww, look at us — just gorgeous. We had no clue." No one ever really mentions that just as we had no clue at the time, there might exist the possibility that we have no clue right now. Captured moments of today are the wistful memories of tomorrow. I guarantee that just as we can look back at a photo from 10 years ago and appreciate ourselves, 10 years from now we will look at a photo from today and think the same damn thing. How come nobody brings this up? Wouldn't this awareness bring us a certain measure of peace? Can you imagine the liberation if we could just appreciate ourselves right now? Who we are, where we are, what we look like? If we could just look in the mirror long enough for a basic once-over and a smile-wink and be done with it? If we were too content and confident to critique?

Ironically, some of my favorite photos are the ones of me in nature. I look happy and comfortable. I never look as bad as I imagined. Then months later I look back on those photos of me on a rock, or me at a waterfall and I feel the powerful surge of those memories coming back to me. That surge doesn't happen with landscape photos. It's not the scenery that triggers pleasure; it's me interacting with nature. I vow to spend more time getting in the picture.

2. Don't Save Your Clothes

The second point comes from Golda Poretsky, a fat-

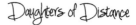

positive body-love coach. Although I am not her target audience, I can relate to her message of body positivity. The majority of us don't present as overweight, but that doesn't mean we don't share many of the same deeply ingrained body acceptance issues. I felt like Golda was speaking to me when she gave this tip.

Golda encourages women to wear what they look and feel best in, as opposed to saving clothes for special occasions. Guilty as charged. I tend to save most of my "best" running clothes for race day, or group run days. When I'm off in the mountains by myself, I tend to pick "lesser" clothes so I don't get my good stuff dirty.

Sometimes this means that I'm uncomfortable on my solo weekly runs in ill-fitting or unflattering clothes. Often, I'll go through several laundry cycles and my "good" clothes are never touched. I saved them for a day that never came. A better goal would be to look and feel my best every day, not just on race day.

Facing the She-Blerch

Every woman is born with a She-Blerch. If you've seen Matthew Ingman/The Oatmeal's comic about The Blerch, you already have an idea of what this is. Matthew drew his Blerch in a comic called The Terrible and Wonderful Reasons Why I Run Long Distances. He confesses that he doesn't believe in "The Wall," that invisible point in a run when your body decides to start shutting down on you. Instead, he believes in The Blerch.

As Matthew tells it:

The Blerch is fat little cherub who follows me when I run. He is a wretched, lazy beast. He tells me to slow down, to walk, to quit. "Blerch" is the sound food makes when it is squeezed from a tube. "Blerch" is the shape of a tummy after a huge meal. If I am sedentary at a time when I have zero excuses for being sedentary, I call this "blerching." The Blerch represents all forms of gluttony, apathy, and indifference that plague my life.

The She-Blerch is sort of the same thing, except she is specially honed into any imperfections. She's like a computer for remembering every unflattering comment anyone has ever made about you, and she keeps those insecurities at the forefront of your mind. She doesn't stop after you're done training. She is with you all day, every day, in season and off-season, whispering and snarling into your poor exhausted ear.

Like a broken record, the She-Blerch replays past experiences that made you feel small. These are usually comments or observations that people made about you, ill-intentioned or not. Usually they are insignificant to anyone besides you and embarrassingly mundane, but the She-Blerch has made them a big deal in your head. They are message you have internalized.

Endurance runner Kathy Vaughn shared her own She-Blerch story with me. Her Blerch-voice spoke the words of her younger brother telling her she was fat back in her teen years. His words were hurtful and hard to let go. Although many years have passed, she still struggles with the weight of his words. "I was never that fat," admits Kathy, "but sometimes on the trail, that concept of me still sneaks through. When I'm having a low point and I feel slow or sluggish, I imagine that I look like a lumbering, obese walrus. I have to tell myself: I am not that girl anymore. I am a new woman. And I think that's how we all need to see ourselves — not as those girls who were called fat, or who didn't quite fit in, or who were hopelessly uncoordinated. We are new women now. We have emerged from our cocoons and we are goddesses."

The old version of Kathy was too shy to even be seen at her husband's ultramarathon events. "I would stay at our car and make his finishing food or hike off on my own, not anywhere near the trail the ultrarunners would be using," she remembers. "I felt like I would stand out as having terrible form, being unfit and not a real runner."

My She-Blerch story also stems from physical insecurities in my late teens and early 20s. For me, it was church girls smugly condescending my choice of clothes and lack of makeup. At one sleepover, they took the opportunity to smother my face in thick, clownish makeup under the ruse of a game and then sat back to laugh at me. When I started dating, they expressed their shock and amazement that anyone could find me attractive. For years, I felt that I was not pretty enough to be successful in anything physical, including sports. Instead, I immersed myself in books and writing. I'd fight back by making them feel intellectually deficient while they kept swinging at me with the ugly bat.

It was through running that I was finally able to rebuild confidence in my physical abilities: every mountain I tackled was a stepping stone reminding me that I was just as strong

111

physically as I was mentally.

Put a Bib on It

Years ago Molly Barker was walking home from work in a skirt when she passed a group of men suited up in business attire. She immediately stepped off the sidewalk and let them pass, then continued on her way. Later on that same day, she passed the same group of men, but this time she was dressed in running gear, dashing down the pavement on a training run. It didn't occur to her to step off the path this time. She ran right through them, head held high and feeling powerful.

Molly Barker went on to found Girls on the Run, an organization that seeks to empower young women through running. She instructs girls on the importance of self-esteem and teaches them to be confident in all their abilities.

The majority of the women I spoke to for this book regarded endurance sports as something that boosted their self-esteem. They reported feeling stronger and more confident after training and competing.

In her book *Running to Extremes*, Lisa Tamati writes:

> The power of running to change people's lives, to put people's lives back together and to help rebuild their self-esteem is another reason I do it. You go through hardships in running but that makes you tougher and shows you what is important in life. It takes you back to basics. You can't be an ultramarathon runner and really arrogant because you're dealing with Mother Nature, and Mother Nature will always give you a hiding. She will also show you your strengths and your vulnerabilities,

your extraordinary abilities and your inherent human weaknesses.

Long-distance swimmer Sally Friedman echoes this sentiment in her book, *Swimming the Channel*. "When we have done something beyond the realm of normal middle-class life, something out of the ordinary, the unexpected, it becomes '[a] secret source of confidence, a private wellspring of originality.'"

In an interview, ultramarathoner Carly Koerner told me: "(Running has) no doubt improved my confidence. Knowing that I can run 100 miles makes me tough. It reminds me that I can do something bigger than myself, by myself. It has also given me the experience of conquering my seemingly insurmountable goals because I believed in myself."

A study by Alison L. Boudreau and Barbro Giorgi of Saybrook University on *The Experience of Self-Discovery and Mental Change in Female Novice Athletes in Connection to Marathon Running* found that women who trained for marathons "underwent a mental change that improved their self-confidence and enhanced relationships with their selves and others." The six factors that emerged were:

- Participants Perception of an Enhancing Outdoor Environment
- Life-Style Changes Resulting in More Openness to Others and Self
- Discoveries Concerning Self-Improvements
- Sustaining a Desired Mental Disposition
- Empowerment in Considering New Possibilities

- Support for Encountering Future Challenges

Imagine how these changes might also affect your family, career and community. Or perhaps you don't need to imagine—you already know. Interestingly, there is little data on the female athlete. The majority of studies tend to focus on male elites, college teams or children: a disturbingly unfortunate oversight.

Other women—a smaller group—confessed to me that endurance did nothing for their self-esteem. In fact, they believed it diminished their confidence.

Remember Neva "Chipmunk" Warren, the youngest female finisher to thru-hike the Appalachian Trail? Many people expected her to be brimming with confidence after completing such a significant feat. They imagined that she would feel empowered and capable of anything, but in fact the opposite was true.

"My hike actually caused my confidence to dip quite a bit," she confessed. "I felt worthless when I wasn't doing a huge adventure. I knew every day wasn't going to be another battle up a mountain with a great view at the top, but I still wasn't quite able to get accustomed to the lifestyle change after my hike. As far as self-esteem goes, that dipped after my hike, too. I immediately felt unhealthy; the cravings for large amounts of junk food remained, but my exercise levels decreased to nearly none. As soon as I completed my journey, I became exponentially more aware of what food I was eating, what I looked like, etc. I didn't feel like I looked good, and I didn't feel good, either. I'm just now starting to get back to eating healthier and exercising regularly, and it's a very hard battle."

One woman didn't fall into either camp. In her book *Arctic Glass*, Jill Homer writes:

> Most of the time, when I am embarking on an adventure that I think of as challenging or even epic, I think I will come back a changed person, or at least different somehow. I always return understanding that I will not change, and I won't be different, but I will have a better realization of who I am.

Although I do feel as though endurance running has improved my confidence, most of the time I feel like Jill. I'm not much different—no more insightful, no more athletic. I'm just me.

The lesson I take away from this is that we are already amazing just the way we are. We don't need the races, the medals, the buckles, the personal records to make us strong, valuable or loved.

Chicking Out and Womaning Up

In my mind, one of the greatest wrongs we can commit against ourselves as females in endurance happens when we "chick out" (a term so new I had to define it on urbandictionary.com). Chicking out is the same thing as chickening out, except this phrase is used when a woman chickens out for woman-reasons. (For all your word nerds, the male equivalent would be "dick out.")

All women have chicked out. Many of us do it regularly. Every time we put away what we *really* want to wear because we don't want to be judged, every time we hold back a comment because we don't want to embarrass a man by sounding smarter than him, every time we avert eye contact because we don't want to appear too aggressive, and every time we drop to an easier race option because we are women — we are chicking out.

This plays a role in our racing and our training as well. It becomes a habit that plants seeds of self-doubt into our performances. It's important to examine the ways we tend to chick out in endurance and how we can woman-up instead:

1. Failing to intend or expect

I recently read a book that transformed the way I train and think about sport. *Elite Minds: Creating the Competitive Advantage* by Stan Beecham is full of mental tips and tricks that top athletes use to gain confidence and to compete.

Stan points out that although many athletes show up to race, few (usually just one) show up intending to and expecting to win. If you're not that athlete, you've already handicapped yourself.

That's not to say you *will* win every time you race, but training to win can make the impossible possible. Stan believes that our goals should have a 60 percent chance of success and a 40 percent chance of failure. Go big or go home.

When Stan writes about winning, he isn't talking about medals, or podium finishes. He writes:

The winning I'm talking about is not about scoreboards, trophies or championships. It's what happens to a person once he or she has the desire to win, the intention to win, the expectation to win. What I am most interested in is helping people perform at their highest level possible — their full potential. The fact of the matter is that people who have a strong desire to win, to be the best at what they do, are more likely to reach their full potential than someone who says, "I don't care if I win or lose, I just want to get better."

Stan suggests starting a daily journal and giving yourself a "W" or an "L" for each day. W is assigned to days where you did your best. Ls are for the days you didn't. You want to avoid two consecutive Ls and aim for six or fewer Ls in a month. It's okay to have a bad day, but you want to learn to recover quickly.

Stan also believes that confidence is a thought, not an emotion. He writes:

> In order to help individuals and improve their confidence, you have to work at the conscious level and address it as a thought. As long as individuals with low confidence view it as a feeling, they will never be able to change their condition. But once individuals with low confidence understand that they have negative and false beliefs about themselves and their abilities, you can begin to help them create a new belief system and a higher self-confidence.

The concepts in Stan's book are much more hardcore than what I'm used to in the run-for-fun mindset that many pack-of-the-packers in the ultrarunning community embrace. For example, Stan doesn't believe in Plan Bs for race day. He says

that anyone with a Plan B is not totally committed to Plan A and they are already planning to fail. Whether or not you're ready to compete at that level, it's still important to remember that confidence is not always being bold and fearless. Often, it involves feeling afraid and insecure, but choosing to go for it anyway. "Fear is your opponent," writes Stan. "No one is better or faster than you—only less afraid."

2. Forgetting to cheer

In Sheryl Sandberg's TED Talk, she tells a story about taking an exam in her senior year of college for a European Intellectual History course. She took it with her brother and her roommate, Carrie. As Sheryl tells it: "Carrie reads all the books in the original Greek and Latin, goes to all the lectures. I read all the books in English and go to most of the lectures. My brother is kind of busy. He reads one book of 12 and goes to a couple of lectures, marches himself up to our room a couple days before the exam to get himself tutored."

At the end of the exam, they all walk out and look at each other. Carrie says, "Boy, I feel like I didn't really draw out the main point on the Hegelian dialectic." Sheryl says, "God, I really wish I had connected John Locke's theory of property with the philosophers who follow." Sheryl's brother looks at them both and says, "I got the top grade in the class."

Regardless of the quality of our actual performances, women generally forget to cheer for themselves. We don't typically ring our own cowbells. Sometimes there are other people around who will do that for us, but not always.

My friend Caity McCardell was the host of a great podcast called Run Barefoot Girl. She worked hard to encourage women to send her stories for a section of the podcast called "Yay Me!" Women would write to her when they had accomplished something, no matter how mundane it seemed, and she would celebrate it on the show. A first marathon, a first barefoot mile, a recovery from an injury: any physical progress was fair game as a Yay Me.

I believe this is how women begin to cheer for themselves: by recognizing, appreciating and praising their small steps. For someone else, those steps might not be so small; for others, they might be miniscule. That doesn't matter. What matters is that we become our own #1 fans. My hope is that we will all be able to echo the sentiment of George Sheehan when he said, "I have met my hero and he is me."

3. Speaking negatively of ourselves

My mom passed away when I was nine years old, so I deeply treasure every single memory I have of her. Unfortunately, one of those memories includes her asking me regularly and obsessively if she was fat.

"Do I look fat to you?" she would squeak as she stood in front of me and pinched at her body.

"No, mama," I would reply. I wasn't just trying to be nice. I really didn't think she was fat. My mom was about 25 years old at the time. She had me when she was 18. She had been a slender teen and I thought she was gorgeous at 25. She had curvy Latin American features and a big beautiful smile. Even if she had had none of those things, she was my mama. I loved her. Of course she was beautiful and not at all fat.

"Are you sure?" my mom would drill me. "You can be honest."

"You're not fat, mama!" I insisted. "Where are you fat? You're not fat at all."

I knew I had convinced her when I saw her smile, and that was that...until the next time she felt insecure about her weight.

I didn't spend much free time thinking about my mom's random interrogations, yet today it's one of my most vivid memories of her. I wish that weren't true. I understand now that the reason those memories stuck in my mind was because that was the first time I understood that there was supposed to be something wrong with my mini-female body. Before that, I had never thought about fat or skinny as good or bad. I wanted to be just like my mama. Would I be fat someday too? Would I have to ask my own daughter to tell me the truth?

It's no secret that women tend to speak out negatively about their bodies in the presence of their friends and families. Too often, we bond with other women by sharing all the details we hate about our own bodies and expressing envy at the physical traits in others. I believe that one of the biggest mistakes a mother can make is to criticize her body in front of her daughters.

Endurance athlete Kristin Armstrong notes the following in her book *Mile Markers*:

> Did you know that studies have shown that the best way to foster positive body image in girls is for their mothers to speak kindly and positively about their own bodies in their company? When I pull on a swimsuit or check out my rearview in a pair of jeans in earshot of my daughters, I make a point to say, "Right on, girl," and

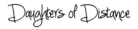

wink at myself in the mirror. After all, if I don't think my own aging booty is cute, how on earth will my girls ever appreciate their own?

It took Kristin a long time to count herself as an athlete. She married famed cyclist Lance Armstrong in 1998 and between her three kids and Lance's rising career, she never saw herself as an athlete. She was the crew, the support, the caring wife and the attentive mother. After her divorce in 2008, she was shattered, but somehow managed to come out of it with a newfound confidence. She had survived the divorce, so she could survive a marathon. "The marathon helped show me that there would be an end to my sadness, just like there is an end to a marathon," she writes. She was no longer an athlete's wife. She *was* an athlete.

Fighting the habit of criticizing ourselves starts with paying attention, stopping ourselves when we realize we're engaging in negative self-talk and replacing those words with positive reinforcements. At first it may feel fake or self-centered, but our perspective will change. Slowly, we'll start to genuinely love and appreciate all our physical details—even the quirky ones.

I find that experimenting with meditation also helps. Meditation is all about controlling your negativity and focusing your mind instead of being carried away by random, runaway thoughts. It takes a lot of practice, but over time, meditation can help condition the mind for goodness and gratitude.

4. Giving the She-Blerch a vote

121

Remember the She-Blerch, that ever-present seed of doubt and shame in our heads? The first time I remember her popping into my life was during my early teens. I was in the car driving to church with my family and I was singing pretty loudly in the backseat. There was no particular reason—I just liked to sing. I wasn't paying much attention to anyone else around me. I was blissfully in my own head.

My thoughts were suddenly jarred by my dad's voice informing me in an annoyed tone that I wasn't much of a singer and I wasn't hitting the right notes. I don't remember his exact words, but the implication was that I shouldn't sing, probably not ever.

I don't believe he intended to hurt my feelings. He probably just wanted some peace and quiet, but I distinctly remember a sudden awareness that other people might be watching me, listening to me and judging me at any given moment. I stopped behaving as if no one's opinion mattered and I started feeling self-conscious. It would be a long time before I would ever sing again. I gave the She-Blerch a vote and she's been with me ever since.

Outrunning the She-Blerch is no easy feat. She is so much a part of us that it can feel like we're killing a part of ourselves. When Krista Cavender set out to run her first 100-mile race, she posted the following words on her blog:

> I've been in the process of killing a part of myself. It's a weird transformation since I'm literally visualizing myself lying on the ground in a violent heap of suffering—on the edge of death or unconsciousness. But the me that's on the ground is a fucking pussy and she

bleeds self-doubt, fear, and negativity. She tries to control me. I want to show her that I won't tolerate her shit-talking anymore. I won't let her build nests of worry in my head anymore. She will not control me. She will no longer tell me what I can and can't do.

Although your style may be less violent than Krista's, visualization still helps. If you imagine the She-Blerch as a thing outside of yourself, a part of you that you don't need, you can start chipping away at her power. Imagine yourself ignoring those judgments and refusing to internalize those negative messages. Imagine yourself crossing that finish line, exhausted but victorious. Imagine a better version of you.

Value Beyond Endurance

When our training is going well, we feel powerful both in body and in mind. It's a high that can carry us through a stressful day and keep us smiling through every obstacle. We learn to believe in ourselves. However, when our training is not progressing as planned, we tend to form negative opinions about ourselves that are not accurate.

Some of us have only run one or two endurance events and don't feel we can call ourselves Daughters of Distance. Maybe we have young kids at home, a few extra pounds on our thighs or an unsupportive spouse. Maybe we can't always train regularly and a sponsorship is not in the cards for us.

That's okay. We are mothers. We are teachers. We are lovers. To many people, we are everything in the whole world. If we did nothing else for the rest of our lives — we would be enough. It's so easy to forget that when we're laid up with an injury or when we miss a workout.

In the first chapter of this book we met Jennifer Benna, the 100-mile champion in waterproof mascara. She told me: "If I never run another step, I will always be able to dig deep and find the confidence running has given me."

It's easy to forget that movement—even slow and pathetic movement—is its own reward. In her book *Honey, Do You Need a Ride? Confessions of a Fat Runner*, Jennifer Graham writes:

> I did not, however, win a race. Didn't even come close. Let's be honest: I never will. But I won something else. Something resembling joy. No, I don't need a ride. I'll never need a ride anywhere again. Abandoning misery and modesty at the same time, I strip off my shirt, bow to the rapturous sun, and dance into another dimension.

Love your movement and love the body that enables you to move. Allow your movements to infuse you with a newfound confidence. Say what you're really thinking and do what you would if nobody were watching. If you feel insecure or embarrassed, fake it 'til you make it. Act like the woman you want to become and watch yourself transform.

Not all of us will get to experience mile 128 at Badwater, but we can all draw confidence from movement. We have all clenched our teeth, pushed through pain and finished. We have learned to conquer instead of cower. Those steps weren't easy. If there were, it wouldn't be endurance.

Marathon runner Kristin Armstrong has a few additional

suggestions. She writes:

Savor yourself. Cut yourself some slack. Appreciate your beauty. Wink at yourself in the mirror. Tell your husband he has nice buns. Tell your wife she's hotter than she was yesterday. Tell your children how you see them. Tell your parents thank you. Remind your friends who they are. After all, 10 years from now, right now will be 10 years ago. Moments are like fireflies. You are a runner, so go chase them. Cup them carefully in your hands and watch the glow seep through your fingers. Don't miss it.

Vanessa Runs

5: That's What (S)He Said (Relationships)

"What good did it do for a man to know that it was only when she was with the mountain that she never had to fake it? And what good did it do for a woman to dwell on how a mountain seemed to be the only thing that was never going to let her down?"

– Andrea Lankford, *Ranger Confidential: Living, Working, and Dying in the National Parks*

It's 4:30 a.m. at the South Kaibab Trailhead of the Grand Canyon and I'm digging through all the clothing in our Rialta RV, looking frantically for extra gloves. A group of about 10 of our friends are descending into the darkness of the Canyon for various distances, ranging from Rim to Rims (South Kaibab to Phantom Ranch and back), up to the imposing bucket-list exploit of the self-supported Rim-to-Rim-to-Rim (South Rim to North Rim, then back), a distance just shy of 50 miles and over 11,000 feet of total elevation gain.

My friends are fidgeting to stay warm and three of them need gloves. I find some extra pairs and distribute them. Knowing the heat and delirium and exhaustion they will face in the next several hours, I don't expect to get them back.

I hand Luis Escobar one pair, and in return he reminds us to tell his wife Beverly that she *must* bring his truck to the Bright Angel Trailhead where they will be finishing.

Back at camp, we prepare for a day of hiking with Luis' better half, the lovely Beverly. We tell her about the truck, but she already knows. Waiting for Luis to finish running is a chore she is all too familiar with.

Before sundown, Beverly drives to the trailhead as instructed, hoping for a best-case-scenario finish time. She waits there several hours until all the battered runners finally crawl out of the Big Hole — delayed and depleted, but alive.

Yes, Beverly knows how to wait, as do countless other endurance runners' wives.

Relationship dynamics in endurance sports is a fascinating topic. I've always been curious about the complexities of the male-female or female-female dynamic, probably because my own past relationships have been mostly disappointing and defined by running.

Relationships are impossible to generalize. Each one is complicated in its own unique way. Sometimes women are doing the running and sometimes they're doing the waiting. Either way, it's hard to describe these challenges as common or normal.

When Only One Partner Runs

I was dating Danny when I first took up running. We had known each other since we were teenagers, and were comfortable together. We started dating under tense circumstances, each of us having recently left our marriages to be together. Leaving my then-husband for Danny was hard on me. It wasn't the divorce itself, but the backlash from our families and religious social circles that wore on us.

In those days, I needed him. I was emotional, hurting and could barely stand on my own two feet. I had limited real world experience and I depended on him. We got along wonderfully.

Then I found running and I became stronger. I started to do things for myself and embraced a new-to-me sense of autonomy. At first Danny was supportive, but as the months wore on I started picking up a disapproving vibe from him and I wasn't sure what had changed.

One seasoned ultrarunning female I spoke with asked to remain anonymous when she told me: "Nowadays men respect a woman who is competitive and has prowess, and can beat the pants off of them, unless they are in a relationship with that woman. Then they've got to find at least one way to become that woman's protector."

Her comments reminded me of Sheryl Sandberg's *Lean In* where she writes:

> ...men's success is viewed not just in absolute terms, but often in comparison to their wives'. The image of a happy couple still includes a husband who is more professionally successful than the wife. If the reverse occurs, it's perceived as threatening to the marriage. People frequently pull me aside to ask sympathetically, "How is Dave? Is he okay with, you know, all your [whispering] success?"

It occurred to me that perhaps my issues with Danny weren't running-related at all. Maybe our disintegration had nothing to do with the fact that I wanted to train for ultras. Rather, I had stopped needing him.

I presented this idea to Kimberly Miller, ultrarunner and wife of Arizona ultrarunner Michael Miller. Her perspective was different. Kimberly happily agreed with the anonymous quote and insisted it wasn't a bad thing.

"I know that he feels like it is his job to protect me," she says. "He goes from being a mellow guy to a mean old man if he feels as if anyone is wronging me...Once on a trail about 20 miles into a run a mountain biker came too close to me without even a warning. Michael chased his ass down. The guy was waiting to give me an apology by the time I caught up with them. A different time he chased a motorcycle for the same reason. That's my man."

On the other side of the coin, women like writer and columnist Lauren Bravo argue that Michael Miller's chivalrous actions actually inhibit the advancement of women. In her *Huffington Post* article *Chivalry is Dead*, she describes chivalrous acts of kindness as "consolation prizes for inequality," representative of an attitude that "smacks of outdated ideals."

Running blogger Rebecca Schaeffer came up with a list of tips to follow in a relationship with a non-runner. Her insights on trailandultrarunning.com are simple, yet so easy to forget in a one-track pursuit of better, faster, stronger and longer events. Her suggestions include:

- Discuss races with your partner *before* you sign up for them;
- Reschedule your training plan if need be;
- Pick a few key races a year;
- Race locally;
- Know they may not ever fully "get it."

The best advice out there? Have plenty of sex with your significant other. In the book *Run Like a Mother: How to Get Moving – and Not Lose Your Family, Job, or Sanity*, one running coach advised a woman training for a marathon to take an iron supplement, relax her arms and have regular sex with her husband. Her client followed these orders, even when feeling drained or disinterested. She found that having sex on Friday night would make her hubby more agreeable to kid-duty just in time for her weekend long run. It was the perfect cross-training.

Kristi is a non-runner who blogs about the art of living with an ultrarunner at ultraspouse.wordpress.com. She assures non-runners that they are not crazy or bad partners, and encourages them to speak up about their needs. Here are some points she feels all one-runner-only couples need to discuss:

- What is reasonable in terms of how much of our money we spend on one person's passion?
- I want us to spend more time together and feel like we don't because training takes up so much time.
- How much of our vacation time should be spent on one person's passion, and how much of it should be spent on things we both enjoy?
- I feel insecure around your fit, awesome running friends.
- I wish I could bond with you on an athletic level and I feel left out.

When important issues get ignored or overlooked, that's when things start to get nasty. For freelance writer Stephanie

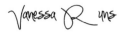

Catudal, they got pretty shaky. On 100milesisnotthatfar.com, Stephanie writes candidly about the struggles of being married to an endurance athlete:

> I fantasized about burning his running shoes. I created elaborate scenarios where his Speedo and goggles would mysteriously fall into the Hawaiian ocean, never to be found again. I dreamed that his bike was stolen from its sacred perch in our already-cramped living room (because we all know that bikes don't live outside.) I thought about all the ways the sport was sabotaging our relationship…

Her feelings had shifted from admiration to resentment. In turn, her husband resented her for not acknowledging his contribution to the family. For Stephanie, a change of perspective and communication helped preserve her mental health and her marriage. She forced herself to look at their issues objectively instead of blaming all their problems on a sport.

The practical changes were that Stephanie became more involved in her husband's athletic pursuits by making training a family event. Her husband made changes too, becoming more flexible with his training schedule, thus setting apart time for Stephanie to pursue her own dreams. "Most importantly, we both began expressing sincere appreciation for each other's sacrifices…Overall, we began to see each other's fears, needs, passions and pursuits as equally valid and important."

Relationships, after all, are feats of endurance.

Stop Holding Me Back

In the heat of the day, Kathy Vaughan has found a piece of shade that is barely bigger than the width and length of her body, created by an old board leaning up against a fence on the Arizona Trail. She lays out her sleeping bag among the thorns, dried-up cow pies and debris, then sits down for much-need rest. In this southern part of the Arizona Trail, shade is a luxury and so are water sources. The land is hot, barren and unforgiving.

Around the corner, Kathy's husband Ras is filling up their water filter bag from a cattle tank and corral. The lower tank is rusty and filled with algae, so Ras is gathering from a fresher, larger one. Kathy feels chills and then deep relaxation. She is so, so grateful for the shade, the water, the rest and the company of her dear Ras.

In the spring of 2014, Altra Ambassador Kathy Vaughan became the first woman to thru-hike (supported) the Arizona Trail, traversing a whopping distance of 800-plus miles in 35 days, five hours, and two minutes alongside her husband Ras "Ultrapedestrian" Vaughan.

The craziest part is that Kathy is no more spectacular, superhuman or athletic than you or me. However, she does have a supportive partner.

Kathy first met her husband in March of 1995 in Anacortes, Washington. Ras was working as a truck driver for Schwan's Frozen Food while Kathy was running a home daycare. When Ras knocked on her door to sell her some frozen food, Kathy was enamored. She ordered stir-fry veggies just so he would come back. His frozen peas had melted her heart.

These days, wherever you take Kathy, you also have to take Ras. It's impossible to overlook his admiration for her. He calls her his Empress and credits her for many of his own awe-inspiring feats, such as his sextuple crossing of the Grand Canyon: three back-to-back Rim-to-Rim-to-Rims, no stopping, no sleeping, and self-supported (except for Kathy's unfaltering moral support, of course).

If you saw her on the street, Kathy would appear unassuming and quiet. If you saw her on the trail, she would be moving happily and efficiently — feeling right at home. She is average in height and weight, but with long, wavy and earthy blonde hair with a preference for pigtail braids. The first thing you notice about Kathy is her arresting smile: a no-holds-barred, cover-my-whole-face, bursting-at-the-seams type of smile. She is a mountain mama, beautiful in every way.

Kathy believes that the difference between a successful endurance athlete and one who just quietly fades away is often a supportive partner — and that goes for both genders.

She speaks about a friend of hers who ran a 50K, felt empowered and signed up for her second ultra. When race day came, she dropped down her distance because she didn't believe that she could finish another 50K. Her husband had been critical of her training, berating her for not pushing herself to exhaustion, scolding her for not running hills and crushing her self-esteem at every turn.

"Women can accomplish great things, but often times we come from an initial sense of insecurity," writes Kathy. "If we have a partner or other support and encouragement, we can push beyond limitations that present themselves. We can be strong and powerful. Without this, the struggle becomes greater."

Kathy considers herself blessed. Her hubby is the first in line to believe in her. He convinced her that she was capable of backpacking for hours on back-to-back days and insisted she could run ultras.

Others are less supported, with partners who don't "allow" them to race longer distances.

When running coach Corrine Wallace first took up running, her husband told her she could try to run a half-marathon but never a full. She ran the full anyway. Although her husband forbade her from running anything longer after that, she took up ultrarunning. Corrine believes her gender is brimming with strong, courageous and loving individuals. She loves being a woman. She also loves that she can do things that some men don't think women should be doing.

In 2012 Jennifer Dicus became one of four women to ever complete the Tahoe Super Triple: a marathon on Friday, a marathon on Saturday and a 72.2 mile ultra on Sunday all the way around Lake Tahoe—124.6 miles in three days.

When I asked Jennifer what her pet peeve was, it was not chafing or poor aid stations. What she hates is fighting with her husband about running. "It annoys me when he does not support me or show up to the finish line of races that are run closer to home with my boys," she writes. Race entry fees have also become an issue.

One of the best ways to show an endurance mother your

support is to bring her children to cheer for her on race day. Although they didn't always demand this detail from their partners, several women did express hidden hurts and secret regrets that their children were not at the finish line.

Sometimes a lack of support can be a deal-breaker. Fitness coach and ultrarunner Holly Miller broke up with a man because he hated her running. She struggled to find a time to run that didn't conflict with his plans. "I knew he would never be okay with me running with other men — so the option of a male pacer was always out," Holly recalls "I tried to run when he was working but that left me with no time for long runs and my training suffered which stressed me out. It just finally got to the point where something had to give."

Some women compromise their running aspirations to accommodate partners while others rise defiantly to new challenges. Our sports are so extreme that when a woman does scale back her training, it's difficult to judge her. Regardless of our level of commitment, it helps to have strong examples of women who could — and did.

Jealousy

A few months ago I woke up to the following status update from Catra Corbett at the top of my newsfeed:

Ladies: For the record, I don't want your boyfriend or your husband. Yes I'm single but would never date or like someone in a relationship. In the past month a few guys I'm friends with were basically banned by their partner from being friends with me. Ladies, be secure with who you are. I would never act inappropriately with a guy who is in a relationship. I don't cross those lines.

Catra is a talented and smoking-hot ultrarunner who rocks an incredible endurance body. My first thought was, "How unfortunate. Such is the price of a woman's beauty — suspicion from other females based on insecurities."

Then I thought of all those trail romances, raging endorphins and beautiful people prancing all over the trails, not to mention the extraordinary amounts of time we spend training with other runners. Fred Lebow, director of the New York City Marathon, once told the story of a female runner with a jealous spouse. The runner's husband accused her of having an affair with a male running partner. She wasn't, but when she got to the finish line of the New York Marathon, her husband was not there to greet her. She figured, "That's it. If I can run New York I can live without him." They were divorced and the woman did end up marrying her running partner.

In the memoir *Honey, Do You Need a Ride? Confessions of a Fat Runner*, Jennifer Graham reveals a dark truth she is deeply ashamed of: starting an inappropriate relationship with a man who revered and took interest in her running while her husband showed little interest in the sport. Here was a new, more athletic man who wanted to not only run with her, but to time her and analyze her splits. He challenged and admired her. They became friends...and then some. Though Jennifer doesn't regret meeting him, she is sorry about the details of how things went down. Her husband is now her ex.

In the book *Run Like a Girl: How Strong Women Make Happy Lives*, Mina Samuels tells the story of Michelle, an avid runner

married to a triathlete. Their busy schedules had them drifting apart, at odds with each other and training separately. He preferred to train with his buddies, all men. "And then somewhere along the line a woman joined them," explains Michelle. "He began to spend more time training with her instead of the guys. And of course they were doing the same races together. We were in marriage counseling at the time, and I just had a feeling."

It all came crashing down when Michelle came home one day to discover candles burned down and romantic CDs in the player. Then the "training partner" mistakenly sent an email to their joint account. Her husband admitted everything and had no interest in saving their marriage. Michelle felt as though she had lost him to triathlons.

After some time, however, she realized how much happier she was without him and felt as though she had dodged a bullet. She even became friends with the "training partner" who is now his new wife.

Although there is no reliable data on this topic, it seems (despite the odd horror story) that infidelity in endurance is still a rare occurrence. On the other hand, there is anecdotal success from couples who have used running together as a means of solving marital issues. Such is the bonding power of running.

When Both Partners Run

I am on mile six of Washington's Adventure Route of the Olympic Discovery Trail. Apart from my dog, Ginger, beside me, there is no one else in sight. My feet are moving as fast as I can make them over the wide packed earth as I glance over my shoulder for Shacky.

Earlier, we had agreed that I would run out with a five-minute lead, then Shacky would try to catch me—speed training turned tag. He's faster than I am, but we rarely push speed on our training runs. I am surprising myself today.

Every once in a while Ginger stops to sniff a bush and I holler at her to catch up. The weather is perfect: breezy, cool, refreshing. I splash through the water crossings—there is no time to tiptoe. I have one more mile before my turnaround, and I want nothing more than to get there before he catches up.

I can almost sense Shacky breathing down my neck, so I pick up the pace. I am flying—a rabbit in survival mode fleeing its predator. I love this feeling. I hit a hill and my stride tightens, but I refuse to slow down. I am so close.

At mile seven I high-five a tree and belt out a victory holler. I am sure Shacky can hear it. I made it! I won.

After catching my breath, I swing around and gallop back proudly, watching for Shacky around every corner...but he's not there. I pass the six-mile mark...five...four miles. Nobody.

Did something happen to him? Is he okay? I'm starting to worry. At three miles and two miles, I am sure something went wrong. I'm almost back at the RV.

I get to the car and find the doors unlocked. Shacky is sprawled out on the bed watching cartoons. He smiles and waves. He never left. My adrenaline high and raging endorphins make it hard to complain. It was my best run of the week.

Over the years I've learned that just the thought of Shacky behind me (or ahead of me) is enough to propel me forward. I am most competitive when I'm trying to beat him, and I can use that as an advantage. It's also extremely convenient to live with your training partner. I rarely have to run alone and I don't need to negotiate or bargain for running time. Racing and training double as quality time.

There are also downsides. Because I love him, it's hard for me to watch him suffer. When he's struggling in a race, I'm more inclined to encourage him to drop than to risk injury. When we're suffering together, dropping out seems like the most reasonable thing in the world. To avoid this, we race separately.

I was intrigued to learn that elite ultrarunner Pam Reed also can't race with her partner. In her memoir *The Extra Mile: One Woman's Personal Journey to Ultrarunning Greatness*, Pam goes into details about the athletic friction between her and husband. Pam prefers that her husband not attend her events.

It all started innocently enough. Two people who loved each other decided to register for the same 100K race and run it together. The problems started when Pam began to pull away, eager to spin her legs and fly at a faster pace. "She'd say something like 'I'm going to run with you for the first 20 miles,'" her husband Jim reports, "but then at mile two some lady would pass her and she'd forget all about me and take off."

So they figured out they couldn't race together. That was fine. Next, her husband tried to crew her. Pam describes his efforts at one 100-mile race as "a big blast of negativity" that

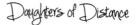

"seems to do a lot more harm than good." She insists it's nothing personal—it's just that his presence represents thoughts and feelings that she'd rather do without at a race.

When a spouse crews you, there is an added challenge because you know that your loved one can take you away from the pain. "It's not just that I want to quit if he's mad at me for not trying hard enough," writes Pam. "I'd also want to quit if he babied me." Pam's husband Jim remains supportive—behind the scenes.

Other couples seem to enjoy a more easy-going and primarily drama-free relationship. Jimmy Dean Freeman and Kate Freeman are one of my favorite power-running couples— both beautiful people, and fast. I asked Kate whether they ever ran into athletic-related friction.

"In the end I don't really think about the man/woman, faster/slower perspective," she said. "I love that I can share this wild hobby with Jimmy, that our lifestyle is active, that we encourage and support one another. It's fun to always have someone to chase."

But for Pam, the struggles are worth it. "When you put a couple of very competitive people in a house together, you're going to have some drama. You're going to have people using one another to motivate themselves, to convince themselves of things they can or can't do, and to blame one another for things they feel guilty about. On the flip side, you'll also see how two people can make each other better and stronger even while they're pulling on the rope in opposite directions. That really can happen, as long as the two of you keep pulling. It's when one stops that you both hit the dirt."

So what makes a relationship between runners work like a well-oiled machine? For Olga King, who met her husband on the trail, it's not the fact that they're both endurance runners, but rather their mutual love for the outdoors. Olga tells their love story on a *Trail Runner Magazine* blog symposium:

It's the fact that both of us love (the trails), and what surrounds them—the solitude, the challenges, the beauty, the views, the camaraderie, the unknown, the simplicity, the nakedness of existence and sharpness of thoughts.

Like most enduring relationships, it's a common passion and belief in something greater than each individual lover.

Same-Sex

I'm standing at the Start/Finish line at a local ultramarathon with a giant cowbell in my hand, waiting for my friend Melissa (not her real name). It's her last lap and she's about to set the course record in this 12-hour race. I'm giddy with anticipation. All day long I have watched her grind out the miles with machine-like focus and tunnel-vision determination.

"Here she comes! Here she comes!"

I'm ringing my cowbell so hard I feel like my wrist is going to snap. I scream until my voice cracks. Melissa smiles, but doesn't break her stride. She is so focused that she is already setting out for another loop, not realizing the race is over. The race director hollers to her. "It's over! You won!" Stunned, Melissa lumbers back. She has no idea how well she's done.

I scan the crowd and pick out all the smiling faces. I am looking for Melissa's partner, but I can't spot her anywhere. Melissa's same-sex spouse of five years is a beautiful woman with a kind face who stands on the sidelines and smiles softly as Melissa glides by. They have been together for 14 years.

After the finish line, the commotion dissipates and Melissa quickly disappears. I assume she's been swept away by her loving wife. But a week later, I get a Facebook message from Melissa telling me that she and her spouse had fought on race day, and her wife left her. Melissa had found herself with a brand new course record that day — and no way to get home.

Melissa's race-day relationship crime had been to talk to the woman in second place, a woman with whom she had previously had an affair and had been forbidden to speak to. Melissa takes full responsibility for the breakup.

I was saddened by Melissa's story, but in speaking with her during the aftermath, it struck me how similar many same-sex issues were with issues in more traditional male-female relationships. Not that we all get abandoned at the finish line by our spouses after smashing course records, but the struggles with compromise, boundaries, trust and jealousy were identical.

So what, if anything, is different in the female-female relationship dynamic as far as endurance racing and training is concerned?

Terran Longacre, an endurance runner I met in California, believes one important difference may be stronger attachment issues in same-sex partnerships than in male-female couples. "One thing I struggled with for many, many years in my

relationship was my wanting to spend more time with my partner and be more attached and giving up running to achieve that," Terran tells me. "This is a dynamic that I would expect to see in a lot of lesbian relationships because it is quite well known that lesbians are more attached and tend to have more issues of codependence. You know the joke: What does a lesbian bring on a second date? *A moving van.*"

Lesbian marathoner and triathlete Tanya Marie Bercu echoes these sentiments. Tanya has been a serious endurance athlete for seven years. She told me about how she bargains with her wife Lela (someone who runs purely for exercise and who doesn't embrace the endurance mindset) about how many races she can do each year, and where. They have agreed that Tanya can race four times a year, and she must try to do it close to home.

In the past, Tanya has heard comments like: "When are you going to make time for me or for the house?" "Another race really? Do you have to do so many?"

Yet when Tanya does race, Lela is always there to support her wholeheartedly. "My frustration is she can be supportive yet not, and so darn emotional at times," Tanya explains to me. "I guess the biggest difference for me in my relationship versus an opposite sex relationship is that women tend to be more vocal and express their emotions and needs on a more intimate level."

Other couples have different experiences. When I spoke to endurance runner Mer Otis, she felt that none of the clingy-jealousy issues resonated with her. "Maybe it's a product of my age [57] or our time together [10 years], but the idea of

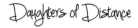

someone allowing me to do something, being jealous or resentful, or acting out as a way of managing conflict is so foreign," confesses Mer. "Maybe it's a woman-woman thing, but that is definitely not a part of our evolutionary dynamic as it relates to my running."

Mer's wife was an avid and rigorous soccer player in her youth, and Mer feels that may contribute to her understanding and appreciation of what it means to commit to a physical goal. "She supports everything endurance that I touch, finds crewing boring for the most part because of all the waiting around (I'm not a front pack chick), but is always willing to be a part of my adventures...I think this has more to do with our evolution as individuals and as a couple than it does with our gender match-up."

Another difference same-sex couples experience—which Terran Longacre argues is a strong advantage—is the non-issue of traditional gender expectations. Lesbians are more likely to take an active role in deciding who does what. "You cannot just fall into a lot of that stuff unconsciously," explains Terran. Divisions of labor are choices.

Jen Wuest describes an ex-husband who was unsupportive in her sport and a current wife who is her #1 cheerleader. On the flip side, Martine Kinkade describes an ex-girlfriend who wrote her a scathing email, lambasting her for ultrarunning compared to the man she is about to marry: a non-runner who believes in her dreams "with every fiber of his being." Obviously, gender in no way determines a partner's ability to love and support.

For the most part, relationship dynamics remain the same.

The budgeting of finances, energy and quality time are just as crucial in any relationship, as are communication and cooperation.

Shangrila Rendon (who describes herself as "engineer, analytical, loves food, cooking, crazy with triathlon, endurance events, loves outdoors, exercises everyday") insists that communication is the most important aspect in her relationship with a wife who isn't physically active. To exercise, Shangrila's wife hops on a rebounder or trampoline for five minutes, three times a week.

Shangrila sometimes wishes her wife were a triathlete, so they could motivate and challenge each other. It would be easier. "There are times that I feel jealous whenever I see couples that train at the same time," she confesses, but she communicates those feelings to her wife. "She listens," Shangrila tells me. "There's really nothing I can do. She is who she is. I do not force her to exercise since she won't be happy that way. It's my love for her that makes me move past this jealousy or wishing that my wife were someone who is into sports. Besides...she has all the other qualities that I want."

Shangrila's wife supports her by showing interest in triathlon, asking questions, attending important races and making optimal, nutritious food for Shangrila to use as fuel.

Shangrila races so often that her wife can't keep up with the schedule. A few times, Shangrila failed to communicate that she needed her wife at the race, then regretted having to make the long drive home alone. Now Shangrila keeps a log of all her races on the computer. She has the important races highlighted, the ones she wants her wife to attend. She also communicates with her wife in advance about getting time off for those events. It's still a bargaining process. Shangrila doesn't want to force her wife to attend events she doesn't want to be at, especially if they're out of town.

When Shangrila's wife is present at a race, she is a "pro-spectator." She studies the course and asks questions. She is also a photographer and comes home with great race shots. She monitors race-day nutrition, drives home and makes a healthy post-race meal.

According to lesbian marathoner Kathleen Erz, communication also includes what you don't share with others. "I make sure that I do not share things with other people that I would not share or have not already shared with [my wife]. When you are running all those hours with people, you do start to talk. Your running friends see you at your worst and your best. You share a lot of really important experiences with them. It's like this weird intimacy: dark a lot of times, no eye contact, so it makes it easier to say embarrassing things. I think that's important for us, so I watch how much I share. I think that helps."

No matter whom you love, relationships can be messy — like dry heaving at mile 75, or being stuck in the woods without any toilet paper. But like most challenges, the rewards are well worth it.

Vanessa Runs

6: Mommy, Don't Go! (Balance & Guilt)

"Show me a woman without guilt and I'll show you a man."
- Marie Wilson

How familiar is this scene:

You are getting ready to go for a run when your young daughter, who had been playing quietly on her own and completely ignoring you, notices you're quietly reaching for your shoes. "Mama? Are you going for a run?" she asks innocently, her eyes growing larger by the minute.

"Yes, just a short one," you reply as nonchalantly as you can. "I'll be back before you know it."

"Noooo!!" she wails, "Don't go!!"

She latches onto your leg with all her strength. It doesn't matter that you've spent all day with her. You've made her breakfast, played games, taught her new things, and now you'd like some time to yourself. It doesn't matter that you'll be back in 30 minutes or that she's in good hands with her loving dad. You can feel the guilt rising and you're pretty sure your neighbors can hear your sweet daughter's screams, but you head for the door anyway. You know that if you don't go now, you never will. And you need this. God, you need this.

I have heard so many different variations of that story from both moms and dads in endurance. They battle every day to achieve a balance between their sport and other responsibilities, with guilt as a common side effect.

When I finished my first mountain 100-mile foot race, Chimera 100, there was a banner at the finish line that read,

"MODERATION HAS ITS PLACE BUT IT AIN'T HERE" Ain't that the truth. And yet we live in and seek to function in a society that preaches moderation and balance. Our extended friends and families may frown on our "extreme" training. Sometimes the guilt comes from those closest to us and sometimes it comes from our own heads.

Although Jennifer Benna has run (and won) some tough races, she insists that finding a balance between work, family and running is the most difficult thing she has ever had to do in her life. "You can fall off the balance pretty quickly," she admits. "I don't blame any women who are raising young families for not running ultras. If I hadn't been an ultrarunner for so much of my life before my daughter, Eva, I'm not sure I would have picked this as the time to start."

Often women are judged harshly for the perceived imbalance. Elite males aren't generally asked how they manage household duties in addition to their sport. In her book *The Extra Mile*, Pam Reed writes:

> An American woman who isn't an Olympic athlete but who really devotes herself to running is likely to be seen as eccentric, to put it kindly. A man is just seen as someone who's devoted to running. Even women themselves can sometimes feel this way.

Researcher Brené Brown points out that you don't have to be a mother to experience mother shame:

> Society views womanhood and motherhood as inextricably bound; therefore our value as women is often determined by where we are in relation to our roles as

mothers or potential mothers. Women are constantly asked why they haven't married or, if they're married, why they haven't had children. Women who are married and have one child are often asked why they haven't had a second child. You've had your kids too far apart? "What were you thinking?" Too close? "Why? That's so unfair to the kids." If you're working outside the home, the first question is "What about the children?" If you're not working, the first question is "What kind of example are you setting for your daughters?" Mother shame is ubiquitous — it's a birthright for girls and women.

Dr. Clarissa Pinkola Estes is an American poet and a Jungian psychoanalyst. She points out that there are few culturally sanctioned antidotes for the female filled with a longing for the wild. "We are taught to feel shame for such a desire..." she writes "But the shadow of Wild Woman still lurks behind us during our days and in our nights. No matter where we are, the shadow that trots behind us is definitely four-footed."

The concepts of balance and guilt intrigue me, and I set out to write this chapter with a series of questions: Are women really busier, or do they just feel more pressure to do everything? Are these pressures legitimate, or imagined and self-enforced? What is it like to struggle with this every day as a female? And finally — how do women who train well and regularly manage their responsibilities? How do they achieve balance in the face of such an extreme sport that is anything but moderate?

The Myth of Moderation

A Team USA basketball trainer named Robert posted a story on Reddit in 2013 about the first time he met basketball star Kobe Bryant. Despite Kobe's off-court issues, it's impossible to ignore his legendary work ethic. This anecdote both shocked and impressed me and I haven't been able to forget it since.

The story, in Robert's words, reads as follows:

I was invited to Las Vegas this past summer to help Team USA with their conditioning before they head off to London, and as we know they would eventually bring home the Gold. I've had the opportunity to work with Carmelo Anthony and Dwyane Wade in the past but this would be my first interaction with Kobe. We first met three days before the first scrimmage, on the day of the first practice, early July. It was a brief conversation where we talked about conditioning, where he would like to be by the end of the summer, and we talked a little bit about the hustle of the Select Team. Then he got my number and I let him know that if he ever wanted some extra training he could hit me up any time.

The night before the first scrimmage I remember I was just watching *Casablanca* for the first time and it was about 3:30 a.m. I lay in bed, slowly fading away when I hear my cell ring. It was Kobe. I nervously picked up.

"Hey, uhh Rob, I hope I'm not disturbing anything right?"

"Uhh no, what's up Kob?"

"Just wondering if you could just help me out with some conditioning work, that's all."

I checked my clock. 4:15 a.m.

"Yeah sure, I'll see you in the facility in a bit."

It took me about twenty minutes to get my gear and out of the hotel. When I arrived and opened the room to the main practice floor I saw Kobe. Alone. He was drenched in sweat as if he had just taken a swim. It wasn't even 5 a.m.

We did some conditioning work for the next hour and fifteen minutes. Then we entered the weight room, where he would do a multitude of strength training exercises for the next 45 minutes. After that we parted ways and he went back to the practice floor to shoot. I went back to the hotel and crashed. Wow.

I was expected to be at the floor again at about 11 a.m. I woke up feeling sleepy, drowsy and pretty much every side effect of sleep deprivation. Thanks, Kobe. I had a bagel and headed to the practice facility.

This next part I remember very vividly. All the Team USA players were there, feeling good for the first scrimmage. LeBron was talking to Carmelo if I remember correctly and Coach Krzyzewski was trying to explain something to Kevin Durant. On the right side of the practice facility was Kobe by himself shooting jumpers. And this is how our next conversation went—I went over to him, patted him on the back and said, "Good work this morning."

"Huh?"

"Like, the conditioning. Good work."

"Oh. Yeah thanks, Rob. I really appreciate it."

"So when did you finish?"

"Finish what?"

"Getting your shots up. What time did you leave the facility?"

"Oh, just now. I wanted 800 makes so yeah, just now."

My jaw dropped. Mother of holy God. It was then that I realized that there's no surprise as to why he's been as effective as he was last season. Every story about his dedication, every quote that he's said about hard work all came together and hit me like a train. It's no surprise to me now that he's dunking on players ten years younger than him and it wasn't a surprise to me earlier this year when he led the league in scoring.

You don't have to follow basketball to appreciate what it means to train harder than your competitors, to stay driven and exceptional.

On one hand, we are criticized and accused of obsession if we practice our sport "too much." On the other hand, if we have any aspirations of greatness, it is clear that moderation is not the way we go. Every highly successful athlete, artist, writer has spent an unbalanced amount of time perfecting their skills to achieve their goals. We look up to these heroes and admire their accomplishments, but what we don't see is the endless practice time we might normally write off as insane or compulsive.

This is true for any career. J.K. Rowling got the idea for Harry Potter in 1990 and spent the next 17 years working on it. She writes nearly every day, sometimes for up to 10 or 11 hours in one day.

Of course, not all of us aspire to become world-class endurance athletes, although even a middle-of-the-pack competitor requires a significant amount of training. Endurance, by its very nature, is unbalanced. These are sports of extremes. To try to achieve perfect balance between our training and work plus family plus leisure time can in some ways be a losing battle.

We can certainly achieve balances that we can sustain and feel comfortable with, yet our activities will still be judged as crazy or neglectful. It helps to remember that perfect moderation (at least in endurance sports) is a myth. It's all a juggling act.

According to Anne-Marie Slaughter, the director of policy planning at the State Department under Hillary Rodham Clinton from 2009 to 2011, it's impossible for women to achieve a balance between work and family (let alone sport) the way economy and society are structured today. In an article titled *Why Women Still Can't Have It All*, Anne-Marie insists that any high-powered job makes it physically impossible for a woman to remain fully present as a parent. It can't be done through meticulous planning, not by marrying the right spouse and not through sheer commitment. It simply can't be done.

This article has been hotly debated, but even without the high-powered job, many of us face an impossible task in trying to balance endurance training with everything else. Perhaps balance should not be the ultimate goal. Instead, we can aim for a compromise that works for those closest to us and for ourselves, balance be damned.

Is Endurance Selfish?

The most "selfish" endurance story I came across while researching this book came courtesy of Moire O'Sullivan. In her book, *Mud, Sweat and Tears*, Moire explains how she was training for the Wicklow Round, a looped course covering 26 peaks in Wicklow, Ireland. The distance totals more than 100K and must be completed within 24 hours.

She trained heavily every weekend with her friend Andrew, to the confusion of her boyfriend, Pete. Whenever Pete would try to take her away for a fun weekend, she flat-out refused. "I can't go away!" she would protest, "I've got a five-hour training run to do with Andrew on Saturday and then Sunday I've got to go orienteering!" Pete would accept her excuse and ask her when she would be free for a weekend trip. Moire's reply was "Never…you see, Andrew and I need to scout the Wicklow Round and we have these long runs that we have to do. And then, towards April the racing season starts, and then this year I want to concentrate on weekend races rather than the Wednesday ones." Pete didn't know what to say, but he stuck by his girlfriend.

One day Moire picked up the book *The Lore of Running* and stumbled across something called the "Selfish Runner's Syndrome." It read: "Running can indeed become an extremely selfish activity…To put racing as the sole reason for living is inappropriate and ultimately detrimental to family life."

Moire was stunned. This was about her! She immediately called Pete and admitted the error of her ways. She writes: "Recognizing this syndrome allows me in turn to forego races or runs for the occasional night out, and opens up a whole new world of activities beyond my running fixation."

Whether or not endurance is selfish is debatable. Despite the long training hours, there are a few significantly unselfish perks that result from it. Some of those perks mentioned by the women I interviewed included:

1. Self-love

When you make yourself a priority, you are valuing yourself and your needs. You invest in your health and happiness. You reduce your stress and become more productive. There is nothing selfish about needing to stay active or taking steps to make sure your body is getting the type of exercise you need and want.

Valuing yourself also benefits others. I have heard this likened to putting your oxygen mask on first in the event of a plane crash. If you don't take care of yourself first, how can you possibly be of use to anyone else?

2. Time management

On days when I'm not that busy, sometimes I'll let the hours slip by and I miss my training. On days when I'm busy, I know I have to schedule in my run and I get it done (usually at the only available time and usually first thing in the morning). I've found the same is true for the busiest women: they usually only have one shot at their workout and they make sure they get it in. They are masters of time management by necessity and remain dedicated to their training.

3. Better parenting

Many women confessed that staying active makes them better moms. They are happier, more patient and more excited to spend time with their kids. A few women reported that when their children sense a sour mood, they demand that mommy go for a run.

Lori Lyons was at a family BBQ one Saturday when somebody asked what her family had on the docket for Sunday. Her husband replied, "I think Oliver and I are going to try to go to church in the morning." Her five-year-old son Oliver immediately piped in and added, "…and Mom will go run in the mountains. That's her church."

4. Self-awareness

As you learn to set a balance that works for you, you also learn about yourself. You know what type of commitment you are most comfortable with, how much training time you need for those endorphins to kick in, and how much is too much for you or your loved ones to handle. Understanding your own needs is vital not only in athletics but also in life.

5. Commitment

Ultimately, we make time for what's important to us. It's okay to admit that some challenges are not worth the effort, but it's also okay to work hard and stay committed to the ones that do matter.

Heather Anderson said in an iRunFar.com interview:

> There's never going to be a time where the stars align and you're suddenly debt-free and commitment-free. That

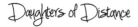

just doesn't happen. You have to make it happen. Nobody's life is so complex that they can't make their dream happen, it just might require more sacrifices than they're willing to give. You will do whatever it is you most want to do.

Remember, making yourself a priority is not the same thing as being selfish. For some women, it's easier to sacrifice their own goals and slowly let their dreams fade than to feel they are putting themselves before their families.

In an iRunFar article, ultrarunner Geoff Roes tackles the question, "Is Running Selfish?" He concludes that running has many positive side effects that seem to far outweigh the time commitment and "selfishness" of endurance. He observes:

> In going out most every day and seeking this balance, joy, passion, and excitement for life through our practice of running, we are most definitely doing good for more than just ourselves. We are spreading an energy and a mindset to everyone we come in contact with that makes each of them just a little bit stronger and a little bit more alive than they were before that interaction.

Critics argue that although positive qualities can be cultivated through running, it is better to discover those traits through relationships instead of lonely, time-consuming activities.

In another iRunFar article entitled *Running and the Small Stuff*, Andy Jones-Wilkins muses on a similar theme. He concludes:

While it's self-absorbed in the moment, it also allows me to be more present for others when I need to be as it blocks out my tendency to be annoyed and obstructed by the small stuff. Maybe, just maybe, running every day makes the small stuff less stressful, less cumbersome, less important and, ultimately, along this long, winding trail of life, it just might make life, and living, more meaningful.

Researcher Crista Scott sent me a study she read while preparing her thesis. The study, *Commitment to Distance Running: Coping Mechanism or Addiction?*, looked at the psychological effects of long distance running. The study's author M. Gail Leedy of Washburn University of Topeka measured and compared anxiety and depression traits found in "Highly Committed" runners and "Recreational Runners." Leedy concluded that "strong dedication to distance running is associated with positive traits rather than with negative aspects of addiction."

If you look up the word "selfish" in the dictionary, you'll find definitions like:

- lacking consideration for others
- concerned chiefly with one's own personal profit or pleasure
- egotistical
- mercenary
- uncharitable

That hardly sounds like the women in endurance that I

know.

Top Tips and Tricks for Parents

I asked endurance parents for their best tips on how to manage training-guilt and being away from their families. More than 100 parents replied. Here are some of the top suggestions:

1. Get up early in the morning while everyone is still sleeping, or go out late at night after everyone has been put to bed. Run during soccer practices or swim lessons or naptime. Run loops around the park while your kids play. Run while the kids are in school. One mother would run on a track while her kids played in the center. Another mother ran loops around the block with a walkie-talkie while her kids slept, just in case they needed to reach her.

2. Bring your kids along. They can ride bikes while you run, or maybe they can run with you even if it's just for a mile. Use single, double, or triple jogging strollers. Carry your children in a kid-friendly backpack for extra weight training. Plant that fitness seed in your kids and set a good example. Your kids will soon learn that daily exercise is normal. (Note: Child carriers are built for walking. The constant bouncing of running with them could be hazardous for a young child.)

3. Fight guilt by reminding yourself that this makes you a better person and a better parent. You need the time to yourself, the physical benefits and the stress relief. Your kids need to see you making yourself a priority and finding enjoyment in a healthy hobby. Don't beat yourself up about it. One mom made a point not to leave the house too early

because she wanted her kids to see her taking time for herself. Another claimed that her kids did better if they could wake up and say goodbye to her before a run.

4. Let your kids try racing if they show an interest, or bring them along to volunteer, crew, or cheer other runners at your races so they can see what you do.

5. Choose races that are meaningful and important to you—don't just sign up for anything and everything. Keep an eye on overnight trips or races that involve travel. Make sure it's worth taking the time away from your family. Long training runs are easier to schedule than races.

6. When you're not training, be 100 percent present for your kids, even when all you want to do is foam roll and take a nap. Focus on quality over quantity.

7. Resort to a little bit of bribing. One mother serves cereal with marshmallows on the days when she has a long run. Another mother promises a movie when she gets back. Another brings home donut holes when she comes back from a long run. The kids look forward to those days.

8. While you're out for a long training run, plan for your kids to spend some quality time with your partner.

9. Turn races into family vacations.

10. Some gyms have good childcare services that will let you squeeze in a solid treadmill run.

11. Run or bike to and from work.

12. If you can only fit in a short workout, make it a speed session or hill training.

13. Sometimes our jobs offer more flexibility than we give them credit for. Don't be afraid to ask for hours that better

complement your family and your training.

14. Don't chain yourself to a training plan. Keep a flexible mindset and remember that some miles are better than no miles. Get it in where you can, even if you have to improvise the training plan.

15. Play a hard game of tag. No "time-outs" allowed. It's just as good as a run.

16. Don't be afraid to hire a babysitter.

17. Cut down the time you spend on other things that don't yield as great of a reward, like surfing the Web (exception: vanessaruns.com). Consider paying for or outsourcing other chores like housework at least occasionally to save your time and mental health.

18. Don't hesitate to break up your longer runs. It's better to do two separate five-mile runs than to plan one ten-mile run that you skip completely.

Spouses and Teammates

It was a Sunday night in mid-April. Leon Lutz had just finished driving home with his family after a trail race and was tucking his two little girls into bed: Lily (4) and her teeny sister Piper Bea (2). The race had been the Hyner View Trail Challenge, one of the toughest 25K races in the Northeastern United States.

It hadn't been a great race day for Leon. Temperatures had dipped unexpectedly into the low 40s accompanied by high winds and a fierce horizontal rain. Leon struggled with every step to climb over the ridge where, to his surprise, he found his family waiting. Leon's mother and stepfather had taken the kids for the weekend and they'd decided to show up and cheer.

The girls were wet, cold, and pretty miserable. Although they did brighten up when they saw their dad, Leon hated to see them upset and pleaded with his mom to get them somewhere warm and dry. "My mother's heart was theoretically in the right place...for me...but, she was asking quite a bit of a two- and a four-year-old," remembers Leon.

The girls had already endured a long car ride to get to the race, and it would be another long drive back. Leon would end up with an Achilles injury that kept him from finishing and would put him on the injured list for the following four weeks.

So it was with a mix of exhaustion and curiosity that little Lily lifted her head toward her daddy that night and asked, "Why do you have to run so much, Daddy?"

It was a question that Leon took seriously. Lily had always been excited about his running. Since he normally trained while she slept, she would wake up in the morning and ask about the details of his run. She had cheered enthusiastically for her daddy at other races, and keenly observed all of her dad's running friends.

In response to Lily's question, Leon wrote a letter. This letter originally appeared on the endurance website iRunFar.com:

> *"Why do you have to run so much, Daddy?"*
>
> My dear Lily (and your little sister, Piper Bea),
>
> If I'm being honest, and for the sake of both you and Piper Bea, I must and will be, I'd seen the question in your

eyes a time or two before you actually spoke the words. More than likely I assigned that look to long days and a child's want to always, always, always move on to the next adventure, hoping that the sentiment existed only on the very surface and lacked actual residence in your worries.

As the words hang there in the air, waiting for me to accept the challenge of offering an acceptable response, I now recognize their sincerity and beginnings rooted more deeply than just in moments of exhaustion or boredom.

At six years of age, you must find two hours waiting for my return to be interminably long. And that, of course, allows for only a short run in comparison to half days, full days, days on end in the backcountry seeking, perhaps, the answer to the very question you just posed. The older I get, the more fleeting hours and even days seem to be, but you haven't yet been saddled with the sobering perspective of aging, the consciousness of expiration dates and a notion of fewer years ahead than behind. Thank goodness. I actually find relief in knowing that this is not yet graspable for you or your sister. I celebrate it and ache at the idea that you both one day will comprehend the ceaseless, unrelenting march of time.

By the look on your face, I can tell that you've decided I wasn't listening or don't have any intention of answering your question, but I do. I'm trying.

Many other children, husbands, wives, partners, parents, friends have asked this very same question of runners scattered all across this enormous (though not so enormous as you might think) planet. Each of them has deserved an honest answer just as each person who is asked the question is equally deserving of his or her right not to provide one. But, for you, I am trying.

Much of my answer lies in the sensations conjured by watching you and Piper Bea race about the backyard. It is the same emotions I experienced the first time you twisted your little newborn hands into my beard and unfurled a yawn seemingly too big for your little body before falling asleep nestled beneath my chin. Witnessing inaugural smiles, first words and teetering, exploratory steps elicited similar feelings. All of those initial revelations and awe-inspiring discoveries were connections to a world so breathtakingly beautiful when uncluttered by all that you at six do not, simply cannot, yet know. How sad it is for me to accept that you will not be and cannot be kept from one day knowing.

When I run and especially when I run long and far, all that I've come to know (or think I know) of the world washes away and I am better, much better, for it. The connections that came so easily at four and six years old, connections that seem nearly impossible to make at 39, become quite possible. Not only do they become possible, Lil, they happen. Bodies that would pass wordlessly on a city street or a suburban neighborhood engage effortlessly in comfortable conversation. Laughter, genuine heart-happy laughter, is the norm amongst ultrarunners and occurs without the reservations of political correctness or the shadowy assessment of present company.

That furrow in your tiny brow reveals your frustration at trying but failing to understand that last sentence but I couldn't be happier that the weight of social constraints is one foreign to you, at least for now.

I'll say it another way. You don't like closed doors, do you? I've watched you approach them with the same disdain I feel, your posture almost demanding access to the other side. Life is full of closed doors, Lily, and I too tire of them. Out on the trails, doors that are closed in our everyday are opened wide. No, that's not quite right. They aren't opened so much as they just aren't there at all.

Please don't mistake my yearning for the outdoors and my passion for running as a need to escape the world on the whole or a suggestion that all of life is constraints, enclosures and nuisance. There is so much to love about our family, our home, our neighbors, school and, yes, even work. You and I have talked quite a lot about balance both in the physical sense of avoiding toppling over on the playground or while riding your bicycle and in the less easy to understand way of keeping from feeling like you're being pushed, jostled and overwhelmed by everything being asked of you by your friends, your teachers or Lindsay and me... Sorry, Mommy and me.

For providing me with that second kind of balance, trail running should be given significant credit. Rather than serving as an escape, my time spent running and exploring keeps me from getting dizzy and losing sight of all that there is to love in a sometimes crazy world. I may lose my physical balance, take a misstep and fall while running, but the rest of life seems to spin a little less out of control thanks to my time spent on the trail.

I suspect that doesn't make much sense either, does it? But it is true.

Remembering how much I love you, your mother and Piper Bea is easy and doesn't require any reminders, but other things can be taken for granted. Mowing the lawn, paying the bills and fixing all the little dings and flaws that need fixing can definitely add up to my not fully appreciating how lovely it is to have our house. Eight, 12, 24 or more hours on my feet and many miles of effort have a funny way of making home seem really, really precious. Solitary runs which I enjoy nearly as much as those shared, if in a different way, make me that much more appreciative of conversation and interaction upon arrival back home and at work. Even the end of long races that included time spent with others brings the promise of reuniting with loved ones or, best of all, receiving big hugs from sign-toting daughters! Long hours on the trail and the freedom from external demands also provide a clear focus, otherwise often lacking, when I go to work day after day, week after week without a break.

All of that perspective is a wondrous benefit of running so much, but it isn't the honest answer to your question. The answer, getting back to my earlier point, is joy. Innocence, sadly, is fleeting. Unrestricted movement and an unfettered engagement of the senses with nature are the closest I've come to reclaiming innocence and restoring the naiveté that makes each new discovery a miracle. Being outside is on its own nearly enough, but coupling the outdoors with running gets me all the way there. When I run, I am not jaded. When I run, all that I see, hear and feel is seen, heard and felt anew, experienced for the first time. For the first time, every time.

When I run, Lily, I *know* joy. I really do. I'm fully immersed in it without any interference. It isn't something that I'm reading about or seeing on a television screen and recognizing as happiness. It is happening right there inside of me. Inside of me and all around me. It's the same unencumbered joy that you experienced (and your adoring parents, too) with those first smiles, first words, first steps. It is the astonishing sparkle in your eye when you waved to me before stepping on the school bus for your first day of kindergarten and the corresponding pride that brought tears to my eyes. Remember how excited you were to show me you could hang upside down from the swing set and do flips underwater at the pool? *That* joy, that's what running gives me. Racing down every new trail (or old, familiar trail for that matter) is like pulling off that first flip or realizing that I'm doing it, I'm *doing* it… I am actually hanging upside down!

It's wonderful, isn't it, Lily?

I don't ever want to miss out on your latest achievement, your newest discovery. More importantly, I do not ever want to be present only to then take any of your joy for granted. The balance of running and all else that life is and can be helps to ensure that I never overlook the things that fill *you* with joy. Maybe you'll even find in time that running is for you too one of its sources, but it doesn't ever need to be, not ever. So long as you find an activity, a person, something, anything that helps you find connection, balance and love, I'll be there to help you celebrate it.

Oh, how I look forward to one day asking you why you do whatever it is you decide you best like doing so much. Even if I think I know the answer.

Love you always and at every moment,
Daddy

Leon's letter sparked emotional responses from parents on both sides of the debate: those who cheered him on and supported his running, and others who condemned him for his selfish hobby. Although issues of balance and guilt are often presented as a female concern, the truth is that many men in endurance grapple with the same struggles. Why not tackle them as a team?

According to Facebook's Sheryl Sandberg, "the single most important career decision that a woman makes is whether she will have a life partner and who that partner is." The same can be said for any woman dedicated to endurance sport. It's not a coincidence that many active women claim they couldn't participate in events without the full support of their spouses. Sheryl tells the story of a man who asked Harvard Business School professor Rosabeth Moss Kanter what he could do to help advance women's leadership. Her reply: "The laundry." Dead on.

Research shows that couples who equally share the division of labor, both outside and inside the home, are more likely to stay together. "In fact, the risk of divorce reduces by about half when a wife earns half the income and a husband does half the housework," reports Sheryl. Furthermore, couples that share domestic duties have more sex. Want to turn a woman on? Do the dishes.

An unequal division of household labor is not always our spouse's fault. Sometimes our partners want to help, but we women have trouble giving up control. We want things like chores and childrearing to be done *our* way and it's difficult to watch someone else take a different approach. This problem has been described as maternal gatekeeping or being a martyr and it's ultimately harmful to any endurance pursuits.

Gatekeeper parenting is a term used to describe the power dynamics in a relationship. It's seen most commonly in first-time parents, divorced, or never-married parents. A gatekeeper parent will try to control and dictate every aspect of the relationship between the child and the other parent. They will criticize or demean the other parent and take on the majority of the childcare responsibilities.

When they do ask for help, they usually provide explicit and detailed instructions to accomplish the task. It's not enough to get things done. Chores must also be done *their* way. These parents usually require a great amount of external validation. It's a stressful and self-inflicted burden. Gatekeeper parents often resort to verbal and psychological abuse, inspiring resentment and a sense of helplessness in their

171

partners.

Utrarunner and author Jason Robillard writes at length about martyr parents. He points out that society often rewards this behavior because it appears selfless and sacrificial, though in reality martyr parents play the role of a victim and suffer from psychological and physiological stress and displaced anger. They ignore their own needs to meet the needs of others, then make others feel guilty for not making the same extreme and unrealistic sacrifices.

It's tough to break the habits of being a martyr parent. A desire to change is always the first step, and Jason also suggests getting the second parent involved to keep the martyr accountable. Communication is key, and so is a decision to put the relationship first (even before the kids). "If we're planning a date night, we go even if our kids cry and beg us to stay," writes Jason. "We need our alone time and we're not about to fall into the martyr trap by putting our kids' 'needs' before our own...If your significant other is playing the martyr role, talk to them. If you're doing it, change. You'll appreciate the results."

Sheryl Sandberg writes:

When it comes to children, fathers often take their cues from mothers. This gives a mother great power to encourage or impede the father's involvement. If she acts as a gatekeeper mother and is reluctant to hand over responsibility, or worse, questions the father's efforts, he does less. Whenever a married woman asks me for advice on co-parenting with a husband, I tell her to let him put the diaper on the baby any way he wants as long as he's doing it himself. And if he gets up to deal with the diaper before being asked, she should smile even if he puts that diaper on the baby's head. Over time, if he does things his way, he'll find the correct end. But if he's forced to do things her way, pretty soon she'll be doing them herself. Anyone who wants her mate to be a true partner must treat him as an equal — and equally capable — partner.

We've come a long way from the societal standards where men were primarily hands-off when it came to childrearing and household duties. Today, more men than ever before are reporting a desire to become more involved in the lives of their children and to spend more time at home. This can be challenging in workplaces that don't always acknowledge a male's need to take time off for their children, or with spouses who may not always recognize a male's contribution in the home.

According to a report from the Families and Work Institute in New York, 59 percent of fathers encounter some level of "work-life conflict," compared to only 45 percent of women. A Boston College study called *The New Dad* suggests that fathers face a bias in the workplace: employers and co-workers assume that male workplace hours and performance should be largely unaffected by children. Men are also struggling for balance, and one of the key mistakes that women make is to underestimate how much their partners can contribute, or assume that female contributions are more valuable in the home.

Endurance: The Balance to Life

When Christine Bilange was asked to pace her friend Stephen at the Angeles Crest 100-Mile Endurance Run, she brought her 15-year-old daughter Lea along to help crew. It wasn't exactly the stereotypical 15-year-old girl's paradise: no clothes shopping, not many boys, no giggling girlfriends. This was the backcountry with rugged trails and unforgiving terrain. They arrived Friday and didn't go home until Sunday afternoon, dirty and tired and exhausted.

A few months later at another race, Christine would overhear Lea instructing a runner at the end of a 50-mile race on endurance nutrition, hydration and cramping prevention. Three years later Lea told her mother out of nowhere, "Mom, that was the best week of my life!"

The crewing experience for Lea had been extreme, yet it provided an important balance to a life otherwise filled with teenaged convenience and conformity. Without such extremes, our own lives could easily turn into overdoses of comfort, far from the call of the wild. We would know nothing of blisters or electrolytes or how to handle ourselves in the backcountry.

Instead of trying to minimize our training time for the sake of balance, maybe we need to acknowledge that extreme endurance *is* the balance to a modern life overflowing with sedentary shortcuts.

In a world where normal involves sitting for more than ten hours a day and consuming copious amounts of highly processed foods, perhaps endurance sport is not the "unhealthy" habit we need to worry about. Save the alarm bells for when people are being hurt or neglected, not when an athlete is aspiring beyond society's "normal."

Endurance athlete Lisa Tamati credits running as the activity that balances her mind, body and soul, yet her weekly training in no way resembles balance to the non-athlete looking in. Lisa is an acclaimed elite, having run the equivalent of three times around the world through the hottest, harshest and highest terrain on the planet. She says that having a single endurance goal is purifying because there is so much going on in her non-running life. "The phone's constantly ringing, emails are coming in, there are a hundred things that need doing—and I have to find a way to balance it all...When I go to a race, I leave all that behind and just focus on the trail."

Jennifer Pharr Davis is another endurance athlete and thru-hiker who has given up the illusion of a daily balance. She has hiked more than 11,000 miles of long distance trails, trekked on six continents and holds endurance records on the Appalachian Trail, Long Trail and Bibbulmun Track. Jennifer is also the first woman to be the overall record holder on the Appalachian Trail, a feat accomplished by hiking the 2,181-mile trail in 46 days, 11 hours and 20 minutes—an average of 46.9 miles per day. How does she make it all work?

It's simple: she plans her life on a yearly basis. "Everything has a season," she explains. "My day-to-day life is not usually balanced, but if you give me 365 days, then I will be able to show you the weeks that I dedicate to work, running and resting with my family." Who says we need to balance every aspect of our lives, every single day? Adopting an annual perspective allows us to train hard within season,

then step back and focus on other things for the rest of the year.

Are these women unhealthy or unbalanced? On the contrary, they have families who love and support them, they run their own businesses and they contribute to their communities.

What Does a Balanced Sport Look Like?

When trail runner Robyn Reed was a little girl, she lived on a lake with a beautiful antique wooden boat. Robyn's dad worked hard to keep his boat in top shape. Together they would take it out on the lake, feeling pretty proud of it. "But," her dad warned her, "There's always someone out there with a bigger boat."

Robyn loves that story because she believes the same is true for endurance. There's always someone who has run more miles, steeper miles, crazier miles, who gets up earlier or trains in more extreme conditions. "And especially in the era of ubiquitous social media, it's easy to find extremes," observes Robyn. Her best advice is: "Think about your season of life and your commitments. Think about how you want to balance things. Acknowledge that someone will have a bigger boat. Then go out and enjoy a long sunrise cruise in your own boat."

What would a truly balanced and guiltless sport look like? Here are some ideas:

1. More women in endurance would rise to the top.

In a backpacking book I read about the Wonderland Trail (a 93-mile loop in Washington around Mount Rainier), I was

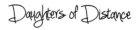

surprised when the author mentioned endurance runners and recommended, "resisting the urge to trip them" as they ran by. She also suggested one of the reasons these runners could travel so fast was because they were pampered with "veal dinners" to greet them at the end of each day. Huh? The runners I know are dirty, tired, sore and hungry. Many of them attempt these amazing feats completely self-supported or on shoestring budgets.

Insinuations like the ones from this author used to cause me to shy away from endurance. I didn't want to be "that woman" flying down the trail, knowing that some people wanted me to fall on my face. In a perfect world, women would no longer feel that sting of condescension that can come with success. They wouldn't be afraid to rise to the top. They would feel free to do their best without threat of anyone wishing to trip them as they run by.

2. Women would reinvent long-standing rules and traditions.

Traditions are lovely, but sometimes they don't work for our lifestyles. Do we really *have* to home-cook every meal? Is dinner with the entire family always necessary? For some it may be, but ideally a woman should feel free to pick and choose the traditions that work for her family. It could be that new traditions are in order, like a family turkey trot or a camping trip in the mountains.

Pam Reed's son, Andrew Koski, said of her: "We usually don't sit down together as a family. Mom feeds Jackson and me and then she and Jim go out to eat. We're all doing our own thing. I like it this way...I remember one Christmas,

when our dinner was turkey and popcorn. No, I think it was pretzels. Something weird. French fries — turkey and French fries."

3. Women would support stay-at-home dads as one of their "own."

Domestic dads are largely unsupported, though they face the same juggling act and struggles as women do. Working within the home is tough for both genders. In a balanced world, gender wouldn't matter. If you're a mommy or a daddy taking care of your kids at home, you would have the same community of support from other parents doing the same thing and sharing your challenges. Gender would be a non-issue, both at home and in the workplace.

4. Women would embrace their right to leisure.

A *Leisure Sciences* study by Catherine A. Roster reported that women don't have the same opportunities to participate in leisure activities as men do. This can be due to time constraints, limited financial resources, the woman's central role in the caring and nurturing of her family, or gender roles in the household (eg. women stay inside and do quilting while men go outside and play golf).

My hope is for women to understand that they are entitled to and fully deserving of leisure time, especially when our "needs" seem like a frivolous run in the woods. I would love to see leisure time for women become a no-questions-asked habit for all females. We have the right, just like any other human, to pursue the passions that interest us without self-condemnation or guilt.

5. Women would embrace the bigger picture.

Our lives have seasons, and perhaps there are some

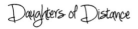

seasons when a six-month thru-hike is not possible. That's okay. Accepting that we will have other opportunities is not the same as making excuses, running away from our dreams or wasting time. Each season has its priorities, and just because another woman is in a different season doesn't mean we will never have the freedom that others seem to enjoy. Plan ahead and expect to do the things you are passionate about, in the timeframe that best fits your priorities.

6. Women would teach their kids that there are no limits.

By shattering expectations and living beyond what "should be" women would teach their kids just how much can be done with a little training and determination.

Rali Roesing sets an example for her kids by running ultra marathons and staying active. She teaches them that "you can do anything, you can start late, you can push the limits and blow yours and everybody's mind. You can be that healthy and eat that well, and go that far. It's possible. My kids have all run several 5Ks, competed in swim meets and ocean swims, and have ridden their bikes farther in a day than anyone they know at school (both sons did a century when they were nine years old on mountain bikes.) There are no limits."

Lori Lyons says: "I've decided kids don't listen much to what you tell them. Lesson: show them. If you want to teach them what hard work looks like, what a healthy body and healthy food look like, what failure and winning and doing your best look like, you don't need to say a word. Just run."

7. "Because I want to" would be a valid reason.

In *Tiny Beautiful Things*, Cheryl Strayed writes:

Doing what one wants to do because one wants to do it is hard for a lot of people, but I think it's particularly hard for women. We are, after all, the gender onto which a giant Here to Serve button has been eternally pinned. We're expected to nurture and give by the very virtue of our femaleness, to consider other people's feelings and needs before our own. I'm not opposed to those traits. The people I most admire are in fact nurturing and generous and considerate. Certainly, an ethical and evolved life entails a whole lot of doing things one doesn't particularly want to do and not doing things one very much does, regardless of gender. But an ethical and evolved life also entails telling the truth about oneself and living out that truth.

Women need to remember that it's still okay to do things just because they interest and challenge you—because you want to. No other explanation is needed.

8. Women would have more fun.

Our sport is supposed to be fun. Although it may be hard to fit in a training session, once we're out there we should enjoy it to the fullest. Don't waste your time worrying about chores or thinking about other obligations. This is your time. Have fun with it. Climb a tree, hop in a lake, stop for ice cream. Most of us do this because we love to be active, not because we're making a ton of money from it. So enjoy your journey fully—that's your payoff.

9. Women would savor the milestones.

Instead of rushing through every challenge to come home

and cook dinner, let's take a minute to savor our milestones. Every small goal accomplished should be a big deal. We only have our "firsts" once: first marathon, first ultra marathon, first triathlon...Let's acknowledge those wins. You don't have to celebrate alone—tell your family what goals you've accomplished and celebrate together. Take them out for a meal or enjoy a special treat at home. Let them see you rejoice in your steps, no matter how minor they may seem. Don't immediately rush into the next challenge—there will be time for that. Celebrate and savor everything before moving on.

10. Women would be kind to themselves.

Two things struck me when I listened to what women had to say about balance in life and running:

a) How much women actually do on a weekly basis (an obscene amount).

b) How unkind we are to ourselves about how much we accomplish, always demanding more and rarely satisfied with what we've done.

I've heard women I deeply admire speak negatively of themselves and criticize their training results, even though they were incredible. Some women were putting in 30 miles of cross training on top of 50 miles of running per week, on top of holding down jobs and cooking dinner every night. They were getting up at 4 a.m. They were making it work...and yet they still felt it was not enough.

If I could send a message to women everywhere it would be this: We do enough. We have enough. We *are* enough. We deserve to be kind to ourselves.

Remember: There are no hard and fast rules for what

balance should look like. Take the tips that best apply to you, or make up your own.

I Am Enough

World-class endurance athlete Lisa Smith-Batchen tells the story of her goal to be the first woman to complete ten Badwater races: 135 miles through the intense heat of Death Valley.

On her tenth race, things didn't go as planned. The day caught up with her and seven miles from the finish line she had to be treated with an IV. Although she did go on to finish the race, she was disqualified as per race rules because of the IV. After the race Lisa ended up spending six days in the hospital in Lone Pine. She accumulated an extra 38 pounds of fluid and was severely ill.

After Lisa left the hospital, a nun named Sister Marybeth reminded Lisa that she had accomplished her goal of becoming the first woman to complete ten Badwater races. Lisa didn't agree, since she had been disqualified on her tenth try, even though she had covered the entire 135 miles. Sister Marybeth said, "Who do you need credit from to be the first woman to have ten Badwaters?" Lisa didn't know what to say, but she thought it over. Did she need official credit from the race? Could she give herself credit?

"God gives you credit, Lisa," Sister Marybeth continued. "His credit is the only one that really matters." It was a lovely thought and Lisa was content with that for a long time. (Eventually, though, she did sign up for Badwater again to chase down that official tenth finish.)

While there's nothing wrong with chasing down our goals with conviction and determination, we can still be kind to ourselves in the process. When I asked the talented ultrarunner Krissy Moehl what advice she would give her 20-year-old self if she could go back in time, her response was: "Smile and limit your expectations of self."

Ultrarunner Carly Koerner had a similar answer: "I'd tell myself to be more patient with life...I'd also tell myself to wear more bikinis."

Endurance mom Lori Barekman is a physical therapist with two kids. She only makes one New Year's resolution every year: "Lower your standards."

Sometimes the fear is that if we put down that whip, we will instantly turn into fat and lazy couch potatoes, but being kind to ourselves is a far cry from letting ourselves go. In fact, the opposite may be true: acceptance may lead to a newfound determination. That's what happened to Marla McGregor at Cuyamaca 100K in Southern California.

At mile 52, Marla had a low moment. She wasn't having fun anymore and she wanted to drop. "But then I had a realization that even if I didn't run another step, I am enough," she told me. "I am good enough just the way I am."

Her epiphany spurred her to finish the race, not because she had to but because she had nothing left to prove. She could finish on her own terms, because she was good enough the way she was, and she wasn't a quitter.

I have heard women say "my training sucks" or "I've been lazy" when I know for a fact that their training and daily responsibilities far surpass those of a typical person. When we

judge ourselves we often do so under the harshest of lights and it doesn't help that so many other women (especially those on social media) seem to have it all together.

Athlete Whitney Richman suggests we take all social media posts with a grain of salt. "Social media plays a huge role in the shift towards extremes," she observes. "It's continuous positive reinforcement. Most people post their successes (or other's success) and rarely post failures. We get a warped sense of all the amazing feats others are completing and feel like we're missing out on an amazing experience. While these posts can be motivating and inspiring, they also encourage us to push the envelope and do something bigger, better, more extreme. When the extreme becomes the norm, then the bar is raised to even more extreme. It's like we're all in kindergarten saying, 'Oh yeah? Well, I can do it better than you!' (complete with tongue sticking out.) I personally love to challenge and compete with myself. It keeps me motivated and I like having goals, but my first one is always to enjoy what I'm doing."

According to Katherine Wintsch, founder and CEO of The Mom Complex, a consulting company that turns the challenges of motherhood into growth opportunities, women (and mothers in particular) will often outright lie about how effortless their lives are. In a TED Talk, Katherine refers to "mommy masks" as propagating false truths and making an already difficult job much harder. "Rather than trying to live up to expectations and doubting ourselves along the way, we should be reveling in the humanity of motherhood and sharing that joy (and the heartache) that is part and parcel of the experience," Katherine writes. "It's messy. That's what keeps it interesting."

If you ever feel down on yourself for not doing enough, try this: write down everything you do. Sometimes we need to see it staring back at us on paper to realize how much we squeeze in. Include every training program, every chore you're in charge of, every child you're raising. Calculate how many hours a day you spend on all these things, and then see if you can still rightly call yourself lazy.

Sometimes I wonder if this is the real reason women excel at endurance sports. Everything we do is an endurance activity—long and challenging, with unexpected obstacles thrown at us. We master tasks like raising children, juggling relationships and building communities. The things we do take forever. There is no finish line.

When Gloria Arlin King comes back from a race, her kids ask her if she has won. Although she explains that she doesn't win races, she just runs them, her kids respond with, "C'mon mama, we know you're the big winner!" And to them, she truly is.

Vanessa Runs

7: Ally Or Adversary? (Competition)

"Play to win, not 'not to lose.'"
- Dondi Scumaci

I am about three miles away from the Javelina Jundred finish line, pacing my friend Holly Miller. She is about to qualify for Western States, a major goal of hers for the year, and Javelina is her last chance to qualify. This is Holly's second 100-miler and we're jogging consistently. We're going to finish well.

It's early Sunday morning and besides the odd runner shuffling along, the world is still. The sun has started to peak for another stunning desert sunrise and the men-shaped cacti are growing shadows. The dawn light opens up the view slowly and cautiously, like a blackfoot daisy fighting to bloom on harsh terrain. Holly fights right alongside them, tired but determined.

Western States legend and founder Gordon Ainsleigh is somewhere on the trail finishing the race himself and inspiring Holly to remember her goal: she is here for Western and she will finish strong.

As we run, we talk about the difficulties of running 100 miles, the value (or lack of value) in a challenge like this, and athleticism in general. I am inspired by Holly's determination to take on this goal, and I am moved—as I always am at races like this—to take on a challenge of my own.

For months now I have been fighting the nagging desire

to train hard for a race. Sure, I've trained before…kind of. I've finished many races. But I've never picked a race, trained specifically for that event, and pushed myself to my limits on race day.

I love endurance and I love the outdoors. I'm a mountain girl trotting along smelling flowers and listening to the birds. I often sign up for races at the last minute and run them on a whim. I am often at the back of the pack, happy and tired but never completely drained. I have never pushed myself to my breaking point, with the deepest part of my heart and soul, risking life and limb. I have never wanted a race finish that badly. I have gone to dark places, but I have never trained to run competitively.

I tell Holly that I want the experience of competition. Fierce competition. I want to push way beyond that point of comfort. I want to set my sights on a specific numerical goal and run my heart out to achieve it.

I don't want to compete all the time, every day, but I do want it once…maybe twice.

Holly encourages me. She believes I can and I should. Still, I mull it over. Is this really what I want? I'm a back-of-the-packer by nature. Most of my friends are back-of-the-packers. We take pictures. We walk. We chat. We push the race cut-offs. That's what I do, but is it who I am?

I feel a competitive drive, but something is holding me back and I realize that it's fear. What if I try and fail? What if I don't measure up? What if I've lost too much fitness? Still, the desire speaks to me. I see a version of myself that is not yet, but could be. I see myself strong and fierce. Dirty and dusty.

Pushing and powerful, caked and crusty with sweat, salt and trail guts. All I need is a little bit of a push to send me toppling over the edge. It's bound to hurt, but it will be a good hurt.

When I think about competitive female endurance runners, Anita Ortiz is at the top of my list. Anita was the U.S. Womens Mountain Running Champion from 2002 to 2004 as well as Masters Runner of the Year for two years. She has more than 100 race wins under her belt and is a force to be reckoned with. She is so used to winning that when she doesn't win, she struggles with mentally processing that unusual fact.

Anita started running in second grade, by herself. She ran loops around her house for fun and wore a path in the grass. She would run home from school every day and won her first race in the sixth grade in a 600-yard run. Since then, Anita has been hooked on winning, and she's damn good at it.

However, she describes her relationship with competition as "an uncomfortable dance." For a long time, Anita couldn't manage the force of her competitive feelings, so she didn't allow herself to race. She even gave up an athletic college scholarship. It was her husband who played a major role in getting her back on the podium.

Her husband Mike describes a turning point in their relationship in *Blood Sport*, a *Trail Runner Magazine* article:

"She's sitting on the bed, shaking like a leaf," he recalls, "so I'm, like, 'Don't worry. You're going to be fine.' And she goes, 'You dummy. I'm not worried about how I'm gonna do. I'm worried about how bad this is gonna hurt. Because if it doesn't hurt, it means I haven't run my best.' And that really

helped our marriage. It helped everything. Because then I understood her."

As an athlete, I want to stand and cheer for Anita to win at all costs, but as a woman there is still a part of Anita that scares me…a part that I never want to see in myself: that blind, ravenous push for the finish, every other competitor be damned and trampled. I'm afraid, that if I get too much Anita in me, I'll be unlikable.

That same *Trail Runner* article tells a chilling Anita story as witnessed by Kami Semick. Anita was coming off her Western States win and trying to repeat as women's masters team champion. At the TransRockies run she was paired with Prudence L'Heureux, the reigning 100K national champion. TransRockies is a stage race where you must finish each leg with your partner or be penalized.

Prudence and Anita had never met, but on paper they were a dream team.

Come race week, Prudence had serious trouble breathing at the elevation of Colorado's trails. Despite their commanding lead, "Ortiz spent much of her days screaming at L'Heureux to move faster…Even when they were that far ahead, Anita couldn't turn it off. She had her hands on her hips and was yelling, `Get your ass up the hill!' And Prudence couldn't breathe."

The last four paragraphs of the *Trail Runner* article broke my heart:

"We'd cross the line after the first three stages, and she wouldn't even look at me," L'Heureux says. "She'd stomp off and go talk to her friends. She just treated me like a bad person. I've never had anyone treat me that way. She didn't seem to have any compassion or human side. She didn't care. And Anita was one of my idols."

Anita describes her drive to do her best as a need. When that best isn't first place, she has a hard time dealing with it. Part of me wants to admire Anita for her fierceness, but a less athletic side wants to shove my smudged glasses up on my pimply face with a pudgy fist, point a finger at her and scream, "Bully!"

As I run with Holly Miller, I realize that my revulsion for this story has nothing to do with Anita at all. This is about my own fears. If I feed my competitive side, will I also soon find myself screaming at women from the side of the trail? Will I also send my teammates home in tears? Could I lose control and lose sight of the woman I want to be? I want to be caring, compassionate, motivating and patient. Will being competitive make me lose sight of that?

Competing Against Men

One morning I rolled out of bed, flipped open my laptop and opened my Facebook page. There at the top of my newsfeed was an all-male pissing contest. The opening topic was pain.

My friend Sean (not his real name) commented: "Why would anyone avoid pain?" As a martial artist and a climber, Sean embraces and adores pain. They are passionate bedmates.

Another friend, a seasoned ultrarunner, assumed Sean

was inexperienced and went on to list his own accolades in endurance—a lengthy and impressive resume. A virtual scrum ensued:

Male 1: "I go longer, faster, and more frequently in everything than anyone I know."

Male 2: "You must not get out much."

Male 1: "Dude, you have no clue."

Male 2: "I write the clues. Come run the next five races with me."

Male 1: "Spend just 12 hours with me one day a week, any day."

Male 2: "Only 12?"

Male 1: "I didn't say I had 12-hour days, I said spend 12 hours with me. Huge difference. I was letting you sleep."

I watched the banter unfold with fascination. Both were seasoned athletes, each incredibly talented in their own sports. Both were relentless, crazy strong and competitive. I understood where they were each coming from, but online it looked like a silly exchange.

The most surprising part of all was that after a few minutes both men were able to neatly wrap up the thread, shake virtual hands and walk away with no hard feelings.

It struck me that women would never display aggression or confidence this way, no matter how talented or competitive they were. And if they did, they certainly wouldn't walk away unharmed.

Women compete differently. Ours is more of a silent, sneaky strength. We don't roar like lions, but we sting like scorpions hidden in the grass, just waiting for your bare feet to stroll by. You won't expect us to be there but we'll take you down, like Pam Smith did when she won the women's race at Western States 100 and nobody saw her coming. Her name had never even been mentioned as a contender.

In a study on Competitiveness Across the Life Span, a *Psychology and Aging* article suggested that competitive preferences may actually be correlated with individual fluctuations in steroid hormones. Athletes with higher levels of testosterone were more competitive than those with lower levels. As we age and our levels of testosterone drop, our competitive spirit also fades.

There's a social and cultural aspect as well. Many women have spoken to me about holding back to nurse a man's ego, be it her husband, boyfriend, friend, training buddy or casual acquaintance. Sometimes we feel life would be easier for us if we didn't directly compete with the men in our lives. Interestingly, some studies have shown that women who are raised in a matriarchal society grow up to be more competitive than women who live under a patriarchy.

In her book, *Run Like a Girl*, Mina Samuels tells the story of hiking Mount Kilamanjaro with her former husband. They were among twelve people on a guided hike with only four people planning to summit: Mina, her husband, and two more.

Mina's husband got hit with altitude sickness pretty early on. He struggled along for a while, but finally shut down and declared he would have to turn back. She agonized over whether she should continue without him. She writes:

We expect men to accomplish things. To overcome

hardship and challenge, to finish at all costs. But I wasn't a man. I was a woman, and that came with its own set of expectations: be a good wife, nurturing, self-sacrificing, protector of the male ego. What would the consequences be if I "bettered" him, if I soldiered on like he would have? I hesitated, deferring to him, waiting for him to decide on my behalf; but he just kept looking at me, inscrutable in the dark. "I'll come back down with you," I said. I wanted to cry…He felt rejuvenated, and I defeated—resentful even. He didn't ask me to retreat. And we never spoke of it. I had caved under the weight of hundreds of years of deep cultural conditioning all by myself.

Other women don't feel the same pressure of this social conditioning. Ultrarunner Victoria Rochat told me: "The best thing about being a female ultrarunner is that usually in a running group there are no more than three women and what feels like a bazillion guys. Whether it is being able to prove yourself, that females *can* run with the guys or just the feeling that we are just as hardcore as, if not more than, the guys are is awesome."

When women do decide to compete against men, some have found themselves coming out on top. As far as Lisa Tamati is concerned, it is the men who should be afraid, not us. "We have usually overcome more obstacles to get where we are. We are fighters. In my opinion, more pain tolerant. Some people think we have a physical advantage. I think the world is our oyster."

Fighting Dirty with Other Women

When Norah Vincent was growing up, she was good at tennis, the best in her class. As she explains in *Self-Made Man*, she was proud of her skills and so was her instructor. He would praise Norah in front of the other girls and set her up as an example for them to emulate. One day a popular girl grew tired of hearing about Norah and announced: "Well, I'd rather look the way I do and serve the way I do than serve the way she does and look the way she does."

Norah compares this to her experience years later in an all-male bowling league, which she joined by disguising herself as a man. The sense of camaraderie she experienced overwhelmed her. She writes:

As men they felt compelled to fix my ineptitude rather than be secretly happy about it and try to abet it under the table, which is what a lot of female athletes of my acquaintance would have done. I remember this from playing sports with and against women all my life. No fellow female athlete ever tried to help me with my game or give me tips. It was every woman for herself. It wasn't enough that you were successful. You wanted to see your sister fail. Girls can be a lot nastier than boys when it comes to someone who stands in the way of what they want.

Although the attitudes of high school girls are not always the same as adult women, similarities sometimes arise.

In *Running Hot*, Lisa Tamati tells the story of a female

thorn in her side at Badwater, a fellow competitor who tried to knock her out of the competition with mind games and misinformation. Firstly, she openly criticized Lisa for going out too fast. Secondly, she told Lisa it was only one mile to the top of a pass, knowing full well that the distance was actually five miles.

In a Skype interview Lisa told me, "There are two types of girls in the ultrarunning scene. One type is all about the sisterhood and supporting each other. And then there are the types who would throw you off your game to get ahead. And I would say they are the minority."

Lisa usually encounters strong women who are supportive and go out of their way to push other women forward. These are the women who will support you, crew you, pace you and cheer you on until they are blue in the face.

In her book *Woman: An Intimate Geography*, Natalie Angier explores this camaraderie/competition duality. She writes:

Women bond with other women, and yet our strongest aggressions and our most frightening hostilities may be directed against other women. We hear about the war between the sexes, but surprisingly few of our aggressive impulses are aimed against men, the putative adversaries in that war. We don't consider men our competitors, even now, in the market free-for-all, when they often are. It is so much easier to feel competitive with another woman, to feel our nerves twitch with anxiety and hyper-attentiveness when another woman enters our visual field. We dress women in fairy white, we dress them in mafia black. We want them around us. We want to be alone among men.

These days women feel they are directly competing against each other not only in races but also for men, jobs, social standing and attention. When there are fewer women at the top, it is assumed that there is only room for one token female.

In 2013, saltyrunning.com posted a women's running showdown that stretched out over several posts. They started with 64 talented female athletes and slowly whittled them down with reader voting to find the "Greatest Woman Runner of All Time."

I normally enjoy the female-positive content on Salty Running, but this series made me wonder about our seemingly obsessive tendency to constantly compare ourselves to one another. Could we not have profiled each of these women individually or as a talented group instead of pitting them against each other? Each woman had her own style of running, her own focus and was talented in her own right. To me, the article spoke of a mistaken female mindset that there can be only one Great Woman Runner. Why can there not be many of us? (Tirunesh Dibaba emerged as the triumphant victor, by the way, only barely ahead of Paula Radcliffe.)

This is an issue that extends far beyond Salty Running. Females compare themselves to other women all the time. How many times have we run behind women and found ourselves taking a mental inventory of all the ways in which all their features compare with ours?

"Wow, her ass is way better than mine," we think. "Why

can't I have calves like that!" we scold ourselves.

Often these comparisons lead to insecurity. That insecurity, if left unchecked, can be the reason we attack other women.

In 2013, *Women's Adventure Magazine* ran a story about a woman who was just starting her fitness journey and who had lost five pounds by taking up cycling and healthy eating. In response, they received a letter from a disgusted reader criticizing the magazine for featuring "unhealthy, overweight women as some type of fitness example" and referred to the cycling female as a "poser." She didn't look good in Spandex so, to that reader, her story didn't matter. She wasn't fit enough or skinny enough to be in the club.

Women's Adventure took the high road and defended their five-pound-lighter cyclist in an article titled "Adventure is Not Just for Sexy People."

When we are critical of others, we are really criticizing ourselves. We call other women fat and ugly because we fear we are those things, or close to becoming them. We call them slutty and lazy because we don't want anyone to notice those qualities in ourselves.

Secretary of State Madeleine Albright once said: "There's a special place in hell for women who don't help each other." If you think that's extreme, consider all the times we have written off female bullying in sports as uncommon or best ignored. Would we dare come to the same conclusions when the aggressors are male?

Imagine for a minute if Anita Ortiz in the TransRockies story had been a man. We describe her as fierce and

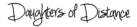

passionate when she screams at another woman and causes her to leave the race in tears. If a man had done the same, the behavior would have been considered highly abusive and unacceptable. Are we letting women get away with too much? Are we writing off real abuse as mere cat-fighting?

When I was a budding ultrarunner in Ontario, Canada, I was excited about moving to California. I had been following a few talented Southern California runners through their blogs and on social media. Although I was excited to meet them all, there was one woman in particular I was looking forward to seeing. Judging from her Facebook posts, she was an experienced trail runner and incredibly talented. She exuded positivity online and I felt I could learn a lot from her.

When I finally met her I was surprised to learn that she was slow—much slower than she had presented herself online—and she rarely stuck through an entire training run, yet wanted everything photographed and documented on Facebook. I found that strange, but figured we could still be friends and support each other. I would soon learn that she had less than zero interest in friendship. She ignored me completely but I was actually lucky—to other women she was downright vile, making snarky comments about their clothing and tearing down their accomplishments. That's what insecurity looks like.

Girl-on-Girl Camaraderie

Self-proclaimed bad feminist Roxane Gay wrote a brilliant essay entitled "How to be Friends with Another Woman."

Her first three points blew me away. Here is an excerpt:

1. Abandon the cultural myth that all female friendships must be bitchy, toxic or competitive. This myth is like heels and purses—pretty but designed to SLOW women down.

a) This is not say that women aren't bitches or toxic or competitive sometimes but rather to say that these are not defining characteristics of female friendship, especially as you get older.

b) If you find that you are feeling bitchy, toxic, or competitive toward the women who are supposed to be your closest friends, look at why and figure out how to fix it and/or find someone who can help you fix it.

2. A lot of ink is given over to mythologizing female friendships as curious, fragile relationships that are always intensely fraught. Stop reading writing that encourages this mythology.

3. If you are the kind of woman who says, "I'm mostly friends with guys," and act like you're proud of that, like that makes you closer to being a man or something and less of a woman as if being a woman is a bad thing, see Item 1b. It's okay if most of your friends are guys, but if you champion this as commentary on the nature of female friendships, well, soul-search a little.

a) If you feel it's hard to be friends with women, consider that maybe women aren't the problem. Maybe it's just you.

I strongly encourage you to look up Roxane's essay or buy her book and read it in its entirety. For most of my life I bragged about having mostly male friends. What does that say about my attitude towards my own gender? This essay woke me up.

Author and outspoken feminist Naomi Wolf shares the same opinion in *The Beauty Myth*. She writes:

> The unknown woman, the myth would like women to believe, is unapproachable; under suspicion before she opens her mouth because she's Another Woman, and beauty thinking urges women to approach one another as possible adversaries until they know they are friends. The look with which strange women sometimes appraise one another says it all: a quick up-and-down, curt and wary, it takes in the picture but leaves out the person; the shoes, the muscle tone, the makeup, are noted accurately, but the eyes glance off one another. Women can tend to resent each other if they look too "good" and dismiss one another if they look too "bad." So women too rarely benefit from the experience that makes men's clubs and organizations hold together: The solidarity of belonging to a group whose members might not be personal friends outside, but who are united in an interest, agenda, or worldview.

But endurance racing and training re-introduces that solidarity, and thanks to trail running I have been able to experience it firsthand.

Sometimes you can tell, just by what a woman is wearing, that she will soon be your new best friend. We may choose our competitors based on first glance impressions, but I also

choose my friends that way. If you've ever run into someone dressed like a runner in a non-running context, perhaps wearing the same shoes (or non-shoes) that you run in, you probably know what I mean. Insta-besties.

Contrary to popular belief, women do not dress up only for men. Women dress for other women. Natalie Angier writes: "Female display also can be affiliative, implying the possibility of an alliance. In that sense, women may have 'chosen' breasts on each other as much as men chose them on women."

That's basically how I met Jess Soco...not that I was looking at her breasts.

Jess looks like everything I would love to be, only I chicken out sometimes and she always has the balls to pull it off. She's trail-fit, super smart, independent, and wears shorts that most women would wear as underwear. She wears buffs that most people would wear as a headband across her chest as a bra. Clearly, she's awesome. To hang out with Jess is to enter a happy place full of mutual admiration and free of ill-will. She is a talented runner and a kind soul.

In Leadville, Colorado, we car-camped together (Jess lives and travels in her van full-time) and shared some 14,000-foot summits. I will never forget one particular summit: Mt. Elbert.

Jess and I got up early with our friends, Toni and Laurie, to tackle Colorado's highest peak at 14,439 feet—also the second highest summit in the lower 48. Jess and I had hiked it once before so we knew we were in for a challenge. After a bumpy ride to the trailhead and a quick trip to the bathroom, we were off.

The first bit was easy. We jogged and chatted and laughed, bumbling our way through the semi-darkness. Then the climb hit and I felt a familiar burn on my legs. I had to take deeper breaths, but I focused on controlling them so I was never panting. The burning, though uncomfortable, was comforting in its familiarity. I knew it would only get steeper from there on in.

"We're not at the hard part yet," I told myself and kept my steady pace. Jess and I were leading the group until we hit the flat section and then a short downhill. Jess and I used the easier terrain to recover and walk, catching our breaths and slowing our heart rates. Toni and Laurie ran ahead, like two giddy schoolgirls just after the bell. I smiled. I had done the exact same thing the first time I climbed this. That downhill is so motivating…until you get to a crazy steep section a few yards ahead.

By the time I hit the steep section I had fully recovered and was able to power hike past Toni and Laurie, Jess right on my heels. We didn't talk much; we were too busy trying to breathe. At the next flat-ish section, Jess and I stopped to wait for the others.

It had been a difficult climb, but we knew the worst was still ahead. We perched ourselves on a log and braced for the climb. Once the others arrived, we made sure they had eaten and recovered before we set off together.

I led the group and found it kept me motivated to keep moving. I picked a pace and pushed to maintain it, even when it felt like my legs were exploding. Hands on thighs, I hiked and hiked and hiked at what felt like a near-90 degree angle,

climbing over rocks and boulders. Toni and Laurie fell behind, taking breaks as needed, just as I had done on my first summit. This time, I had no plans to stop until I was at the top. Jess kept pace behind me and I was grateful for the silent company.

"Almost there, almost there, almost there..." I kept telling myself. There was no one else ahead of us — we had passed all the hikers on the mountain. I thought of poems and songs to distract me from the difficult terrain and, as always, peeking behind to see Jess a short ways behind me drove me forward.

When I reached the top with Jess by my side, it was a glorious moment. I wasn't wearing a GPS but I knew we had summited much faster than our first time. Jess and I huddled behind some rocks for relief from the high winds and freezing temperatures. I was wearing all my layers and still I was cold. Jess had an extra layer in her pack that she gave me, but I couldn't stop shivering.

We both ate some food and waited...five minutes...ten minutes...fifteen minutes. There was no sign of Toni and Laurie. Jess and I decided we should run down before we froze to death and hopefully meet up with them on the way down. Maybe they had turned back?

It felt good to run. My limbs loosened up and I started feeling warmth again. I was almost warmed up when we caught up to the others. They were giving it all they had and they weren't far from the summit. Toni gave Jess her car keys and we agreed to wait for them in the car.

Knowing a warm car was waiting for us, Jess and I picked up speed, sometimes talking, sometimes walking, sometimes running hard. Downhill, we finally had enough breath to chat. We discussed pacing and crewing duties for Leadville 100, future running adventures and praised each other's athletic prowess and body types.

I had always admired Jess' build, but it didn't occur to me that someone might admire mine. This still sticks out in my mind as one of the most genuine and soul-building conversations. No cattiness, no jealousy, no games—just two good friends being open, honest and caring with each other.

The trail flew by under our feet and by the time we reached the car, we had set a summit PR and were feeling great. We used the bathroom and settled into the car to nap and wait for the others.

As we drove back to Greg's house that day, I couldn't help but think, "This is what's awesome about women." For every female who is pretentious and fake, there are ten more in the endurance community who are eager to share, love, learn and run together. Jess Soco is on the cover of this book to represent that type of friendship.

Women are beautiful, complicated and fascinating creatures. Even women we dislike have stories we can relate to. Many of our experiences are common themes both within and outside of endurance. Most of us have struggled with safety, relationships, children, harassment and social expectations. If we would freely share our knowledge and experiences with each other, that transparency would bond us.

Too often we are surprised that someone is going through, or has gone through the exact same thing that we are. Let's reach out to each other. Let's ask for advice and guidance. Let's get to know the women around us.

Runner Kristin Armstrong believes that female friendships are not a luxury, something we should indulge in our spare time and when life allows. Friendship and community are mandatory for optimal health and happiness, and we need to schedule time for them. We need each other.

She writes:

The funny thing is, no one ever wins — because, ladies, we are all on the same team. Can you imagine if we acted like it? If we treated each other like it?...Because regardless of who we are, what our bank account has in it or doesn't, what we do for a living or don't, if we are married or not, if we are emotionally broken or healed, if we breastfeed or not, if we eat meat or not, if our hair color is real or not, if we believe in God or not, if we are sullen and introspective or freewheeling and hilarious...there has to be a place to just be. And in a sport that requires only shorts, a jog bra, a shirt, socks, shoes and some heart, we are probably about as equal as we are going to be. Why not enjoy and appreciate each other for once, plainly?

The Solitude Advantage

In 2009 Angie Piskorski was working as a supervisor in a female adolescent residential treatment program when a 13-year-old girl threw her against a wooden bed — twice. The suicidal teen had placed a strap around her neck and became violent when Angie tried to remove it. Both times, Angie's head slammed against the bed. Later at the hospital, the doctors told Angie that she had suffered from a severe concussion and had injured four regions of her brain.

An avid gym rat, Angie soon found that her gym overstimulated her with noise, lights and people moving in different directions. Her workouts would often end in tears of disappointment and frustration. That's when she stumbled onto trail running and a light bulb went off: everyone was running in the same direction. She could do this!

"We live in a world where everyone is hustle and bustle, living in the electronic era of getting things done at a faster rate, and my brain can't keep up," writes Angie. "It burns out quickly and needs time to recharge before entering the fast-pace flow of life. Running helps me clear all the chatter." Angie runs to silence her world and to be alone.

Although not every woman has suffered a brain injury, many understand the simplicity of a single-track trail. We crave an escape from the fast lane and some quiet time to think our own thoughts. In the quest for solitude, Angie is far from alone. Many of the most competitive athletes I interviewed reported a passion for solitude.

Even the youngest athletes share her opinions. Neva "Chipmunk" Warren says, "I hike to have alone time. If you look on most teenagers' blogs, they'll tell you how happy they are when they're left home alone for a few hours. Between school, and parents, and going out with friends, people my age don't often get the time they need to be alone with themselves, not being judged or criticized. While hiking, I realized how nice it was to be alone with my thoughts, and not mindlessly chatting with everyone in my life. I enjoy others' company, but hiking gives me the chance to enjoy my own."

In a society that lumps solitude with loneliness and a lack of confidence, I was surprised that so many women linked solitude as vital to staying competitive. Solitude is about the development and understanding of self. It is not something imposed, but rather chosen and protected. It is the freedom to not only be ourselves, but to think without distractions and develop valuable mental training strategies. According to an article in *Psychology Today,* "solitude suggests peacefulness stemming from a state of inner richness."

Solitude seems to give women a competitive edge. The endurance runner *must* thrive in solitude. Often, top athletes "perform" for hours on end in complete solitude, miles away from cheering crowds and screaming fans, if not on race day at least in training. I have witnessed many social butterflies drop out of races—not because of injury or lack of training— but because they could not handle the suffocating solitude of a lonely course.

Men have also long pursued a state of solitude. Edward Abbey in *Desert Solitaire* describes his reliance on isolation from others for a more complete connection to the outside world. Countless other books by avid outdoorsmen and athletes express similar sentiments, but Suzanne Roberts, author of *Almost Somewhere: Twenty-Eight Days on the John Muir Trail*, believes there is a gender distinction in the way we approach nature: "Often people say they hike mountains because they are there. Even though some women have taken on this attitude, it seems to me that it is an internalization of man's view of nature." Suzanne suggests that instead of checking off peak-bagging conquests, women prefer to feel a connection to movement in the outdoors.

By moving swiftly through nature, women can take a break from being givers. There is no one around to ask them for help or a quick favor. Their time is their own; they can feel free and comfortable in their own skins. Part of the secret to a female's competitive success may well lie in her joy of sweating it out solo.

Aversion to Competition

The year I volunteered as a coach for the non-profit Girls on the Run, I was working once a week with a group of middle school girls in a program called Girls on Track. Most girls in this program were third to fifth graders, but our girls were in grades six to eight. The dynamics of working with these girls was different than with the younger crowd. They were cliquey and interested in things that were "cool." Too often, it was uncool to care or participate in group activities.

We had one eager-to-please outcast who was up for doing anything for coach approval: a poor, rail-thin girl with greasy stringy hair and ratty shoes. We also had a bunch of cooler, more developed girls with the right clothes who couldn't be bothered to run. As a lifelong nerd from a poor neighborhood, I immediately bonded with the thin girl and we'd run laps together while the other coaches talked to the girls who mostly refused to move.

I was one of four coaches assigned to work with Girls on Track, and one day we all got together to brainstorm how to best motivate these older girls. We came up with the idea of introducing some friendly competition. The girls already seemed competitive, so we thought we could channel some of that pre-teen competitive vibe into something more positive and inclusive. This would involve some minor changes to the program.

When we approached the administration with our ideas, we were immediately shut down. Girls on the Run operates on a non-competitive approach. Everyone participates, everyone wins and everyone has fun. Nobody competes, ever.

I had a hard time accepting this. Wasn't this just another way of demonizing competition among women? Weren't we squelching a female's natural competitive vibe, teaching her that she's not actually allowed to win?

According to an article on *Psych Central* by Dr. Lynn Margolies, women may become catty when their innate competitive spirit is stifled. A woman, like a man, is competitive by nature but society often convinces her that she cannot express competitive aggression. When a woman's healthy competitive spirit goes underground, it can turn into envy, insecurity, guilt and shame. She is still innately competitive, but she is more sly and sneaky about expressing it.

When I began talking to women in endurance, I was shocked to learn that all of them, even the slow ones, viewed themselves as incredibly competitive. Though most weren't out there winning races, they were there to do their best at every single event. Even my back-of-the-pack friends who I assumed were running for the scenery and sunrises and selfies confessed to putting their game face on.

My friend Desi Klaar told me, "I look around and I see some well-groomed and beautiful women showing up in their strategically matched outfits. I also see another group which doesn't care about makeup, ever. Some are afraid to run alone, some like me are okay with nature and all its glory. Each of these ladies has an inherent desire to kick the other's ass out there."

Lynette McDougal, who had never been a frontrunner, had a coach scream at her once during a 50-mile race. It was enough to make something click and she pushed herself to stay with the first-place female for an exhilarating second place finish. After that she went on to finish her first 100-miler in less than 24 hours.

On her second try at Western States 100, Mary Lou Lackey came into the mile 85 aid station just a few minutes after cutoff. She had hoped to slip quietly through, but was unfortunately pulled from the course. A well-meaning volunteer said to her, "Just think, now you don't have to run the last 15 miles!" Mary Lou remembers that comment bitterly. "The captain of the aid station knew better than to say something so insensitive," she told me. "He turned his head away with a tear in his eye and cut my bracelet off. He knew how I felt."

Other women have taken risks to stay competitive, like Michelle Roy who ran the Vermont 50 so hard that she passed out at mile 37 and woke up to strangers rubbing down her naked body in a desperate effort to warm her up. Or like Ashley Walsh who went directly from collapsing on the Fort Clinch 100 course to intensive care with a bad case of

rhabdomyolysis, a breakdown of muscle fibers that causes kidney damage. As they were dragging her off the trail, she was screaming that she wouldn't quit (although she doesn't remember doing that). All these women cared deeply about competing, and they cared about finishing.

While I was finishing up Javelina Jundred with Holly Miller, little Teagan Redden was also finishing her race on the same course. She was running a distance of 100K with her mother, Sabrina. Teagan is nine years old.

I first saw Teagan at a race called Across the Years in Phoenix, Arizona where she covered 50K with her brother. Both of Teagan's parents are ultrarunners. This girl loves to run. Every time I saw her she was looking joyful and fresh. Although the child-runner debate is an issue in itself entirely, it's impossible to ignore Teagan's passion for endurance.

In 2014 I interviewed Teagan's parents for *The Natural Running Network Live*, a podcast I was co-hosting at the time. Sabrina talked about Teagan's fierce sense of competition. This was not a sport her parents drove her to do. Rather, there was a drive within her that made her want to run long and far.

However, several studies have suggested that cooperative sports trump competitive sports when it comes to enhancing the physical abilities and self-concepts of young girls. Cooperative sports seem to encourage girls to develop their own skills instead of focusing on making others look bad.

This is the focus of Girls on the Run and I can't deny that they have been highly successful. Coaches are trained to not only run with the girls but prioritize life skills above all. The program mission is "to educate and prepare girls for a life time of self-respect and healthy living."

While this approach has been effective among developing young girls, is it useful for grown women with an aversion to competition?

According to a 2003 study on competition aversion, a female's decision to enter competition does not reflect her talent or abilities. "While fast young men are almost certain to enter the highly competitive race, a sizable minority of the fast young women do not choose to do so."

Women are reluctant to compete unless they are fairly certain they can win. If they have a chance, but aren't sure they will win, they don't often take it. Some evidence suggests that women tend to compete harder against other women, but hold back when competing with men. Although we are born equally competitive, the gender gap has been noted as early as age five, suggesting a social learning factor. This isn't exactly a surprise.

In 2012, Run Rabbit Run 100 in Colorado offered prize money to the top five females to finish the race, but only four women stepped up to compete and finish. The fourth and final runner, Salynda Fleury, was running her first 100-miler and finished in 29:42. Any other female coming in after her could have won prize money, but the competition was not there.

In an interview with *Trail Runner Magazine*, former Olympic marathoner Magdalena Boulet said, "There are plenty of women out there who could excel at multiple distances, but they don't try them. Either they enjoy what they're doing, or prefer to stay within their comfort zone."

How will we know what we're capable of if we don't try?

I ask this question more to myself than to anyone else. I'm back on the Javelina Jundred course, debating with Holly about whether or not I should train more competitively. Well, I'm the only one debating. Holly is encouraging me. I have visited that Javelina course several times in my mind since then, wondering if I should, if I *could* step it up.

In the fall of 2013, Shacky and I were driving across Canada. We stopped in beautiful Banff, Alberta, and walked into a quaint little tourist shop. There, I fell in love with some Varua Good Spirit dolls. They were little keychain-sized charms, each bearing a different reminder.

Shacky chose the Ninja Sheriff with a message: "Together we will go in search of action and not be afraid." I picked Rock On: a spunky redhead with wild hair, rocking out to her own beat. Her message: "I will give you the confidence to show off your talents." I attached her to my running hydration pack.

This doll speaks to one of my deep fears, solidified after years of being called a show off, a suck up and an overachiever. The fear of showing off my talents. The fear of truly doing my best. The fear of being unapologetically awesome. It is self-censorship in an effort to blend in with a less-exceptional crowd.

After all these years, I'm still that preteen girl pretending she didn't do her homework when in fact she did it very well. When I slow down, I want it to be because I'm enjoying a view but never ever because I'm afraid.

8: Rapists And Other Creepers (Safety & Fear)

"The one emotion that this hobby has helped me understand over all others is fear. I was once gripped by fear, nearly paralyzed by it — now I feel that I have some control over this largely irrational emotion. For me, endurance sports have always been about looking fear and weakness in the face and pressing forward anyway."
– Jill Homer, *arcticglass.blogspot.com*

In April 2013, Felecia Dora Moran started her thru-hike of the Pacific Crest Trail, a 2,668-mile trek from Mexico to Canada. Accompanied by another solo female hiker with the trail-name of Midget, Felecia had just reached Walker Pass, the last desert re-supply stretch before Kennedy Meadows in Inyokern, California.

She was facing the beginning of the High Sierras, a major milestone. Walker Pass is a small camping area on the side of the highway, easily accessible by car. Normally, it is crawling with trail angels (non-thru-hikers who provide "trail magic" in the form of food, drinks, and support) and impromptu BBQs. However, this was a warm desert morning and still early in the season. They found Walker Pass abandoned.

Midget was out of food, so the plan was to hitchhike into Lake Isabella, California for supplies. It would be a 40-mile hitch, the longest ride of the entire trail. Felicia had been averaging a weekly hitchhike to re-supply — a common and welcomed practice for thru-hikers.

Thumbs out and packs on, the women stood on the side of Route 178, chatting and laughing while they waited patiently for a ride. "A happy-looking hitchhiker is much more easily picked up than if you're out there looking miserable," Felicia explains, and the trail guidebook had warned that rides to Lake Isabella were hard to find. However, as two attractive women in their 20s, their chances were higher than most.

Fifteen minutes later—which can seem like a long time when you're standing on the side of an Interstate—they caught the attention of the driver of a grey, well-used Buick Oldsmobile, a man in his early 70s. He eagerly jumped out of the car, stuck his hand out for a shake and introduced himself as Billy Ray from West Virginia, "...But you can call me Hillbilly..."

Midget shot Felicia a this-could-be-interesting glance, but it was getting hot and the lure of food was strong. They opted to accept the ride. Felicia took the front passenger seat and in no time Hillbilly was chugging along at 35 mph. It would be a long ride.

It took Hillbilly ten minutes to cover his entire life story. Born in West Virginia, he had joined the military, married, had a few kids and been widowed. He was now dating a "hot 30-something who has four kids from four different men." He described himself as her sugar daddy and went on about how much he hates men but "treats women real nice!"

It only got creepier from there. Hillbilly transitioned into asking, "Do you girls like having sex?" Felicia was dumbfounded. "I am a lady and am not going to discuss my sex life with you!" she shot back. "Not until marriage," Midget contributed, laughing nervously in the backseat.

Hillbilly ignored their replies and followed up with, "Do you like having sex with women? You know that doesn't make you gay. Women having sex with women is great…"

Was this the horror-movie hitchhike of every worst nightmare? Felicia could feel herself getting angry, but Hillbilly wasn't finished.

"Have you girls ever been raped?"

Felicia bit her tongue. "I wanted to tell the pervert to go fuck himself and pull the car over to let us out, but my better judgment told me not to piss this creep off," she recalls. Instead, she visualized stabbing his leg with her pocketknife and leaping from the car. She was comforted by the fact that he was a frail old man and that she was confident she could take him down.

Felicia and Midget opted to ignore him while he described the vast number of women he knew who had been raped. Men were bad, he explained, except for him. He was a "good, good man."

A few times, Hillbilly placed his hand on Felicia's left thigh. She would smack it away and glare out the window. The truck was now crawling at 30 mph and Felicia's blood was boiling with rage and adrenaline. All she wanted was to get to Lake Isabella.

They arrived after 50 excruciating minutes. Hillbilly pulled into a gas station, stopped the engine, and looked straight into Felicia's eyes. "If you would like to have sex with me, that could be arranged," was his generous goodbye. The open invitation came with an offer of $20 for each of them and pre-made maps to his house in Ridgecrest, California.

Felicia leaped out of the truck and mumbled, "I would rather die…"

In the end, the hikers laughed it off. Hillbilly had been a pervert, but not a real threat. Hitchhiking is still one of Felicia's favorite modes of transportation. "You meet the most kind, generous, interesting people," she promises. "The Billy Rays of the world are the one percent." Nothing like that ever happened to Felicia again.

In researching this book, I asked hundreds of women about the barriers that prevent females from participating in endurance challenges. Many of the answers revolved around some sort of fear or safety issue. Basically: we're afraid to. The women who trained regularly complained about constantly having to justify to others why they were taking "dangerous risks."

Show me a female endurance athlete and I'll show you a woman who has, multiple times, been told that she is "very brave."

I followed with great interest the iRunFar.com article where Ellie Greenwood asks why more women aren't running ultras. One commenter wrote: "For me the biggest things are: fear of running in the woods by myself, with all the creeps out there…fear of getting lost on the trails by myself, with all the creeps out there…"

When I did an article search for "women+trail", here are the immediate hits that came back:

- Woman sexually assaulted on Maple Ridge walking trail

- Woman dragged by attacker on Vancouver park trail
- Man charged with murder of woman found near Burke-Gilman Trail

I couldn't find a single positive article about females in the outdoors, and frankly that didn't surprise me.

While it's true that there are some inherent dangers in endurance — getting lost, getting caught in the elements, wildlife encounters — in this chapter I focus on the issues that don't typically apply to men. Are there special, extra dangers for females? And if so, what are they? Most importantly, what are we so afraid of?

The Rapist At the Trailhead

Heather Wiatrowski was eight miles into her first 50K race, a beginner-friendly event in New England, when she heard two middle-aged men run up a few feet behind her, keeping her pace. She couldn't turn to see them clearly, but she could hear every word of their conversation. They were discussing how much they would like to "pound," "drill" and "nail" her private parts. There were no other competitors in sight.

Terrified, Heather picked up the pace, but the men stayed right on her tail. Near-sprinting through the forest on an isolated course, she describes the experience as "the stuff of nightmares."

As a newbie ultrarunner, Heather remembered learning the term "pace booty" to describe a situation in which one runner uses the attractive behind of the runner in front of him/her as motivation. Heather had used this tactic herself to

get through a hard run, but why the violent language? Was this friendly (if inappropriate) banter, or a real intention to rape her?

Heather is a scientist, so her mathematical mind started sorting through the data: "One in six of women in the US are the victims of rape," she told herself. "According to the psychologist David Lisak of UMass Boston, among unincarcerated men, one in sixteen men has raped a woman. Most of these men have raped more than one woman and the vast majority of them do not get caught." Heather calculated that with approximately 150 men registered for this race, that should put nine rapists on the trail today.

"Is today my unlucky day?" Heather agonized. It was a question that had crept into her mind during many training runs—any time she passed an occupied, parked car or a strange man.

Heather wanted to report these men, but when she finally made it to the aid station after what seemed like an eternity, she found it was being staffed by a group of enthusiastic teenage girls. Her heart sank. There were no grizzled ultrarunners or race officials in sight.

Heather lingered at the aid station for a few minutes, hoping the men would leave without her. They didn't. Still terrified, she ran into a nearby porta-potty and hid there—amid the stench. After two minutes had passed, she cracked open the door and peered out. They were still there, waiting and staring. She locked herself back inside and sat in that sweltering poop-smell for ten more minutes.

Finally, they were gone.

Heather didn't know the names of these men and couldn't remember their bib numbers. It turned out they had dropped out of the race, DNFed.

Although Heather's story seems extreme, she wonders if it's really that unusual. The ultrarunning community is so tight and feel-good that she suspects some women are afraid of reporting similar experiences. Will they be shunned for speaking out? Will anyone believe them? Will race officials defend a seasoned male runner over a newbie female? Will they claim she just doesn't understand the free-spirited anything-goes trail culture?

"While everyone is saying how wonderfully supportive the ultrarunning community is—and it is—I can't shake the feeling that I'm in an old boys club," laments Heather, "...with old boys rules and no penalties for harassing women." Even if Heather's experience is uncommon, once is already too much.

Today, Heather refuses to register for races with historically low female participation. This is unfortunate because she prefers challenging, technical courses with lots of elevation change, the kinds that don't typically boast large female fields. Instead, she opts for larger-scale, beginner-friendly courses where she can usually keep another woman in her sights at all times.

"I'll never know whether those men intended to assault me or were just fantasizing about it," Heather confesses, "but I'm reluctant to put myself in that position again."

The constant and all-consuming fear of male predators is a daily reality for many women. Sadly, these fears are not always unfounded. Whether we are training in the city, in the

wilderness, at the pool or at the gym, the potential attack of a male predator follows us like a shadow. It transcends our sport.

That's not to say we can't or don't enjoy the outdoors, but rather that it is nearly impossible for us to walk out the door without somehow, in the back of our minds, wondering if we'll be returning safely. Many women understand that there are things she must prepare for that most men do not ever have to consider.

In her memoir about thru-hiking the John Muir Trail, Suzanne Roberts speaks for most of her gender when she says that as a woman, she can never escape the fear of violation. She writes that the gravity of that fear is as real as the weight of her own body:

"Muir rejoiced in his freedom in nature, but at the same time he took his personal safety for granted," Suzanne insists. "He could fall from a tree or into a crevasse, though either way, he retained a semblance of control. Nature doesn't provide a proving ground to women in quite the same way as it does for men because we are often too wrapped up in wondering whether or not we will be threatened out there. Women cannot control what men might do to them in the wilderness."

Potential Solutions
What steps can we take to help women feel safer in the endurance community? Here are a few proposals:
1. One experienced adult at every aid station
One aspect (of many) that disturbed me about Heather's

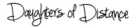

story was the aid station run by inexperienced teens. I have also had the misfortune of running into aid stations filled with teens in the later miles of my first 100-mile race, and it was equally inappropriate. Not only did they not understand the needs of an endurance athlete (or were too busy flirting with each other to care), it was also impossible for them to provide any sort of medical aid, advice or assessment. At that point, it becomes a safety issue.

While I can understand the challenge of recruiting race volunteers for the many long hours of an endurance race, it seems like we could be making more of an effort. The minimum standard should be at least one responsible adult present at every single aid station.

The races I have run in Southern California have excelled at this: every aid station has a captain with full, race-director authority. They are responsible for all the other volunteers and any tough decisions that need to be made. These people are seasoned, experienced athletes. Any one of them would have been in a position to help Heather.

No volunteers? Opt for a water drop or an unmanned aid station. Better yet, don't put on a race without the support.

2. Zero tolerance for sexual harassment

I suggest a publicly stated (on the race website or registration site) zero-tolerance policy for harassment on the course. Many trail races already have a zero-tolerance policy for littering or cheating—go ahead and add harassment to the list. This is a serious offense that should come with serious consequences.

Just so there is no grey area, sexual harassment should

also be defined on the race website, waiver or registration site. Below are a couple of good definitions from the book *Gender and Sport, Changes and Challenges* by Gertrud Pfister and Mari Kristin Sisjord:

According to International Olympic Committee:

Sexual harassment refers to behavior towards an individual or group that involves sexualized verbal, non-verbal or physical behavior, whether intended or unintended, legal or illegal, that is based upon an abuse of power and trust that is considered by the victim or bystander to be unwanted or coerced.

According to Women Sport International, Sexual Harassment Task Force brochure:

Sexual harassment is unwanted, often persistent, sexual attention. It may include: written or verbal abuse or threats; sexually oriented comments; jokes, lewd comments or sexual innuendoes; taunts about body, dress, marital status or sexuality; shouting and/or bullying; ridiculing or undermining of performance or self-respect; sexual or homophobic graffiti; practical jokes based on sex; intimidating sexual remarks, invitations or familiarity; domination of meetings, training sessions or equipment; condescending or patronizing behavior; physical contact, fondling, pinching or kissing; sex-related vandalism; offensive phone calls or photos; as well as bullying on the basis of sex.

3. Female-only training runs

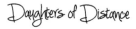

In some cases, an all-female training group may ease more women into the outdoors. Jo Brichetoo and Gretel Fortman are the founders of the Summit Sisters in Australia, a community of all-female trail runners with a passion for sharing wellness and adventure with other women. These groups can act as a female mentorship program to motivate and support women who would otherwise feel unsafe.

Jo believes that community building is the key to facilitating a shift of women to running trails. In an interview with ultra168.com, she said: "It requires a non-threatening environment where women feel safe and without pressure to be of a certain speed or ability. Having group runs that are done to time (e.g. 30 minutes out and 30 minutes back) takes away the pressure for people to keep up. Having online 'closed' groups for women to arrange training runs also helps women feel safer when planning runs."

Other practices she adopts involve introducing women to trails via fire roads to allow them to build confidence without investing money in trail-specific gear. "As the confidence builds, we can help to educate women about the realities of trail running, as well as start discussions within the community about training, gear etc."

4. Female-on-female support

If you are a female in endurance, do not for one second underestimate your influence on other women who are newer at the sport, or looking to join. From afar or up close, other women look up to you. Extend a hand, sport a kind face and present an encouraging voice. The majority of criticisms that bring women down seem to come at the hands of other women—or at least the ones that hurt the most.

Stay approachable and honest about your experiences and limitations. Be vocal about welcoming questions or concerns, and attempt to stay in touch with the women who reach out.

To date, I have been approached with questions about everything from what type of underwear I run in to how I handle my periods to managing vaginal discharge on the trail—personal topics that some might balk at. I don't want to be seen as a super-human, ultra-brave female. I would like women to look at me and feel like they could do this too.

5. Female pacers

When I was much newer to the endurance community, Shacky convinced me to look for a pacing gig at our local 100-mile race, The San Diego 100-Mile Endurance Run. I didn't want to. I was nervous and uncertain. I had never paced before. I wasn't that fast of a runner—what if I let my runner down? Not one to back away solely from my lack of confidence, I put the word out that I was available.

Within a day, I was put in contact with Jay Danek, an incredibly talented runner and author who was shooting for a 20-hour finish. I wanted to back out immediately. That pace was *way* faster than anything I was used to, but Shacky encouraged me to give it a shot, so I did.

On race day I met Jay at the Sweetwater aid station after dark. His wife blurted out some verbal instructions about how often he needed to eat, and then we were off. It was an uphill stretch that Jay mostly hiked, but with his lanky and purposeful gait I found myself jogging to keep up. I was stressed about whether I would be a good pacer, but Jay was easygoing and pleasurable company.

In those short miles, I learned so much from him and was deeply inspired by what he was about to accomplish. It occurred to me—what better way to introduce someone to trail and ultrarunning than having them pace for part of a 100-mile race?

When it came time for me to run my next endurance event, I wanted to give that opportunity to a woman. At Zion 100, I lined up a female pacer I didn't know and who was less experienced than my normal posse of ultra friends. Although I didn't share much time with her, I could tell that this opportunity infused her with some serious trail love.

If you run endurance events on a regular basis, why not solicit more endurance-curious women to work as pacers or crew? Ultrarunner Lori Barekman feels that women should feel capable of doing any sport well, so she chooses female pacers. "I am choosing pacers who are women because I want them to have the opportunity to do this even if they are not as experienced as some of the men that I run with," she explains.

Although the obvious tried-and-true route involves getting good friends and experienced athletes to pace you, a detour from that may be the "in" that a woman needs to find out how much she loves your sport.

6. Self-defense (but don't count on it)

What about learning some sort of self-defense or martial art to boost our confidence and help us protect ourselves? According to author Jason Robillard, that actually could backfire. Yes, it does boost our sense of confidence, but possibly to our own detriment.

Jason wrote an article entitled *How to Avoid Being Robbed, Beaten, and Raped* following a discussion with his wife Shelly, also an ultrarunner. Jason argues that self-defense classes may actually give women a false sense of security. He describes one woman who was adamant that she could defeat any potential attackers after one year of taking karate lessons. In real life, an attack would have likely rendered her training useless, and her false sense of comfort might actually cause her demise.

The safest option in a sticky situation is always to run and/or avoid confrontation at all costs. Even better, take steps to never appear like a victim. The issue is more about situational awareness rather than seeing danger around every corner.

"It's sort of like driving a car," Jason explains. "The act itself is dangerous statistically, but that's not a reason not to drive. Just avoid the stuff that's really dangerous, like tailgating or drunk driving. Same deal with running. A few simple things can be avoided that will make you a lot less desirable as a target." The keys are being aware of your surroundings and making eye contact with the people around you.

Jason's concerns about runner safety began during chats with his wife when they noticed the number of runners who were oblivious to their surroundings. "They fail to notice people, sounds, smells...If the same car drives by three times, an internal alarm should be going off...same deal if an approaching person suddenly changes body language. This happens in the wilderness, too. If the birds stop chirping suddenly, there's a reason. Most people just don't have an awareness of their surroundings. This awareness shouldn't cause stress...ideally it's occurring below our conscious awareness. That takes practice, though. It's like an external manifestation of the inner awareness ultrarunners develop. It's not too far off from the Buddhist idea of awareness in the present."

Are safety issues over-sensationalized for women? Jason believes they are when people are trying to sell a defense product like classes, a weapon, or an ID bracelet. He insists that our time and energy would be better spent learning wilderness survival and first aid.

He recommends Wildlife First Responders classes. Survival skills can be very location-specific, but there are some basics that are worth picking up.

Jason adds: "For what it's worth, I don't like how it's always framed as a female issue. Dudes get jumped, too...and often make the exact same dumb mistakes. Runners are in a good spot, though. They're constantly training to do the most effective self-defense measure — running."

The intent of this chapter is not to scare women from going outside, but to demonstrate that this is a real problem for many females and a strong deterrent from enjoying nature or pursuing a sport. The purpose is to open a thread of conversation that asks, "How can we fix this?"

A Word to Men

Nathaniel Wolfe is a transgendered male. Born a woman, he now enjoys an active life as a strapping male in his 40s. His unique perspective allows him to eloquently express deep insights about the main difference between male versus female sexual attention.

The stock response to issues like these is usually that not all men are like this, and of course that's true. Unfortunately, that's poor consolation for a woman who is being leered at. She has no way of knowing which man is just kidding around, and which one intends to do her serious harm.

Nathaniel once posted an old photo of himself on Facebook from when he was a beautiful 20-year-old female. The comments he received were teasing, playful and highly sexual. This sparked some analysis on his part and I'd like to let his words conclude this section.

In his blog post, *A Tale of Two Titties*, Nathaniel writes:

[This] brings me back to the "I'd hit that" comments on my thread regarding my 20-year-old self. It is because my friends see me as a man that they said that to me. It is locker room talk. It is common locker room talk. It is regular verbiage between men regarding sexual objects. When my body is objectified by men and women through the images of me as a man, it does not threaten me because the power differential is not there. As a man, my NO is taken seriously. Even my "meh" is taken seriously as a no.

When we do this to women, as men, the power differential is not only present, it is all-present. It happens to all women every day. It is never out of a woman's mind. It was never out of mine, until I started living as a white male in our society.

So, you can tell me how much you want to fuck me

all day long and I won't feel threatened by it. And there is that part of me who does enjoy the fact that my physicality elicits desire in others (still doesn't give anyone the right to force themselves on me). The huge difference is that as a man in this society, I am the one with power to stop you if you attack me or if I don't want your attention. I can walk away very easily. I'm not saying it's impossible to be raped as a grown man—it is— but it's not highly likely in everyday life. The same is not true for any woman or child.

So, what do we do? How do we stop this? Well, I think, for one, we, as men, have to recognize it in ourselves when we objectify anyone for any reason. We as men need to stand up to our brothers and address the realities in our locker rooms, in our clubs, in our man caves. I'm not saying sexual flirtations, jokes, etc. are off limits, I think the realities of individual relationships should be the guiding factors behind our engagements with each other. In lieu of actual relationship, common courtesy should be employed.

"I'd hit that" negates any personhood of the "that" and takes away even the idea that "that" might not want to be "hit." In a society that didn't have this underlying tone of women as possessions, the default compliment on my post giving the same intent I am sure my friends meant would have been something like this, maybe: "You look like someone I might have been interested in, I would have asked you out to dinner."

The "Brave" Ones

It is worth noting that not all women are intimidated by the sport, seek mentorship, fear getting lost or want to run with other women. There are women who feel right at home in their sport of choice.

Lizzy Hawker, for example, is known for her solo multi-day runs. In the Great Himalaya Trail in 2011, she found herself alone, lost and stranded in a remote forest for three nights after misplacing her bag with her satellite phone, maps, compass, camera and journey permits. She had enough food and water to survive, and eventually stumbled her way to a nearby village with almost no provisions and "a very strong feeling that everything would be fine."

In an article for *The Telegraph*, she was asked whether there was anything she had changed to prevent this predicament from happening a second time. "Not really," she shrugged. "People know when to expect me back. But I don't have any day-to-day contact and I'm comfortable with that."

Endurance athlete Catra Corbett also laughs in the face of death. In an *Ultra Runner* podcast interview, she said: "If it's my day to die, I'm where I want to be."

Catra runs without knives, guns, emergency gear, or weapons of any kind. She carries a small knife on her fastpacking trips, "but that's not going to hurt anyone," she chuckles. "I could maybe file my nails…"

Other women, like endurance junkie and journalist Jill Homer, use their fear for personal growth. They go ahead and feel afraid…but they still perform. In her post titled *Is There Enough?* Jill writes in a comment:

In many ways, the "bigger, longer, harder" drive has little to do with numbers and more to do with facing new fears and encountering new heights of joy. It doesn't actually need to be longer or more physically difficult, although it often is—but the main drive is something that's more mentally or emotionally challenging….the fear of being alone in the wilderness has yielded to strength and joy, and thus sparks continuing passion.

Kyra Sundance feels the same way. Despite several random medical scares (choking on a vitamin pill, back sciatic spasm, stomach flu), she forces herself to get back out there despite the fear of being in the wilderness alone. "If I didn't," she confesses, "I would turn into a fearful person."

Cheryl Strayed, the author of *Wild (From Lost to Found on the Pacific Crest Trail)*, uses positive thinking to overcome fear. In her book, she writes:

Fear, to a great extent, is born of a story we tell ourselves, and so I chose to tell myself a different story from the one women are told. I decided I was safe. I was strong. I was brave. Nothing could vanquish me. Insisting on this story was a form of mind control, but for the most part, it worked. Every time I heard a sound of unknown origin or felt something horrible cohering in my imagination, I pushed it away. I simply did not let myself become afraid. Fear begets fear. Power begets power. I willed myself to beget power. And it wasn't long before I actually wasn't afraid.

Vanessa R__ms

Fear is an emotion often charged with femininity and portrayed negatively. To run like a girl, hike like a girl, or throw like a girl means to do so clumsily, fearfully and not very skillfully.

Extreme skier Lynsey Dyer says that one of her biggest mistakes in her sport was adopting the idea that women were weak and emotional, and that she should be anything but that. Lynsey went to great lengths to avoid being called a girl, until she realized that her fear and intuition were actually her greatest strengths.

In a TEDx Talk, Lynsey explains how she now uses fear as a tool to pick her challenges: "I would look up at the mountain (what most would call a pretty challenging arena). If in my first instinct there was something that looked inspiring or exciting, I would take note of that, and right behind that, it was very subtle, the fear would come, and I would let it come, all the potential consequences, the what ifs, the potential death even. I would let that come. And I would look back up in the mountain and if that hint of excitement was still there, I would go and do it." Today, Lynsey skis like a girl by accepting her intuition and feeling her fear.

Martine Sesma, on the other hand, couldn't be less scared of endurance running. In comparison to the rest of her life, it's one of the safest situations she has endured:

Growing up on the US-Mexico border surrounded by drug and human trafficking (and I don't use the term "surrounded" lightly...), I never felt safe as a child. I was also extremely poor, so I had no hyper-inflated sense of white-privilege to go with my then-blonde hair and blue eyes. Instead, my physical appearance was a daily hindrance to me...I was hated for being white, unable to blend in at all for protection, and ridiculed frequently for being poor. I was also molested and assaulted regularly, and often told it was because I looked like I wanted the attention.

Martine feels safest when training solo on the trails, alone and hours from anywhere. Whenever she starts to feel afraid in nature, she experiences a flashback to her own painful youth. "And just like that, fear gone. Back to the dirt, back to the stars, back to the love of the trail."

Vanessa Runs

9: Ew, My Thighs Are Touching! (Disorders & Addiction)

"What passes for 'normalcy' seems to be the absence of real devotion, not to mention passion. Where would that leave the people who have been the greats in any field? When you have a gift, there is often a dark side… One of the biggest challenges of my life has been making sure that the dark side doesn't win."
- Pam Reed, *The Extra Mile: One Woman's Personal Journey to Ultrarunning Greatness*

When I worked as an editor for active.com, I was always in search of new stories to tell. We were expected to create 10 to 15 new links per week—content for which I tried to maintain a high standard. Although the goals were lofty, I wanted each article to be useful and engaging.

That's when I stumbled on Valerie's story. Valerie was a runner who had suffered from an eating disorder for most of her life. Long distance running had taught her to care for her body. She put on weight, took on ultra distances and renewed her outlook on life. I fell in love with her story and asked her to allow me to share it. I assured her that her experience was important and would be well received. I was envisioning a feel-good, success story that could inspire others.

When the article went live, it was posted on social media, and the comments started pouring in. To my surprise, her story wasn't well received at all. Many of the comments were condescending, snarky, judgmental or just downright cruel.

People accused her of trading one obsessive activity for another, ultrarunning in exchange for her eating disorder.

Poor Valerie hopped on Active's Facebook page and tried to defend her sport as politely as possible. I had been so sure that others would see what I saw: a strong, resilient woman who had overcome her demons. I had encouraged her to share her story and I had exposed her to this backlash.

I was angry with the Active community for trashing her. The last thing in the world Valerie needed was more condescension and negativity. Valerie was a class act. She never responded in anger and she certainly never blamed me, but I felt responsible for the sting of those negative words.

If I had known then what I know now — that some form of disordered eating is actually quite common among female runners — I would have been more irate. When I wrote about Valerie, I believed that her experience was unique. As I began interviewing women for this book, however, one woman mentioned overcoming an eating disorder through endurance sports...then another...and another. The list of women who had used running to battle an eating disorder got longer and longer.

These women were not embarrassed or shy about describing their experiences, and I wondered why these conversations weren't more out in the open. Maybe I just hadn't been listening?

Eating Disorders & Weight Obsession

According to *The Beauty Myth* by Naomi Wolf, 90 to 95 percent of anorexics and bulimics are women. "America, which has the greatest number of women who have made it into the male sphere, also leads the world with female anorexia," Naomi concludes. "Women's magazines report that there are up to a million American anorexics, but the American Anorexia and Bulimia Association states that anorexia and bulimia strike a million American women every year."

Studies on this topic can be contradictory: some conclude that athletes are at lower risks of developing disorders, while others say the risk is higher. We do know that among female athletes, those most at risk are the ones who engage in sports where a lower body weight is an advantage. This includes gymnastics, figure skating and distance running. Incidentally, many of these female athletes also tend to have personalities driven by competition, discipline and achievement—all great qualities that can also work against them to fuel a disorder.

It's virtually impossible to pinpoint exactly why some athletes develop a disorder while others don't, although I suspect the history of family dynamics and abuse may provide some clues. A study about anorexia and abuse published in the *Journal of Loss and Trauma* tells the story of a woman named Beth. Beth is a competitive distance runner who was abused by her coach. In addition, from the time Beth was eight years old, her mother had been telling her she looked pregnant. Beth reasoned that if she made herself ill, her parents might not hate her as much. Tragically, Beth's story is not uncommon.

Eating disorders boast the highest fatality rates for a mental illness and there is evidence that in college campuses,

eating disorders have become the norm while healthy eaters are now a rare exception. However, as common as it has become, it's still extremely difficult to spot disorders in athletic women.

Pam Reed has always been vocal in the running media about her struggle with anorexia. In her memoir, she goes into great detail about her haunted past. Her hardships with food began during puberty and were fueled by her athletic ambitions. Pam wanted to be a world-famous, competitive gymnast—as good as Olga Korbut. To her, this meant looking exactly like Olga: "small, wiry, flat as a board." In a desperate effort to stall her own physical development, Pam stopped eating. Studies confirm that this is not an unusual reason for female athletes to adopt anorexia. The mantra? "Thin is going to win!"

It wasn't until she took up endurance racing that Pam realized she needed food to remain competitive. She began learning how to fuel her body and went on to win Badwater twice. Pam is also a two-time national champion in the 24-hour run, as well as the national women's age-group (40 to 44) record-holder in the 48-hour run.

Pam identifies a condition known as anorexia athletica and goes on to measure her progress against its characteristics. They include:

- Repeated exercising beyond the requirements for good health;
- Fanatical attention to weight and diet;
- Stealing exercise time from work and relationships;
- Focusing on the challenge, and forgetting that exercise

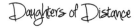

can be fun;

- Defining self-worth in terms of performance;
- Being rarely or never satisfied with athletic achievements;
- Not savoring victory;
- Justifying excessive behavior by defining self as an elite athlete.

For Pam, healing came in the context of endurance. "When running (which I very much wanted to do) came into conflict with eating (which still made me uncomfortable), something had to give," she writes. Pam's book is well worth a read if you have any interest in athletes and anorexia.

Mimi Anderson is another ultrarunner and world record holder who has spoken publicly about her experience with anorexia.

Mimi's battle began at age 14, but she doesn't believe it is something that ever goes away. She started running at the age of 36 because someone told her it was the best way to change the shape of her legs. Mimi credits the sport with boosting her self-esteem as well as returning her pride. Despite these women's powerful stories, their actions and lives are analyzed and criticized.

One blogger recovering from anorexia compares Mimi's efforts to an "ex-alcoholic [doing] a drink-a-thon to support Mothers Against Drunk Driving" and questions the logic behind an eat-to-run mentality for an anorexic, since extreme running is also a way to purge calories.

Some of these criticisms contain valid points. Sadly, many are expressed in harsh and judgmental tones. This doesn't stop

Pam or Mimi from speaking out—and with a little digging I discovered more women who were also telling their stories.

When Rachel Spatz attempted her first ultramarathon, she was still struggling with an eating disorder. She was a different woman then: a self-described loner who greatly disliked the person she was becoming. She failed to finish her first ultra, but fell in love with the trails, the endurance vibe and the strong community of runners. Today, Rachel has completed seven 100-mile foot races (plus more than 25 shorter ultra distance events), and five triathlons (including two Ironman). She is currently training for Western States 100.

I was also touched by Shannon Stone's story. Shannon was 13 when she first became anorexic and it haunted her for the next 20 years of her life. She felt lost, worthless and never able to accept herself. Eventually, anorexia became her identity. It was the one thing that made her special, and she clung to it for fear that without it, she would just be a nobody. Running, instead of helping, was an accomplice to her self-destruction.

"I walked the fence between health and disorder, not willing to give up the one thing I had called my own for so long," recalls Shannon. "And, although I hate to admit it, with ultrarunning, I thought I had found the perfect solution that would allow me to keep my identity, yet disguise it through the lens of 'health.' For, I wasn't 'anorexic' anymore, I was just an 'ultrarunner.'"

Everything came crashing down in 2012 when Shannon suffered a string of running injuries and lost the ability to run. Her poor health caught up to her and she developed early-onset osteoporosis. She had run almost her entire lifetime without a menstrual cycle due to poor fueling. Shannon's sense of identity was slipping away and she spiraled into depression.

It was a harsh wake-up call, but Shannon realized that if she didn't make drastic changes, she would lose ultrarunning forever. "It was at this point where I stopped talking about change and starting acting on it," Shannon confesses. "I had to fight the lies that I let myself believe for too long and had to start fueling my body so that I could get back to the sport I loved…the one thing that was going to save me from myself was running."

Though she still struggles with old thoughts, Shannon's entire outlook has been transformed. "Every time my foot hits the trail I am reminded of how blessed I am to have a body that can partake in nature's playground. If I want to continue this journey, I must feed my body and treat it with respect."

There are endless resources online for helping friends (or you) overcome an eating disorder. I won't go into those details here but encourage you to dig deeper for more. Here is a link to a free and anonymous screening test from the National Eating Disorders Association:

https://www.mentalhealthscreening.org/screening/NEDA

Obsession and Addiction

When Jennifer Pharr Davis announced an attempt to set the record for the fastest hike of the Appalachian Trail, she was asked in a skeptical tone how she would prevent a

passion for running from turning into an obsession. (I wonder whether a man would have been asked that same question?)

Davis answered that she would rely on the accountability of her small crew of supporters—her husband, her pacers, her family and close friends. She also knew that her thru-hike, as obsessive as it seemed, was a short-term endeavor. It had been planned in advance and had a foreseeable end. "This hike only represented a season of our lives and did not ultimately define who we were," wrote Davis in her memoir *Called Again*. Her next adventure? Having children.

In the eyes of society, there is something off-putting about a woman who invests an "extreme" amount of time training her body. An acceptable societal standard for women seems to be 30 minutes of physical activity two or three times a week—and if you're already skinny, why exercise at all? Athletic dedication can be hard for our friends and family to understand, especially when it isn't making a lot of money.

In *The Extra Mile*, Pam Reed argues that one distinguishing trait of an addictive individual is the way in which he or she answer the following question: "If pushing a magic button would forever eliminate your desire for your addictive activity, would you push that button?"

Addicted people answer yes—their addictions are burdens that interfere with important aspects of their lives. Addiction is defined as "physically and mentally dependent on a particular substance, and unable to stop taking it without incurring adverse effects."

However, Pam (and many runners) would answer that question with a resounding no. "I love this. I would not want to have a life in which I wasn't able to do my sport or did not have the desire to take part in it," she writes.

In 1964, the Diagnostic and Statistical Manual of Mental Disorders dropped the word "addiction" and now refers to substance "dependence." It describes dependence as "a cluster of cognitive, behavioral, and physiological symptoms indicating that the individual continues use of the substance despite significant substance-related problems."

To prove a negative running addiction, one must show that running results in impairments, and that running continues despite these impairments. Evidence for this is limited. The typical runner characteristics that work against us include running while injured and moodiness when we miss a workout, though there is no clear evidence whether this moodiness is an indication of withdrawal.

Running a lot does not imply addiction. Running past the point of physical benefit does not imply addiction. In fact, the mere mention of the word "addiction" outside the context of a medical or clinical discussion is usually not much more than an opinion. It cannot be quantified in mileage and is a word too easily thrown around. (Heck, Brooks sells a woman's running shoe called Addiction.) However, one woman's addiction can be another woman's passion, priority, physical expression of joy or mode of transportation.

Keep in mind that a person whose body is not conditioned to endurance (for example: the body of the critic) may overestimate the amount of pain and difficulty we experience. They know that for *them*, running one mile hurts. So they may assume we are hurting for hours, and that's

Vanessa Runs

inaccurate.

It is also unfair to make a judgment call on whether or not a woman is addicted without considering her priorities. There are seasons in a woman's life where running can rightfully and healthfully become a high priority—when she is training for an athletic accomplishment, for example.

While addictions tend to limit us, endurance running can expand our potential, sharpen our focus and drive us to become a better version of ourselves. Besides, it's hard to achieve greatness through moderation.

10: Boobs, Babies And Other Bumps In The Road (Life Stages)

"I learned that my body can do good work. That if I am patient, if I note its limits, tend its frailties, and push past them when I have the hunch it's right, my body is not just a partner I can trust. It's actually me. Both a tool and a home."
- Christine Byl, *Dirt Work: An Education in the Woods*

It's mid-morning and we are nearing the peak of Mount Baldy in San Bernadino County, California. My friends Elizabeth and Christine have paused to shed a layer of clothes while I sit on a nearby rock and wait. My layers came off miles ago even though it's still relatively cool just after 6 a.m. It's not the sun but the effort of the climb that has me drenched in sweat.

We're hiking hard but still keeping a conversation pace. And converse we do—as women do—about anything and everything. Years ago as a teenager trying to assert my status as a tomboy, I would snub my nose at girl talk. These days I seek it out, revel in it and use it as a qualifying standard of a "good run."

The truth is, we are barely running. This is more of a trudge at approximately 1,000 feet of elevation gain per mile. By the time we reach the summit at 10,068 feet, we are fighting piercing winds and talking about birth control. On the descent we talked about our mothers, our daughters, our sisters and our periods.

I need girl talk primarily as a gauge of my own normality as a running female. Something is happening with my body — is it happening to you too? Did it happen to you at my age? What other changes can I expect running into the next ten, twenty, thirty years?

It's information-sharing at its best. Better than the Internet, or at least I trust it more. It's honest, well-intentioned and anecdotal. Luckily for me, women in endurance love to share. If there are subjects that are off the table, I haven't found them yet. This type of conversation is never gross or inappropriate, but rather refreshing and deeply bonding.

This chapter is my best effort to recreate some of that girl talk. These are topics that women don't generally feel comfortable broaching around men, and unfortunately that sometimes means they are never discussed at all. There is much benefit from women sharing their experiences when it comes to the nitty-gritty details around menstruation, pregnancy and breastfeeding.

If you are a woman, I hope you will relate to some of these themes and learn from the stories and tips that others have shared with me. If you are a man, prepare to enter an inner sanctuary of female openness as you've probably never experienced before.

Periods and Personal Bests

For many girls, menstruation is the first bodily function that may be accompanied by a gross lack of information, as it is still seen as a taboo topic. Sex education classes in schools do some of the work, but it has nothing on honest and genuine female-to-female conversations—not to mention the stories of our experiences and struggles when it comes to juggling menstruation issues as endurance athletes.

Periods are hard enough as they are, but add training and racing to the mix and something is bound to get a little bit messy. One of my favorite period stories comes from Cami Ostman in her book *Second Wind*. In this memoir Cami tells the story of her mid-life quest to run seven marathons on seven continents.

In Panama City, Cami experienced every woman's worst nightmare: she got her period in the middle of a race. She was about 17 miles into her marathon when she began to feel distinct drops of something wet on her legs. Sweat? Rain? She looked around—there wasn't a cloud in the sky. When she looked down at her thighs she was horrified to see her legs covered in blood almost down to her knees.

(If you are squeamish, skip over the next few paragraphs now.)

As she tells it:

Long streaks of coagulated, blotchy blood streamed down from my crotch. There was a thick, dried red line of it just below where my shorts stopped above my knees. This scabby ring was stopping the blood from flowing farther down my legs.

Omigod, omigod, omigod, I thought.

Dread surged up from my stomach to my throat. A brief wave of nausea came and went, and I felt my face go red. I looked around at the volunteers. It was clear people were staring at me and registering what was going on.

I was apparently the only one perplexed about the situation. I was having my period—that much I knew, of course. I'd started the day before and was prepared for my cycle as I knew it, which generally involved a tampon change every six hours or so. So what the hell was happening? Was I hemorrhaging?

I felt fine, outside of my total mortification. It couldn't be dangerous if there was no discomfort, I hoped. Then it occurred to me—something the doctor had told me when she had inserted my IUD: "Your flow will be heavier than usual." Lady, that was the understatement of a lifetime, I thought, as I grabbed a packet of water from a green-shirted young man and dared him with my eyes to look at my legs.

This wasn't a heavy period; this was a gush. I reached around to the running pack on my backside and unzipped the pouch. I had come prepared for a change, but I had only one extra tampon. I pulled it out of the pouch and saw with dismay that the humidity and my own sweat had expanded it. It was wide and wet, already used up, and probably impossible to insert. Anyhow, there was not a port-o-potty, not a phone booth, not a palm tree to hide behind, anywhere within eyeshot.

What was I supposed to do?

The irony was that Cami had just started to embrace a strong sense of girl-power before this incident. She was starting to shed her shame at being born a girl, and had been working through the embarrassment and awkwardness that had plagued her most of her life.

Yet there she was: exposed, vulnerable, bleeding.

She thought about quitting. Certainly people would understand. Women were not supposed to expose the public (and especially men) to their periods. Quitting the race would be acceptable and yet she didn't want to quit. Despite the blood, she felt great, but when she tried to wash the blood off with water, she only succeeding in spreading it around. The race course volunteers started to leer at her and, dejected, she walked off the course.

Again in Cami's words:

A taxi driver honked at me, wanting me to get a move on and out of his way. I saw his expression as he looked me up and down, judging, mocking. He smiled and winked at me suggestively, running his tongue along his lips. As we locked eyes, he honked again. I studied his face, so superior and contemptuous.

In the energy of the exchange between us, my faithful protector, the Bitch, spoke up loudly and full of indignant pride. *Screw you, asshole!* she said to the taxi driver. I'm in the middle of a marathon! To me she said, Pull yourself together. What are you, afraid of your own body? Move it. Pick up the pace. We have a goal here!

"Right!" I said out loud. She'd brought me to my senses. What was I thinking? I'd come here for a marathon.

Fact: I was a woman. Fact: Women bleed. Fact: I was a bleeding woman running a marathon. Double fact: I needed to get a move on. Sticky, sweaty, salty and bloody,

I picked up my pace and got back on the course (but not before making the taxi driver wait until I was good and ready).

Cami got back on the course and refused to clean her legs. Instead, she smiled at the volunteers and bystanders. She had found her pride.

A few minutes later there was a sudden flash and the skies opened up. Rain poured all around her, over her head, shoulders, arms, back and legs. It washed away her red warrior stripes. She was sad to see them go.

"I got more than a medal that day," writes Cami. "I threw off all apologies for being born female and received my reward: success as defined by me alone. And I did it all while running like a girl."

In 1946, Walt Disney came out with a 10-minute film about periods called *The Story of Menstruation*. In it, a woman with a soothing, motherly voice presents a scientific explanation of periods, completely avoiding the subject of sex. The menstrual flow is shown as white instead of red, and this is believed to be the first film to ever use the word "vagina."

The clip was rumored to be banned and although there is no evidence of this, such wariness reflects the social taboo around menstruation at the time. Many years later there is still much stigma, fear and disgust associated with periods.

In the book *Flow: The Cultural Story of Menstruation*, authors Elissa Stein and Susan Kim uncover the troubling history of our beliefs around periods. In 77 A.D. it was widely accepted that menstrual blood could make seeds infertile, kill insects, flowers, bees, grass, and cause fruit to fall off trees. Periods were also blamed for dulling razors, driving dogs mad and causing horses to miscarry. Contact with menstrual blood could cause another woman to lose her child and men were strongly cautioned to not have sex with a menstruating female. These theories went unchallenged until 1492, more than a thousand years later.

You would think things got better after that, but not by much. The book describes a 1928 ad for a commercial douche featuring "the wife sobbing as her husband, coat in hand, storms out the door in a huff, nauseated and offended by having to actually breathe the same air in the apartment as her vagina."

These days we know the world "douche" as a synonym for an asshat, a cock-waffle or a plain old-fashioned jerk. Back in those days, a douche was primarily known as a current of water sometimes containing a dissolved cleansing agent for hygienic purposes.

Douche manufacturers rarely tested the harsh chemicals their products would contain. One product marketed from the 1920s to the early 1960s contained a high dose of Lysol and water. It managed to stay on the market despite causing countless vaginal infections and internal burning in many women.

One thing that hasn't changed after all these years is the implication that there's something filthy about the vagina and the blood that comes out of it. In fact, menstrual blood is no different or dirtier than any other blood and a healthy vagina is one of the cleanest spots on the body. (If you're looking for

something filthy, check your mouth, which is statistically dirtier than your anus.)

Still, the difficulties of getting your period as an athlete are very real. Out of all the negatives mentioned by female endurance athletes about being a woman in sport, these monthly visits were the #1 downfall.

Environmental Concerns

When I spoke to women about their periods, many would guide the conversation to one sub-topic: bleeding responsibly.

What were the effects of menstruation products on the environment, and what could they do to eliminate or reduce this footprint? It was a serious concern for females who felt passionate about the outdoors and spent as much time as they could in the wilderness. One woman even went off the Pill when she started trail running because she didn't want to pollute the wilds with the hormones in her pee. Instead, she would plan her runs around her periods and reported it was a small price to pay to keep the wilderness healthy.

Here are some of the tips I gathered from women on the trails with the goal of leaving no trace:

1. Mind the wrappers.

A large portion of the waste we send to landfills is made up of packaging. You can do your part by choosing products with minimum packaging. (Do this with everything else you buy, too.) Since feminine care products aren't sterile they don't require extra wrapping. You can find pads that aren't individually wrapped or tampons that don't include the plastic applicators. Buying in bulk may also help reduce extra waste.

2. Choose menstrual cups.

The environmental superhero of period protection seems to be the menstrual cup. Moon Cup is popular but there are several other brands such as Diva Cup and the Keeper. The cups are inserted like a tampon, removed and emptied when full, then reinserted. You can use the same cup for years and they've been around since the 1930s. One runner reported wearing it comfortably for up to 12 hours without needing to rinse it off. They are easy to clean, hold fluid well and feel comfortable. Several women reported training and racing with menstrual cups successfully, although it may require a learning curve as far as insertion. You can buy versions made of natural latex or silicon.

3. Try reusable pads.

Soft, reusable pads like Tree Hugger, Lunapads and GladRags are all machine-washable fabric maxi pads. Remember to use an energy-efficient washing regimen.

4. Use a baggie.

What's the best way to pack out a tampon in the wilderness? One woman I spoke to reported carrying doggie bags to tie up her used tampons. Another mentioned Ziploc bags. The last suggestion was a surgical glove trick: put on the glove, take out your tampon, then remove the glove by turning it inside out with the tampon inside. Tie up the end of the glove and toss it in your pack for later disposal. No mess, no blood on your hands, and no trash on the trails.

Not every woman will be comfortable with all these options, but the point is that we *have* options. Make the best choice you can to protect the wild places you train and play.

Period Hacks

Every woman is affected differently by her period, but a wide variety of side effects can be inconvenient for endurance training. The women I spoke to reported everything from intense pain and negative self-talk to feeling light-headed and passing out on the trails.

Although it's a myth that women should avoid strenuous activity during their periods, some side effects make it difficult to get out there. Over the years, women have developed their own period hacks to make their lives just a little bit more manageable. Here are a few that were shared with me:

1. Pill Manipulation

If you're due to get your period on race day and you'd rather not, you can push your cycle back a week (or several weeks) if you're on birth control pills. Simply skip the fourth week of pills (when you typically get your period) and start right into the next month's cycle. As long as you do this, your period can be held off indefinitely. Women have reported doing this for long runs, races or vacation time. Since women on the Pill do not experience uterine build-up, they technically don't need to have a period to shed the lining. The bleeding that does occur while on the pill is not a "real" period. Some basic research or a chat with your health care provider can offer more insight into the biology behind this trick.

2. IUD

IUDs are a favorite option for endurance females. This small device inserted directly into the uterus can provide up to

12 years of birth control. Once inserted, you can forget about it. The biggest selling feature mentioned to me: no periods. Many women stop getting them.

Even when a woman manages to master her own cycle, she can still fear things outside her own body...things in the wild that she cannot control.

Blood and Bears and Sharks! Oh my!

"Special precautions apply to women! For their protection, women should refrain from wilderness travel during their menstrual periods! Bears and other large carnivores have attacked women in this physiological condition!"

That quote is from an old U.S. Parks Department flyer distributed for years to campers. The fear was based on the idea that hungry bears could pick up the scent of a woman menstruating, putting her at a higher risk of attack. Although there was no direct link between bear attacks and menstruating females, women were warned just in case—for their own protection, of course.

This myth—yes, it is definitely a myth—originated on the evening of August 13, 1967. Two women were killed by grizzly bears in Glacier National Park. When no causes were found for the attack, it was speculated that perhaps both women had been on their periods. Years passed without any legitimate investigation and the period-fears morphed into an unfounded but generally accepted warning.

Some feminists argue that this is a perfect example of how women are discriminated against in the outdoors. In general,

they are seen as weaker in the wilderness, less able to handle themselves and in need of careful protection.

It wasn't until 1991 that the bear myth was finally put to rest in a National Park Service study involving grizzly bears, black bears, polar bears and used tampons collected from 26 different women. Then NSP also considered data from various different studies and couldn't find a single incident of menstruation-induced bear attacks. They also failed to find a single situation in which black bears or grizzly bears were even attracted to used tampons.

Polar bears, however, presented a bit of an exception. A 1983 study found that four captive polar bears responded to menstrual odors. Wild polar bears were also found to consume used tampons while ignoring unused ones.

The bear myth is still prevalent today. A 1997 pamphlet titled *Backcountry Bear Basics* out of Glacier National Park read: "Although the evidence is inconclusive, menstrual odors and human sexual activity may attract bears."

A similar and equally prevalent myth is that menstruating women shouldn't go into the ocean because of the risk of a shark attack. While it's true that sharks are capable of detecting blood, they can also detect any other human excretion such as sweat or urine. Menstrual blood doesn't put women at any additional risk.

Ralph S. Collier is a shark behavior expert who has been documenting shark attacks since 1963. In the late 1960s, he conducted a study with fellow shark expert H. David Bladridge. They introduced several human body fluids to wild sharks in open ocean pens and examined the response. The only fluid that was found to cause a reaction was peritoneal fluid, a liquid found in the human abdominal cavity.

Marie Levine, founder and executive director for the Shark Research Institute, claims she has been diving for decades and even got her period while underwater with a school of hammerhead sharks. The sharks did not show the least bit of interest. On the contrary, she claims she had to work hard to get close to them. Interestingly, 90 percent of recorded shark attacks involve men.

Baby on Board

If a woman manages to escape the ravenous clutches of wild animals, she may actually live long enough to procreate. Is the pain of running 100 miles similar to the pain of childbirth—one of the greatest pains known to man or, in this case, woman? Jennifer Benna not only believes this is true, but also that the entire experience of being pregnant is like a 100-mile endurance run: each trimester parallels the different stages of the race.

This is how she breaks it down in her blog, *A Girl's Guide to Trail Running*:

First trimester and first 30 miles of the race

You on the start line, feeling hopeful, excited and amazed in wonderment of what's ahead. Attached immediately to the life inside you, you are connected to the little heartbeat that your blood feeds. The adrenaline then soon wears off and you feel overwhelmed. What have I done? I have a long way to go. Fatigue, exhaustion, hunger can set in. Adjustments must be made. Perhaps more care is needed. You hit the first aid station; you assess and move forward. You hear the heartbeat for the first time. You are in love. You don't question anything anymore. It's time to settle in. This will be an awesome race.

Second trimester and miles 30 to 60

You are taking good care of yourself now. You may have slowed down some in your pacing, but you feel steady. Food is key here. Not too much or too little. You feel the flutter in your abdomen below, reminding you often of the life you sustain inside. Not just your life, but a precious little life that you will soon meet. The race speeds up. You find your clip, your sweet spot. You have energy, renewed purpose and you breathe easily. You know there is a lot of running left to do, but you are over the halfway mark. You search for a headlamp. You search for your husband's hand to let him feel the child moving. You are inspired to stay positive. You are loving the trail, loving the journey.

Third trimester and miles 60 to 90

Proportionally, the last third of the journey feels longer. Fatigue sets in and sometimes darkness too. Your friends are racing; they are up ahead and you wish to join them, but you are tired. You know you must drink, eat and rest when you need to. The last ten miles are magical. They are a place where you find out who you really are. You wish to get there, so you stay upbeat. Your friends and family check in with you. How are you feeling? When are you due? You think, not soon enough. But all the while, this little person grows and stretches and is sustained by all that you do. You keep moving and finding your footing as the sun sets.

The finish, the birth, the last few miles

The pain begins. A rippling in your every being. You breathe, sometimes cry, but keep moving. Food tastes awful, you don't want any more. You just want to get to the finish, but it seems to be taking forever. You are hurting, but anxious. Your pacer offers advice, encouragement, but you are deep in the place in your head where you can barely hear him. Something instinctual kicks in and your work to finish gets real. You push, despite how much it hurts. You want to remember everything now. You can't wait to see the finish, to hold your baby. Only one more push, only one more mile.

Birth and finish line

It's sweeter than you could have imagined. To hear her cry for the first time, to hold this tiny person in your arms. You are smitten. Life is different now. You are relieved, tired and thankful your body let you run 100 miles. You are proud. You need to sit down and just savor this moment. You realize you love this feeling, hurt and all. You would do again, but just not tomorrow.

While pregnancy was previously considered a weakened state, we now observe pregnant women rising in the ranks and staying active late into their pregnancies. The athletic accomplishments of some pregnant runners have been outstanding.

Generally considered the poster girl for pregnant running, marathon world-record holder Paula Radcliffe ran 14 miles a day while pregnant. She won the New York City Marathon 10 months after delivery. Similarly, marathoner Kara Goucher also ran while pregnant, training up to 80 miles a week. Pam Reed never stopped running throughout her three pregnancies and ran within a few days after each birth.

Another example is Kasie Enman from the small town of Huntington, Vermont. Kasie was the World Mountain Running Champion in 2011 as well as podium finisher in the 2012 SkyRunning Series before becoming pregnant with her second child. Salomon Running TV's short film *The Mother* features Kasie running through her pregnancy. She ran right until the day she went into labor and in the film she notes parallels between competing athletically and motherhood.

Kasie runs to get fresh air, to unwind and because running is one of the few times when the physical discomforts of being pregnant seem to go away. Kasie wants to share her experience with others to help eliminate misconceptions about running while pregnant. She says, "getting it out in the open can help provide more role models when you're trying to make choices for yourself."

Liz McColgan won the gold medal at the Tokyo World Championships in 1991, less than a year after giving birth to her first child (she went on to have four more).

Pregnant women have excelled at shorter distances as well. Alysia Montano ran the 800 meters at the U.S. Track and Field Championships in 2 minutes, 32.13 seconds. She was nearly eight months pregnant at the time.

Some things to consider if you are running or plan to run while pregnant, courtesy of your fellow pregnant women in endurance:

1. Perceived Exertion

It used to be that doctors recommended heart rate restrictions for active pregnant women, usually frowning on anything over 140. The American College of OB/GYNs (ACOG) has since replaced those restrictions with a perceived exertion self-gauge since individual heart rates vary so widely in response to exercise. The ACOG now recommends that pregnant women keep their exertion levels within the "somewhat hard" category. This is equivalent to an elevated heart rate and breathing pattern, but where it is not too difficult to carry on a conversation.

2. Potential Falls

One of the main concerns presented for pregnant runners who frequent trails are tripping hazards over technical terrain. Although most trail-running moms prioritize their baby's safety and take the necessary precautions of slowing down, it also helps to know that the amniotic sack is designed to serve as a protective barrier for accidental falls.

Alix Shutello, founder of *Runners Illustrated* and *Endurance Racing Magazine*, started her writing career through her pregnancy-focused blog. In a podcast about running while pregnant, she said: "You could fall down, but the old wives tale about falling down and causing a miscarriage is not true. It's always good to learn how to fall, but especially if you're pregnant, you may not be able to fall in a way that's preventative of anything. Your body is meant to withstand

that kind of fall. It's not like you fell out of a building. It's really not as big of an impact as I think people would suggest. If a woman does fall during pregnancy and falls on her belly, it's a good idea to call your doctor."

If women feel apprehensive on technical terrain or steep grades, it is always best to opt for more gentle trails. During pregnancy a woman's body produces the hormone relaxin, which loosens the joints and ligaments. Additionally, the widening of hips may change biomechanics and shift the center of gravity so pregnant women are advised to go by their current feel instead of what they have been used to.

Another thing to watch out for on the trail is exposure to tick bites. You don't want to contract anything while pregnant. It also helps to know where the bathroom stops are. Listen to your gut, but know that there's no good reason to say off the trails completely.

3. Strength Work

Strength training through pregnancy and post-partum is one of the best ways to keep your body endurance-ready, aiding in both injury prevention and building your speed back up quickly. If you've never lifted before, make sure you work with someone who can guide you and get the green light from your health practitioner before beginning a new regimen.

4. Judgment from Others

You will be judged. It doesn't matter if you're perfectly healthy and capable. It doesn't matter if you've been cleared by your doctor. It doesn't matter that we now know that pregnancy is not a sedentary sentence. You won't just be judged by non-runners or by men. You'll be judged by other women and by fellow runners. Expect it and be gracious. Educate others were you can, but take it in stride as part of the experience.

Even those who mean well will judge. In one book with the goal of empowering mothers, the author confesses rolling her eyes at "Paula Radcliffe wannabes" and congratulating them while thinking to herself, "Hope a little sleep deprivation doesn't interfere with training for your umpteenth marathon, Ms. Overachiever."

Although the author was trying to bond with women who are not able to run through their pregnancies, attacking running mothers is not the way to do it. Let's stop drawing battle lines and support each other, regardless of how, when and why we train.

5. Judgment from Yourself

We are often our worst critics, aren't we? A woman's ability to run through pregnancy in no way reflects her mental strength, athleticism or physical resilience. It largely depends on her physiology and structure. Some women can do it. Others can't. The ones who can are no better, no more fit or healthy or strong. It just depends.

As with most things in life, it's useless to compare yourself to other pregnant moms. Your changes as far as weight, feet and center of gravity will vary. Embrace your own body and accept its limitations. Keep an eye on your own progress and listen to your body carefully. And above all, don't compare yourself to your former self.

Postpartum and Breastfeeding

In April of 2012 Martine Kinkade made a life-changing decision. She determined to become the strong, healthy momma that her 9-month-old boy deserved. To her, this meant training hard, and training with him. She decided to train for and run a marathon.

Martine bought a jogging stroller at a yard sale for $20 and got to work immediately. Six months later, she found herself at the starting line of the Long Beach Marathon in California with her signature jogger and mini training buddy in tow. She had her heart set on a sub five-hour finish.

Martine nursed her son, emptying her reservoirs from both sides. The plan was to finish the race while her son slept, then nurse him again after crossing the finish line.

Martine ran her heart out that day. By mile 18 she had developed terrible blisters, so she finished the final 8.2 miles barefoot on hot asphalt. She finished in 5:02, just barely missing her goal. It was a victory nonetheless.

As she tore across the finish line, the race announcer hollered, "Holy crap, it's a mom pushing a stroller, and she's...barefoot!?"

Just as Martine collapsed on the grass at the finish line, her son woke up asking to be fed. Her post-race recovery photo is one where she is seated on the grass wearing a red, sweaty, happy grin, and nursing her chubby toddler. Her first marathon medal is tossed on the grass beside her, glittering in the Southern California sun.

Martine went on to run another marathon and two ultramarathons in the next 15 months while continuing to breastfeed her son. These days, her son has been weaned and

Martine has given birth to her second baby boy. She is still running.

Women like Martine can make it look easy, but nursing mamas face real training challenges. In his best-selling book Born to Run, Christopher McDougall calls our attention to amazing running mamas like Kami Semick and Emily Baer, while commenting that "caring for kids on the fly isn't that hard."

Wrong.

According to the nursing moms, it is hard—as hard as a nipple in a snowstorm. McDougall's intention was to encourage women to participate fully in endurance sport, but let's take a closer look at what training is really like for nursing moms.

Milk-dispensing Mamas

There's a photo of endurance trail runner Emma Roca with her three children at a cross-country ski resort in France that strikes me as a raw image of motherhood.

Emma is in full racing gear sitting in what appears to be the back of a car. She's wearing a Buff company jersey, a buff on her head, sunglasses on top of her buff, and GPS strapped to her wrist. She is obviously ready to run.

Except...her shirt is halfway up her chest and her breasts are exposed with two beautiful half-asleep babies feeding on both sides. Peeking out underneath her cleavage is a heart rate monitor strap. Emma is wearing a huge, makeup-less smile with one more golden-haired, droopy-eyed toddler hanging contentedly off her neck. Emma's husband, David, was out

training when this photo was taken. Right after him, Emma trained.

As serene and iconic as Emma Roca's photo is, the real story isn't how easy she makes it look, but how hard it really is. When iRunFar asked Emma what the hardest and most fulfilling experiences in her athletic career were, she said it was training while breastfeeding.

Keep in mind: this is from a woman who has raced in extreme cold and extreme heat, pushing through hallucinations and severe sleep deprivation. She has suffered from a foot infection and has broken her wrist only to continue cycling (a teammate had to change the gears for her). She has raced duathlons, triathlons and adventure races. She has won world championships. She describes some of these experiences as difficult, and then puts breastfeeding at the top of the list.

To keep her production of milk going, Emma would pump her breasts during adventure races, then drink her own milk. She would tell her team it was her magic potion. Other women reported using fenugreek to maintain or increase milk production.

Some other examples of breastfeeding trail mamas include:

1. Emily Baer

This ultrarunner was mentioned in *Born to Run* for her feat at the 2007 Hardrock 100: she completed the race while stopping at every aid station to breastfeed her infant son. Despite the delay, she still finished eighth overall, besting ninety other infant-less men and women.

2. Jennifer Benna

268

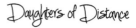

For the entire running season of 2011, Jennifer had a tiny breast-seeking infant nearby. She ran the Way Too Cool 50K at five months post-partum, and during the Tahoe Rim Trail 100 she instructed her dad to meet her with a breast pump so she could race near the front of the pack. She remained competitive despite the sleep deprivation of being a new mom and the stress of moving to a new city. Jennifer found herself running faster so she could get home to her baby girl.

3. Liza Howard

At the age of 42, Liza Howard set a course record at the Umstead 100 by running a 15:07 while stopping several times to use a breast pump on the floor of an outhouse. Liza stayed close to her baby during training by running up to 40 miles on a treadmill in her garage. She started her 40-miler at 9 p.m. and marked off every mile on a white board.

4. Jennifer Pinarski

Jennifer Pinarski ran the Winnipeg Birds Hill Sprint Triathlon when her son was five months old. She nursed him ten minutes before the start, although trying to breastfeed in a wet suit was a challenge. By the end of her race, her breasts were sore from being crammed into racing gear but she managed to clock a personal record.

5. Kelly Gould

Kelly Gould took on the challenge of Ragnar SoCal when her son was 17 months old. She covered a 200-mile relay with a team of 12 other mothers. They called themselves Team RIOT Moms. Kelly had to leave for her race before her baby was awake, so she pumped before she left. Her husband then met her at designated points along the course so she could

nurse and she continued pumping in the team van. Team RIOT moms completed 200 miles from Huntington Beach to San Diego in 32 hours.

6. Barbara Olmer

Barbara finished the Rocky Racoon 100 in 2013 while stopping to pump every 20 miles. She estimates she lost about 20 minutes of running time at every pump break. She struggled with nutrient depletion and a pulled groin, but when she finished she was presented with an award for "Most Miles Breastfed." Her Rocky Raccoon finish now means more to her than her Hardrock buckle. Barbara writes, "All you new mothers—go run and fear not; the mind will take you places you never imagined and the body will follow suit."

There are many stories just like these.

The DO's of Being a Nursing-Running Mama

The following tips are courtesy of several active and nursing moms:

1. DO carry a lightweight handheld pump on long runs, or learn how to hand express milk for mid-run relief

2. DO drain both breasts completely at least 30 minutes before a long run or race to avoid engorgement and blocked ducts during your run.

3. DO have a battery operated pump waiting at an aid station mid-race to drain again if you're going to be out there for more than just a few hours.

4. DO arrange for someone to bring your baby to a mid-race aid station if possible for proper nursing, especially during longer events.

5. DO hydrate more than you're used to. Stay on top of your calories and make sure you're eating enough (way more than you normally would).

6. DO invest in a running stroller. It will save you.

7. DO pack a wet washcloth in a Ziploc bag if you're planning to nurse immediately after running. Use it to wipe your breasts down. Some babies are picky about sweaty and salty flavors. Change out of a sweaty bra as soon as you can.

8. DO stake out a couple of nice logs or rocks that you can sit on to nurse in the middle of a run. Having pre-selected spots will save you time.

9. DO remember to be patient with yourself. Opt for shorter trail races if you need to. You will have low moments—that's normal. Don't panic if your supply drops slightly after a race. Rest as often as needed. You will bounce back in time.

10. DO invest in a good, supportive sports bra. It's worth it.

11. DO stick to a training plan, but be flexible. It's okay to run at a different time, switch up days, or push a baby jogger.

12. DO announce to TSA agents that you are traveling with a breast pump if you are getting on a plane for your event. Pull the pump out and make sure it's clearly visible (apparently some breast pumps resemble the TSA's training manual diagrams of a bomb). Remember, pumped breast milk is one of the exemptions from the carry-on liquids rule at airports, even if you are not traveling with the baby.

13. DO look to other running mamas for inspiration. Ask for help, advice, feedback—chances are another woman has

gone through the same thing.

14. DO set goals for yourself, even ambitious ones. After giving birth, endurance training may seem trivial. You have a different perspective on life now, and that makes you stronger, but it's still okay to work towards something you are passionate about.

15. DO maintain a calm and focused state of mind while running. Some women report that worrying too much about their babies causes milk let down during training.

In whatever capacity you choose to stay active, don't be afraid to latch on to your favorite sport and let it nourish you.

Infant-Sized Advantage?

I have wondered if mothers, as a result of the experience of pregnancy, might in some ways be better suited for endurance racing.

This is not a new thought. It has been suggested and mused over before, and although there are no studies or concrete proof around the advantages a mother may carry, the most common advantage suggested is a higher pain tolerance.

Stephanie Catudal, a freelance writer living in Flagstaff, Arizona with her husband and daughter, understands this. She writes:

> As with so many things in life, we often search for the path of least resistance, or an easy out when things get tough. But, like the freaks of human nature they are, endurance athletes seek for the most treacherous path and will put themselves through the most grueling situations. Similarly, many women enter into pregnancy

knowing that the baby's exit route is perhaps the most physically and mentally difficult thing that a human can endure, but they do it anyway. Often times, more than once.

The biggest compliment Stephanie's husband ever paid her was shortly after the birth of their daughter. After twelve hours of labor with no medication to numb the pain, her ultrarunning husband looked over at her and whispered in complete awe, "I've been searching my whole life for feats of physical endurance, and the ability to endure pain. All of them pale in comparison to this. Seriously."

There are no aid stations or drop options when you're in labor. There is no way to just collapse and say, "Screw this. Take my bib and get me home."

Then there is the advantage of sleep deprivation "training." Moms know what exhaustion feels like and how to get through the day anyway. This comes in handy when you hit the wall several times during a race.

Mothers are also used to adapting and problem-solving — great skills for race day. A few nursing mothers mentioned that the pumping and nursing breaks force them to slow down during a race, thus aiding with pacing and helping them conserve energy to finish strong.

If a mother trained through her pregnancy, she may find herself with extra stamina after childbirth, similar to having training with a weighted vest for nine months.

Lastly, there is a key shift in perspective. While some mothers reported feeling stressed or anxious about race

performances before children, many of them go into events with a calmer demeanor post-childbirth and they find this improves their racing. They understand that a race is just a race. It isn't going to define their life and frankly, there are more important things to worry about. New mothers don't have the time to overthink their races or dwell on performance anxiety. This perspective allows them to approach their events with a positive mindset and often put up strong performances.

On a biological level, there is evidence that pregnancy increases the number of red blood cells, which improves oxygen capacity. Also, in the third trimester a woman's ligaments begin to relax and allow her to lengthen her stride.

There is no clear evidence to suggest that these physical changes definitely enhance performance, but there has been much speculation. Some countries were rumored to use a pregnancy hormone (human choroid gonadotropin or HCG) on their athletes as a performance-enhancing drug.

The anecdotal evidence among female athletes still stands: some mothers return to their sport post-birth feeling stronger than ever.

Breasts: Nature's Airbags

At the age of 22, Deva Lingemann got a boob job. She would have had it much earlier, but thought it would be wise to wait until her body had finished developing. Unlike other girls her age, she didn't opt for the perkier Playboy Double Whoppers. What Deva wanted more than anything was a breast reduction.

At a size 36DDDF, Deva was uncomfortable running in

public. People would shout at her as she shuffled by. More than once, someone yelled, "Watch out! You'll put your eye out with those things!"

Deva opted for a large C size and no one noticed her surgery. Sometimes people would look at her curiously and ask whether she had lost weight. Others would compliment her posture, and rightly so—Deva was indeed standing taller. The pain in her back and shoulders was gone. The bottoms of her breasts were no longer black and blue (and sometimes bloody). She could wear one bra instead of three. Her confidence soared.

Although her running times didn't initially improve, the weight off her chest literally inspired her to run harder, and in public. She felt confident enough to start running road marathons, and eventually got fast enough to qualify for Boston. "Having the reduction was one of the best choices I've ever made," Deva confirms "...for both my physical and mental well-being."

The challenge of breast-bound movement is something few male endurance athletes understand. Although this detail may seem inconsequential, for some women it can be a severe handicap. Breasts can not only weigh heavily on the back and shoulders but can also impede gait, arm swing and hydration packs. Some women report sensitive protruding nipples, chafing and the fact that finding a good sports bra fit can be as hard as finding a spot to pee in a field of cholla cacti.

To the untrained ear, this may sound like whining and excuses, but consider this: breasts, regardless of size, can bounce eight inches in just one direction when we run.

Additionally, breasts also wiggle from side to side and in and out. Our feet aren't the only body parts accumulating mileage and defying gravity. This wear and tear can be significant. In *Run Like a Mother*, post-nursing breasts are described as empty tube socks with the resiliency of taffy.

The science behind the athletic disadvantage of breasts is fascinating but limited. According to an ESPN article "a typical A-cup boob weighs in at 0.43 of a pound. Every additional cup size adds another 0.44 of a pound. That means a hurdler with a double-D chest carries more than four pounds of additional weight with her on every leap. And when they get moving, the nipples on a C- or D-cup breast can accelerate up to 45 mph in one second—faster than a Ferrari. In an hour of moderate jogging, a pair of breasts will bounce several thousand times."

There are some things we don't know, like exactly how much our chesticles are slowing us down. What we do know is that young, active female athletes start bouncing out of their sports as soon as their breasts begin to develop. They report feeling embarrassed and uncomfortable. Certain sports become practically out of reach, such as ballet or gymnastics. Is it a coincidence that many of the most talented female runners have chests that more closely resemble bee stings than bazookas?

If you want to get a female endurance athlete ranting, bring up the topic of sports bras. The sports bra market is shockingly underdeveloped. In her book, *As Good as Gold*, cyclist Kathryn Bertine complains about the "yogafication" of sports bras as excluding the "impact-oriented athlete."

During a standard breast exam, Kathryn had one nurse compliment her on her breast surgery, but Kathryn's scars were not from surgery at all. They were from years of incisions from poorly-made sports bras. "The effect of Adidas' sports bras, with their logo of three vertical stripes—and their six seams—is still visible on my breast pit," Kathryn reports. "Today, it is actually easier to find a supportive, comfortable, non-chafing lasting relationship with a man than it is with a sports bra."

When Kathrine Switzer ran the Boston Marathon in 1967, the sports bra hadn't been invented yet. The original "bra" consisted of two jock straps sewn together. Ouch.

A further hindering factor is the social handicap of breast shaming. Although half the world has breasts, a slip of the nip still has the power to cast a dark shadow over a female athlete's career.

Young Nebiat Habtemariam suffered a wardrobe malfunction in a borrowed singlet during the qualifying heat for the women's 5,000-meter run at the 1997 world championships. It was an 18-minute nipple flash and Nebiat spent the next few days hiding in her hotel room in shame. There is tremendous pressure to keep our running buddies under control, and there are social consequences if we can't.

Even if our womanly speed bumps are neatly tucked away, nipple shaming is still a thing. I asked every woman I interviewed for this book what the worst thing about being a female endurance athlete was. Several of them mentioned the stress of trying to hide those pesky protruding nipples under their running tops. Between the bouncing, limited sports bra

options, sweating and gentle breezes, this is practically a losing battle.

It doesn't matter that every woman's nipples will naturally protrude at some point during her workout, we still feel like we've done something wrong if and when they do. We are ashamed, and it's not just the old white men ruling the world who make us feel this way. We do it to ourselves and to other women.

In one running book the female author scolds other females for wearing spaghetti straps on a run. She describes the natural female bounce as disrespectful, especially on a particular female who has the gall to thrust confidently in the author's own neighborhood. This, my lumpy ladies, is a tragedy.

11: Respect Your Masters (Aging)

"If you have a life that's full of laughter — you are going to have wrinkles. If you play, enjoy and spend time outdoors, you're going to freckle...you aren't going to have an expressionless, lineless, photoshopped face. You will be real."
- Kate Bartolotta

It's almost midnight and we're running into Pedro Fages, the last aid station of the Cuyamaca 100K in California. My friend Christine Bilange is behind me and we can see the aid station lights twinkling from the road, just up a small rolling hill.

Christine, a bubbly French-American, is known for her quick wit, strong French accent, and easy smile. She's tough as nails. Ultrarunning legend Gordon Ainsleigh calls her "The Dominatrix" and, when her friends race, they fight over her as a pacer because she doesn't put up with your bullshit—she'll drive you to the finish, whether you want to finish or not.

Today, it's Christine's turn to race. I'm pacing her for the last 18-mile loop and she's about to hit the farthest mileage she has ever run.

I'm excited for her and I remind her of this milestone. Wisely, she delays her celebrations until the race is over. Sixty-two miles first, and then she'll celebrate with a beer that has been chilling in a red cooler for nearly 18 hours.

That doesn't hold back my celebrations, though. I love this. The moon is glorious, not quite full, but unobscured and

dusting the trail in front of me. The singletrack is smooth, like butter under my soles.

My gig as a pacer tonight is easy. Christine is highly self-motivated and has more years of trail experience than I do. She knows her body. She knows when to eat, when to drink, and she's on top of it all. It's a rare thrill to have front row seats when someone breaks a mileage record, smashing all the faux limitations we place on ourselves. Christine is better, stronger and faster than she ever thought possible.

There is always one point in every endurance race when you know — it just hits you — that you're going to make it. It's a glorious epiphany, and this is it for Christine. I can hear her behind me, mumbling to herself. "I'm going to make it! *Allez*, Christine! 50 years old! I'm going to make it! 50 years old! *Allez, allez!*"

I'm proud of her. We're so close.

My thoughts are disrupted by a blast of frigid air. It's near-freezing here. In a stretch of a single mile, the temperature has dropped about 15 degrees. My teeth are starting to chatter — I'm wet with sweat and the winds are uncomfortably harsh. I think about the jacket in my hydration pack. I must remember to put it on, but only when Christine stops for aid. I won't do anything to delay her progress.

Our friends at Paso Picacho are warm and so is the chicken broth. I grab some watermelon (I can't resist it, even in the cold) while Christine opts for warmer food.

A few weeks ago Christine celebrated her 50th birthday with a 50-mile run. She used each mile to meditate on what she was doing on each respective year of her life: mile one for age one, all to way to mile (and age) 50.

The memories brought her to tears: marriage, the birth of her two beautiful daughters, moving to the USA from France, a divorce, and several trail races. By her next birthday she plans to have run a 100-mile race.

The trail ends and we turn a sharp right onto a dirt road. A small sign on the corner reads FINISH: ONE MORE MILE. Christine starts to run. We pass another runner and her pacer, and then the road gradually starts to incline. We're running uphill after 62 miles. (Christine got some bonus miles when she had to run back to an aid station to retrieve a water bottle she had forgotten).

The views have disappeared and it's just a straight, all-business road ahead. Christine has a look of determination on her face and she's waiting for the dirt beneath our feet to turn to pavement. When it does, we'll be a sprint away from the finish.

The runner behind us makes her move, inching toward Christine. Christine will not have this. She immediately speeds up. There's a gate straight ahead and just past that is the pavement. We hit it and Christine shoots off like a bullet. I try to keep up, but she's too fast. My legs are tired. I'm only in my 30s, after all. Christine finishes, beautiful and strong. Age has not held her back.

In the endurance community there is a large number of master runners breaking records and running better than they ever did in their younger years. And yet, mainstream society still considers aging a disease, something that must be fought off with pills and cosmetic surgery.

What motivates these endurance folks? How are they accomplishing these amazing feats? What do they know that their other, more sedentary peers don't?

The day after the race we gather at Christine's house to watch the San Diego Charger's football game, lounge on her incredibly comfortable sofa, and stuff our faces with her boyfriend's delicious homemade chili. Christine and her boyfriend Bill cuddle and tease each other like young lovers. At some point we giggle at the ridiculousness of older women with Botoxed faces and fancy clothes, desperately clinging to an already-lost youth.

Christine is still wearing her compression sleeves and rocking her wrinkles. She has embraced her age but is not defined by it, much like our running rockstar Catra Corbett.

At the age most of us consider "over the hill," Catra is indeed going over hills—and mountains and valleys and summits, for hundreds and hundreds of miles. If you miss her at the start line of a race, you may be colorblind.

Catra wears short running skirts, the brighter the better. Her hair is flaming red and often in pigtails. In one photo she is leaning against a bridge with a grey, white and pink plaid skirt hiked up to reveal a thundering quad. Her bright red shirt matches red and white polkadot arm sleeves and black and white striped knee-high socks. She is covered in tattoos, coloring in most of her exposed skin. Catra once showed up to a Halloween race and won a costume contest—dressed as herself.

Catra has completed more than one hundred 100-mile races in addition to countless shorter-distance ultramarathons.

She was the second American woman to complete the Marathon des Sables in 2002, a brutal six-day race through the Sahara Desert. She holds the "yo-yo" speed record for women on the 212-mile John Muir Trail, from Yosemite to Mt. Whitney. She completed it once, then turned around and ran back, covering 424 miles in 12 days, 4 hours, and 57 minutes.

Every year, Catra celebrates her age with a birthday run. While most endurance runners cover their age in years, she runs her age in hours. These years she is running for 50+ hours and covering hundreds of miles, self-supported. Few can keep up.

I once commented on one of Catra's birthday photos: "If this is 50, I don't want to be 30." Catra wrote back. She confirmed that her body was the result of many years of hard and consistent work. In a way, you *need* to be 50 to have a body that amazing.

Catra in her 20s was a different person. Instead of colors, she wore black. Black hair, black clothes, black shoes, black makeup. She didn't run. She didn't smile for pictures. She had turned to drugs for a synthetic high and her future looked just as dark as her reflection. The wake-up call came after she got arrested and spent the night in jail. The next day she ditched all her friends and hit the gym.

Although Catra may seem like an outlier, there are others like her. Harriette Thompson, a ten-time grandmother from North Carolina, completed a marathon at the age of 91. Andjelina Andjelic didn't start running until age 55. She has since raced distances of up to 100 kilometers.

Helen Klein also started running at age 55. She loved it so

much she sold her home and belongings and moved from the Midwest to California so she could race more frequently. Every morning like clockwork Helen gets up at 4 a.m. and heads out for a two-hour run. By the time she turned 84, she had completed 143 ultramarathon distances of 50 miles or more, plus 70 marathons. She has completed the Western States 100 Mile Endurance Run several times.

Triathlon and cycling have their own examples. Joan Joesting-Mahoney, who passed away at age 76, was an ultra-cyclist and four-time Ironman finisher. In her lifetime, she managed to nail the record for most perimeters cycled, completing perimeters of at least 24 countries as well as counties, lakes and islands all across North America. Joan was also the indoor rowing record-holder for 100K and 24 hours (60 to 69 female lightweight), as well as the longest continuous row by a woman of any age or weight class (30 hours). At age 67, she was a power lifter.

Last but not least, consider Ida Keeling, a 99-year-old great-great-grandmother from New York. Ida is the 95 to 99 age group world record holder in the 100-meter run with a time of 59.8 seconds. She started running competitively at the ripe old age of 67.

In the non-endurance crowd, old age is a time to slow down, take naps and conserve your energy. You'll need most of it just to get of bed in the morning. Lower your expectations and cancel your plans—you'll be lucky if you can stand up in the shower. The following quote from a book published in 1796 still reflects some commonly-held beliefs about aging:

The strongest, especially if they are older, are most

commonly hurt by heavy burdens and feats of activity. The fatal effects of running and the like can be seen daily and should deter such practices. (William Buchan, *Domestic Medicine*)

If only William Buchan could have seen the master athletes of today. Not only are older runners exceeding the performances of their younger peers, there is some evidence that older athletes may have an endurance advantage. Recent studies suggest that the fastest 24-hour runners achieve their peak performances as master athletes (over the age of 35) while ultramarathoners don't peak in their performance for the 100K distance until age 39 to 40.

A study by Martin Hoffman and Eswar Krishnan tracked the health and injury status of more than 1,200 ultrarunners and found that 77 percent of them reported at least one injury in the previous year, but those who remained healthy were, on average, two years older and had two more years of endurance running experience.

So why exactly are older runners so darned good at endurance? Here is what the women themselves say:

Getting older has changed my state of mind, because I have the confidence to finish things that I never thought I could...I love being part of a community that values character and experiences over appearance, and where laugh lines, scars, and weathered skin are celebrated over flawless complexions. Sometimes the creases around my eyes and mouth make me feel old. This morning instead they made me laugh as I reflected on what they truly

represent. Get out there and make wrinkles. Laugh and
wrinkle on!

- Missy Berkel

Ageing slows everything down, but at the moment
I'm the strongest I've ever been. I'm still doing personal
bests and I've gotten to know my body and how much it
can handle more than I have before.

- Lisa Tamati, *Running Hot*

It's like a fine wine that gets better with age. I'm more
aware. I think aging is a benefit to endurance running
because we have learned the value of dedication,
persistence and commitment. In addition, we have the
ability to listen, respond and support our bodies as
needed to succeed at any long-distance mileage.

- Angie Piskorski

I feel like a goddess out there. I am completely free in
every sense of the word. Free from stress, work,
obligations. I listen to Mother Nature and tap into what
she is teaching. She humbles you when you are in her
world climbing huge peaks, and she gives you great gifts
of beauty and inspiration when you are fortunate to run
in breathtaking scenery.

- Molly Sheridan

That's not to say that there's nothing lost when it comes to
aging and staying competitive. In an iRunFar article on the

effects of aging and the endurance athlete, Sarah Vlach, MD, Board Certified in Physical Medicine and Rehabilitation, breaks down some numbers for us: "There is a decrease in total muscle mass, and decreased muscle fiber number and size. Vo2max decreases by nine to 10 percent per decade. Muscle mass decreases 1.25 percent per year after age 35."

Essentially, with age, our strength diminishes. Although the strength of each muscle fiber remains the same, the overall body strength is reduced due to the smaller cross-sectional area of each muscle group. Regular resistance training is the key here, reducing losses by as much as half.

Our cardio is affected as well. Writer and coach Matt Hart writes:

Our maximum heart rate starts to decrease as we age, losing its ability to pump blood to working muscles. Upstream from that, as we age our lungs lose intake capacity, as well as their ability to move oxygen to the bloodstream.

Most of these changes happen so slowly they may go unnoticed. If you are feeling the effects, Sarah and Matt recommend appropriate sleep, intelligent training, quality nutrition and strength work to reduce the impact of aging.

Regardless of the bumps in the road, there is still much to be gained by staying active in old age. If you're on social media, you've probably seen the photos from a study on master-level athletes. The image shows three cross-sections:

- A thigh from a 40-year-old triathlete
- A thigh from a 70-year-old triathlete

- A thigh from a 74-year-old sedentary man

The thighs of the two triathletes are identical, regardless of their age: healthy, strong, muscular. The 74-year-old sedentary man's thighs are a pitiful sight: full of fat and shriveled muscles. The study concludes that "chronic exercise preserves lean muscle mass in masters athletes" and suggests that a decline in vitality may have more to do with lifestyle choices than musculoskeletal aging.

A study by Scott Trappe at the Human Performance Laboratory in Indiana examined the aging effects on marathon runners. He found that "years of distance running can maintain the oxidative capacity of skeletal muscle at high levels." While it's true that single muscle fibers grow smaller and weaker, and contract faster with less power, this may actually be an advantage for distance runners. Smaller muscle fibers allow for a shorter diffusion distance of oxygen and long-distance athletes have little use for high strength or power output.

In addition to these adaptations, many aging endurance athletes appear to compensate for their deteriorating bodies with bang-on nutrition, a healthy and sustainable pace, an impressive mental resilience and an overwhelmingly positive attitude.

In many cases, older athletes focus on goals and ambitions that play specifically to their strengths, whether it be flat races, mountain races, looped courses, hot weather, cold weather, elevation, self-supported challenges, etc. They stick to the types of races they excel at instead of sampling a variety of everything the way a younger person might.

The aging process seems to slow on their faces too. Seasoned ultrarunner Meghan Arbogast told iRunFar:

> For athletes who take care of their bodies and adopt a lifestyle that supports their activities, the aging process is much slower than the inactive human. Most fit athletes that I know look ten or more years younger than their chronological age, and I believe have the physiology of someone much younger as well.

Why Them and Not My Mother?

When Lori Lyons discovered I was writing this chapter on aging, she asked me to answer this for her:

> What gives (aging endurance athletes) grit? Because they all seem to have it. It would be much easier to take up golf and cut coupons. My mother is 68 and I can't even convince her to go to the gym or walk everyday. She never exercised growing up. What is inside the 68-year-old men and women that are, for example, ultra racing, that does not exist in my mother?

Her question intrigued me and I turned to several endurance athletes over the age of 50 for their opinions on where that grit for endurance come from. Although I gathered several replies, there were recurring themes:

1. They just forgot to act their age.

At heart, older endurance athletes are goofy goobers. They were born that way. They have always been adventurous, fun-loving, up for anything. They have a zest and passion for life. They have always been physically active

and they see no reason to stop. They may have a few extra wrinkles, but their bodies still take them all the places they want to go—wild, beautiful and challenging places. Their playful spirit keeps them in the company of younger folks. Being sedentary feels like—and has always felt like—a total waste of time. They just never grew up and they never will. One runner said, "I still feel like I'm 18..."

2. They are facing mortality.

A few people listed fear as their central motivator: fear of aging, fear of dying, fear of breaking down, fear of exclusion. The clock is ticking and they are overcome with a gnawing realization that they have little time left. Pounding away at endurance sport is their way of keeping the Grim Reaper at bay. You can't really die doing a marathon, can you?...Can you??

3. They are realistically confident.

In our youth, we are full of ego, believing we can tackle things we may not be ready for. We are overconfident but not necessarily skilled. As we age, we come to understand exactly what our bodies are capable of, and that's often a lot. Older runners are realistically confident. Their confidence is based on life experiences and they know they have everything they need to meet their goals.

4. They are unwilling to put up with bullshit, including their own.

When you sense you are running out of time on this earth, you become less willing to put up with bullshit. Bullshit comes in all forms: unsupportive and toxic relationships, negative life influences, trying to please others, pretending you're someone you're not and personal weakness. Older runners aren't going

290

to be held back by nagging doubts, cop-out excuses or society's expectations. They may not get another chance. They will plow ahead. They will meet their goals. They will finish the race.

5. They are determined to cash in on well-earned "me" time.

Many older runners have spent a lifetime working for and under others, raising kids, investing in a family, securing their futures, and making sure their kids become functioning members of society. They have worked hard and they have held out for the "me" time society promised them. They are also financially stable and have more free time than they did in the past. Many put their dreams on hold until retirement and God help anyone who tries to tell them they're now too frail to do exactly what they want. This is their time.

6. They prefer to keep it simple.

Older runners are drawn to the simplicity of running. They don't have to rely on anyone else or expensive equipment to get it done. Running for them is a no-fuss, no-muss activity they can enjoy for years to come. Simple as that.

7. They understand real suffering.

When you have experienced health issues or watched the people you love slowly suffer and die, an endurance race by comparison seems pretty easy. Watching time pass, dealing with the loss of parents and the maturation of children puts everything into perspective. Sweating it out in a race is nothing. Pushing mentally and physically is nothing. They know what real pain is.

8. They respect their bodies.

Instead of mindlessly plodding ahead, older runners

understand exactly what they need for top performance. They take great care of their bodies because they have to. They can't get away with terrible eating habits or sleep deprivation. They are no longer interested in filling their bodies with toxins. Long-term quality of life becomes much more important. They give their bodies the best ingredients and their bodies respond with strength and resilience.

9. They grew up with a strong work ethic.

This particular generation didn't grow up getting a medal just for showing up. Their parents and peers and teachers were hard on them. They were expected to put in a respectable effort and extra work if they wanted to excel. Older runners aren't afraid to put in the long training hours, to fit in some cross-training, or to push themselves to the edge. Quitting for them is never an option. They were raised to never give up.

An interview on Fittish with ultrarunning legend Gordon Ainsleigh helps shed some further light on this topic. Gordy said:

> There are two philosophies of aging: "Take kindly the counsel of the years, gracefully surrendering the things of youth" (Desiderata, 1927), or Dylan Thomas: "Do not go gentle into that good night, Old age should burn and rave at close of day; Rage, rage against the dying of the light." I'm on Thomas' side.

Maybe all of us who live, play, work and breathe these sports are on Thomas' side. Maybe we're just wired to push our bodies longer, faster, stronger...or die trying.

Menopause and the Aging Athlete

Shelly (not her real name) sat in the car with her boyfriend, driving home from a wonderful play at the Dorothy Chandler Pavillion in downtown Los Angeles. Although the evening was pleasant, the conversation in the car was not. It had veered severely and hopelessly off course. Shelly could feel her blood pressure rising as she got angrier and angrier. Out of the blue her boyfriend asked, "Have you gone through menopause yet?" Shelly was stunned. She was only 47.

"What the hell kind of question is that?" she snapped.

"Well, my ex-wife went through that," he replied weakly.

Shelly's boyfriend realized too late that he was walking on a minefield. When they arrived back at his house, Shelly grabbed her things and stormed out. Before leaving, she spun around one last time. "Hey, I know you haven't dated in 20 years, but to ask a woman if she has gone through menopause is not exactly going to rate real high in winning you points!" (She may or may not have slammed the door on her way out.)

His question had struck a nerve. It made Shelly feel old and unloved. At the time, Shelly had been recovering from a difficult breakup, while her current boyfriend was going through a contentious divorce. He was an ultrarunner and had introduced her to the wonders of endurance.

Shelly had been slowly increasing her mileage and training hard, but feeling exhausted. She attributed her fatigue to the added mileage and the stress of her breakup, but she was also experiencing off-the-charts mood swings (think: Jekyll and Hyde). She had lost her sex drive (not like her) while gaining vaginal dryness and discomfort during sex.

Her boyfriend was patient and understanding. He showered her with gifts, which Shelly loved…sometimes. Other times she felt ambivalent or annoyed. She liked him. Then she didn't. Then she did. Same thing with running.

A few weeks later, they broke up for good. Shelly's mood swings continued to get worse and now that she didn't have the relationship to blame, she had to face the reality that perhaps her boyfriend's tactless question made sense. Could this possibly be menopause?

After much contemplation, Shelly reluctantly visited her OB/GYN and had tests done. She learned that she had entered full-blown perimenopause and was put on a program of medications. Her symptoms subsided almost immediately. Her sleep improved, her diet got better and her running took off.

Since then she has raced numerous ultramarathons and has tried to get back together with her ex who first suggested menopause. Unfortunately, that ship had sailed. He was and remains unwilling to try again. Shelly feels she lost a valuable relationship at the hands of her hormones. She's moved on now, but wishes she could have understood her symptoms sooner. Today, she advises any female athlete in her forties to be mindful of menopause since it may be the root cause of many training and relationship woes.

Shelly is not alone. Several of the women I spoke to reported going into menopause with little to no understanding of what was happening to them biologically, especially in an endurance or training context.

Sally Hulbert had been running for 33 years when she found herself struggling with pre- and post-menopausal issues. She searched for information on the topic of running and menopause, but found nothing. She battled for months with lethargy, dizziness and short-term memory loss so bad that the symptoms scared her. When she finally had blood work done, Sally was shocked to discover that her body was already three-quarters of the way through menopause. She also uncovered a thyroid imbalance. That knowledge changed her training approach and gave her some much-needed peace of mind.

Even in this Internet age of over-sharing, there is a glaring lack of information about active women and menopause. In one study, women undergoing menopause listed the fictional character Edith Bunker of *All in the Family* as their chief source of information about what to expect. Another reported that when she asked her doctor about menopause he replied, "Ask your mother."

This section consists of details that women like Shelly and Sally wish they had known.

The Basics (and a Little Horrifying History)

Menopause is tricky because the symptoms vary wildly and so do scientific studies. Although hot flashes and night sweats are the most common symptoms associated with menopause, there are hundreds more. Many of these can directly affect training and endurance. Some include:

- sore joints
- trouble sleeping

- crashing fatigue
- weight gain
- heart palpitations
- nausea
- brittle fingernails
- feelings of dread
- disorientation
- gastrointestinal distress
- vertigo
- panic attacks
- lethargy
- flatulence
- changes in body odor

It's like a bad race.

Medically speaking, menopause is the one-year anniversary of a woman's last period—just that one day. Perimenopause describes the years (on average, five of them) of fluctuating fertility and irregular periods a woman experiences before officially undergoing "the change."

We now know that aging comes from the ovaries. In the article *A Natural History of Menopause*, writer Nancy Marie Brown explains it this way:

A girl is born with upwards of a million follicles in her ovaries. Like the cells in the brain and the eye, these follicles are never replaced when they die. Unlike brain cells, dying off is what follicles do naturally: by the time a girl reaches puberty and her hormones kick in, she will have lost all but some 100,000 of them. Every month after that, a dozen or more follicles will begin to grow, only one of which is usually selected to mature and be released at ovulation. By the time she is 45 (at least according to the handful of studies that have been done using autopsy cases or ovaries that had to be surgically removed), a woman's follicles will number only about a thousand.

Once we've run out of follicles, all the hormonal feedback is removed and the result is menopause.

Of course, we didn't always know this. Every woman alive today should thank her lucky stars she was not born in the Victorian era, when menopause was still considered a mental disorder. For treatment, some women were institutionalized. Others were operated on.

In 1824, Dr. John Lizards, an Edinburgh surgeon and lecturer in anatomy and physiology, was the first person to perform an ovariotomy surgery to treat menopause by removing the ovaries. His patient survived, but the next three did not.

Thirty-one years later, 89 women had died on the operating table in attempts to remove their ovaries. Anesthesia was not introduced until the late 1840s and it would be another 100 years after that before synthetic estrogen was developed.

Victorian physicians believed in a link between the womb and the brain, which predisposed women to insanity. Basically, ovaries were evil little walnuts that caused nymphomania and hysteria, among other terrors. (The term "hysteria" comes from the Greek word "hysterus," meaning womb.) One myth warned that the more "badly behaved" a

woman had been in her youth, the more menopause would affect her. Hormones were not officially "discovered" until 1902.

Women today are better at sharing information. Here are some tips I gathered from female endurance athletes who have been there, done that:

Menopause Management Tips for the Active Endurance Athlete

1. Familiarize yourself with the symptoms, and not just the common ones. This will save you the grief of blaming yourself for hiccups in training that may have a biological root. Symptoms of menopause can easily be mistaken for signs of overtraining.

2. Get a blood test to rule out thyroid imbalances. Thyroid issues are common and can be helped with a proper diagnosis.

3. Listen to your body and don't be afraid to lower your mileage when you need a break. Your hormones, muscles and bones are changing. Even your sleep patterns may be changing. One of the biggest lessons in menopause is accepting yourself for who you are. Go ahead and set lofty goals, but go easy on the self-judgment.

4. Try herbs and natural supplements. A few women swore by black cohosh and red clover in copious amounts. The ancient Chinese also used dong quai and acupuncture techniques to treat menstrual and hormonal irregularities.

5. Drink, drink, drink. If you experience hot flashes and night sweats, you may be underestimating how much water you're losing in a 24-hour period. The amount of water that used to suffice in the past may not cut it anymore. Also keep a

close eye on dehydrating beverages like alcohol or caffeine.

6. Keep tabs on weight changes brought on by hormonal shifts. It is estimated that nine out of ten American menopausal women gain weight. Your metabolism is shifting and you may find yourself with a reduced ability to get away with junk food, refined sugars and/or alcohol.

7. Start a body journal. Keep track of your diet, your symptoms and your training to spot patterns and learn how your body is responding. Knowledge is power.

The good news is that running and menopause seem to be good companions, according to several anecdotes. Women reported that long distance running helped them vent excess sexual energy, manage their weight, improve sleep quality and stabilize mood swings. One woman reported that wearing pretty running skirts helped her channel her inner girly-ness while long group trail runs helped her bond with other older women going through similar life challenges.

According to one study, exercise can also reduce the metabolic risks associated with declining estrogen and offset the decline of bone mineral density. The ideal exercise prescription includes endurance aerobic training, strength work and balance exercises.

Women in endurance can and do remain highly competitive in their later years. When I asked active women online how they deal with menopause, Lisa Bliss jokingly typed: "I don't pause for men; I try to run them down."

Vanessa Runs

12: Final Words

When I started writing this book I thought it would be a much shorter project. Now I realize it could have been longer. There is a lot that still needs to be said and many stories that were omitted. I urge you to continue the journey.

If you remember nothing else from this book, take away these two things:

1. Be kind to yourself.

This doesn't have to include pampering, though it certainly can. I'm talking about not berating ourselves for whatever we feel we are lacking. Most men don't have it all together either but that doesn't stop them from thinking they're the shit. We are the shit too. Let's act shitty! (You know what I mean.)

2. Don't apologize for your experiences, opinions and struggles.

In 2014, athlete Shannon Payne wrote about gender inequality on her blog. She explained that if you podium at the WMRA Championships, as she did, you're in for Team USA at next year's WMRA Championships. The 2015 Championships were to be held at the Zermatt Marathon in Switzerland and the LOC for Zermatt was funding 75 percent of the team's travel expenses. However, there was a catch: although all three men would be funded, only one woman would benefit. Neither Shannon nor Morgan Arritola would receive a dime. Why fund three men and only one woman?

Shannon's points were valid, clear and factual. Her

questions were fair and powerful, yet she still felt the need to "throw in a massive and extremely long-winded disclaimer," part of which was: "I don't really know 100 percent what I'm talking about."

This is not a Shannon thing; many women are full of apologies. One woman I spoke to apologized for not being able to pee standing up (an ultra trail runner's trick that some women are lucky enough to master).

Why do we form valid opinions, then turn around and attack ourselves for having them? Let's work on this. (By the way, the WMRA Council has addressed the issue of funding for women and is moving forward with a new contract that will reflect equal money for the top three men and women.)

We also tend to dismiss our concerns for sport equality as "first world problems." We need to stop this. Just because we aren't dealing with famine or abuse does not mean we don't get a voice or that our struggles do not matter. We are not insensitive to the plights of others by speaking up for ourselves. Our rights do not retard another woman's rights and we can advance on both fronts at the same time. Sport does matter.

And sport can make a difference to world issues. In her book, *A Life Without Limits*, Chrissie Wellington wrote about how she used sports to support international development:

I worked as a swimming teacher at a day school in Boston, and I saw firsthand what a difference sport can make to children's lives. And again in Nepal, where sport was one thing that could bring conflict-affected communities together. Sport has a tremendous power, and can be a force for considerable change.

Wild Dreams for a Brighter Future

I want to close this book with some of my own ideas and hopes. This is my go-to list if I ever become the god of sport and can do whatever I want.

(In writing this, I had to stop myself from describing these points as silly, crazy, probably not going to happen anytime soon, maybe not even a great idea, logistically. In other words, "I don't really know 100 percent what I'm talking about." See how easy it is to do that?)

1. Gender-free Podiums

One of my comedy heroes, Tina Fey, wrote in her book *Bossypants*:

> My dream for the future is that sketch comedy shows become a gender-blind meritocracy of whoever is really the funniest. You might see four women and two men. You might see five men and a YouTube video of a kitten sneezing. Once we know we're really open to all the options, we can proceed with "Whatever's the Funniest"… which will probably involve farts.

What if we looked at endurance the same way? What if we did away with female wins or male wins and threw everyone into one big human pot? No shortcuts and no handicaps. Isn't it ridiculous to demand equal pay and equal opportunity while embracing segregated events and prizes?

I believe women should compete with men on the same day and on the same course across every endurance sport.

Women have already proven time and again that they are capable of keeping up and winning outright. Yet it is still generally accepted that women are weaker, hence our own divisions and our own sets of prizes.

Yes, males have certain biological advantages, but those advantages have little to no relevance in endurance. Upper body strength in long distance running is practically a non-issue. The longer the run, the more true this becomes. The biological strengths of women (higher body fat percentages, smaller frames and strong mental drives) put females in a competitive position.

I don't believe it was a coincidence that Pam Reed won Badwater twice. I don't believe Pam is super-human. Let's up our competition. If that sounds crazy, keep in mind that at one time the ideas that women could work and vote were considered insane.

If categories must be set, let's use height, weight or body fat percentage divisions, but always allow women to compete with men.

2. Shame-Free Bodies

As I'm writing this, I'm at Across the Years in Arizona, a six-day event that involves running a one-mile loop around a sports facility for anywhere from 24 hours to six days. This morning I slipped into the showers to wash up and I met a woman who was registered for the six-day event. She was getting ready for her first shower.

This woman had never raced anything like this before and was eager to chat. The more we talked, the more layers of clothes she peeled off until she was standing in front of me nearly naked and still gabbing.

Although her breasts were exposed, the conversation was comfortable. I promised to keep an eye out for her on the course. How could I not be friends with this woman? I had already seen her naked.

Endurance athletes should not have to invest any time or energy into worrying about stray nipples or peek-a-boo glutes. It should be no big deal to pop a squat in the woods when nature calls. Our bodies are tools and incredible machines, not sources of shame.

3. Human Rights (Not Just Women's Rights)

One well-meaning article I read about "getting more women into ultrarunning" suggested that perhaps some women were put off from the "swaths of testosterone" and the "male egos" at the start line. "And who could blame them," the author wrote. "Us men can be real idiots at times!"

We need to stop pretending that women are exalted when men are belittled. Writing off our men as idiots or clueless does not help the female cause, and the rise of women is not linked to the fall of men. Equality is not a limited resource; there is enough to go around.

Another flaw is the "women and children" mentality. This assumes that women are the fairer or weaker sex who needs protection, just as children do. Shedding this concept means shedding certain female privileges and crutches. It involves putting on the big girl panties.

Why weren't women allowed to run the marathon? To protect them. Why aren't women currently allowed to cycle longer distances? To protect them. In the past, women have also been protected from reading and learning.

What else are we being protected from today?

Even chivalry is based on the concept that females are especially fragile. That doesn't mean you shouldn't hold open doors or elevators. It means you should hold them open for both men and women.

Finally, gender-focused discussions ignore the experiences of transsexuals and others who don't identify with a single or traditionally defined gender. Let's advocate for human rights above all, with women definitely but not exclusively included. Women are not our enemies. Men are not our enemies. Our worst enemy is ignorance.

George Sheehan was right when he identified running as a bonding activity between the genders. He wrote:

The truth is that sports, and that includes men running against women, may well be the salvation of the man-woman relationship, the answer to our marriage problem, the solution to the eternal discord between what is masculine and what is feminine.

Endurance should unite, not separate us.

4. Flawed Feminism

Essayist Roxane Gay (the self-described bad feminist) likes pink. She dances to music that is degrading to women. Yet she is passionate about women's rights.

I feel the same way. I'm a bad feminist and a bad athlete. I love sexist jokes and I objectify pretty girls. If I could run around in pink panties and pigtails all day, that would be my job.

I'm a bad athlete, too. I'm too slow to win anything and

half the time I don't even want it. Truth be told, I'm not a huge fan of sweating. Running hurts. Mostly, I took up trail running to be alone. I like reading. I like wood stoves. I love to eat, especially breakfast foods.

I realize and have realized with every stroke of my pen (er, cursor) that I'm probably not the best woman to write this book, but if we always waited until we were the best women for the job, the dudes would just do everything.

The point is, we're all flawed but that doesn't mean we can't play. Let's be flawed feminists together.

5. Outdoor Industry Attention

Shacky and I live in a 22-foot Rialta RV. We each have two small shelves for our clothing, but my shelf always seems to be bulging with clothes whereas there is enough extra space on his to store a small Dutch oven.

On an annual basis, I spend twice as much on outdoor clothing and gear as he does. Other couples also experience this female purchasing power slant.

The outdoor industry is beginning to notice women, but we still have a long way to go.

"Shrinking and pinking" is still too common. This refers to a company's tendency to shrink a men's size and make it in a "feminine" color to sell to women. This is irritating and inefficient. Women are not shaped like mini-men. We need more breast-friendly hydration packs and backpacks. For the love of god—make better sports bra options.

It has also been wonderful to see some companies use real female athletes as promoters as opposed to non-running models who simply look pretty. We need more of this. Women pay attention to what other women wear. We talk about gear and we always share what works for us. We talk about products in person and on social media. Women want function, not just frills. And we don't want to be an afterthought.

6. Girls Outside

We are greatly failing our young girls when it comes to getting them outside and keeping them active. Adolescent girls are dropping off the sports radar like flies. Research has shown that although overall outdoor participation is growing among adults, girls between the ages of 13 and 17 are participating much less. We need to wake up and pay attention to this if we want a future in female endurance.

It's not fair to assume that teen girls don't want to get dirty or break their nails. It's time to consider that perhaps sports are simply not including younger females.

If you are a woman in sport, seriously consider becoming a role model, mentor or coach for a young girl. This can be as easy as talking about your sport, sharing stories, taking a teen girl hiking, sending them postcards or writing them letters. Show up. Be present in their lives. Make sure they know what you're doing and why you do it.

I've already mentioned Girls on the Run, an organization dedicated to this. The 100 Mile Club is another great charity committed to keeping kids active.

Goals and Goodbyes

This book is not an authoritative conclusion on these topics, but a conversation starter kit. Can you relate to some of these themes? Strongly disagree or agree with something in this book? Share your own story. Carry on the torch and keep these topics alive. I bet you'll find other women who share your opinions.

Many of the women I interviewed felt they were alone, fighting private struggles as female athletes, when in reality our experiences are so similar. It just takes one woman to open up and share.

The best we can all do is to continue learning, reading, sharing and listening to women.

We can continue the conversation on my blog at vanessaruns.com or on the Daughters of Distance Facebook page at facebook.com/daughtersofdistance. You can also email me directly at vanessaruns@gmail.com.

If you enjoyed this book, please take the time to leave an Amazon review online.

Vanessa Runs

Acknowlegements

It would be impossible for me to list the hundreds of women who helped make this book a reality. This book is for you and by you.

A special shout-out goes out to my amazing research assistant Crista Scott and photographer Luis Escobar for the cover shot. Thanks to Trisha Reeves for designing a fabulous cover and my editors Susan Fish and Meghan Hicks who brought years of expertise into my manuscript. Thanks to Jimmy Dean Freeman for planting this book idea in my head with his crazy ideas.

Thanks to my little sisters who inspire me every day to be the best woman I can be and thanks to you, the reader, for thinking and caring about women in endurance.

Onward.

Vanessa Runs

References

Intro

"PLANET WORK Women in Sports: How Level Is the Playing Field?" *PLANET WORK Women in Sports: How Level Is the Playing Field?* N.p., 01 Apr. 2006. Web. 17 Feb. 2015.

"Difference Between Men's & Women's Basketball." *LIVESTRONG.COM*. LIVESTRONG.COM, 12 Mar. 2014. Web. 16 Feb. 2015. http://www.livestrong.com/article/122406-difference-between-mens-womens/.

"Tennis' Gender Pay Gap Problem Looms On The Sidelines." *Forbes*. Forbes Magazine, n.d. Web. 17 Feb. 2015. http://www.forbes.com/sites/miguelmorales/2014/02/21/tennis-gender-pay-gap-problem-looms-on-the-sidelines/.

"National Committee on Pay Equity NCPE." *National Committee on Pay Equity NCPE*. N.p., 17 Feb. 2015. Web. 17 Feb. 2015. http://www.pay-equity.org

Chapter 1: Is My Mascara Running?

Khanna, Madhu. "Nature As Feminine: Ancient Vision of Geopiety and Goddess Ecology." IGNCA. May 2011. Web. 16 Feb. 2015. http://www.ignca.nic.in/ps_05011.htm/.

"Why Are These Teens So Fast?" *Runner's World & Running Times*. N.p., 29 Apr. 2014. Web. 17 Feb. 2015. http://www.runnersworld.com/high-school-racing/why-are-these-teens-so-fast?page=single/.

Ensler, Eve. *I Am an Emotional Creature: The Secret Life of Girls around the World*. New York, NY: Villard, 2010. Print.

Sosienski, Shanti. *Women Who Run*. Emeryville, CA: Seal, 2006. Print.

Samuels, Mina. *Run like a Girl: How Strong Women Make Happy Lives*. Berkeley, CA: Seal, 2011. Print.

Friedan, Betty. *The Feminine Mystique*. New York, NY: W.W. Norton, 1963. Print.

Kalbfleisch, Pamela J., and Michael J. Cody. *Gender, Power, and Communication in Human Relationships*. Hillsdale, NJ: Erlbaum, 1995. Print.

Serano, Julia. *Whipping Girl: A Transsexual Woman on Sexism and the Scapegoating of Femininity*. Emeryville, CA: Seal, 2007. Print.

Brown, William. *Art of Shoe Making*. Chandni Chowk, Delhi: Global Media, 2007. Print.

Kremer, William. "Why Did Men Stop Wearing High Heels?" *BBC News*. N.p., n.d. Web. 12 Feb. 2015. http://www.bbc.co.uk/news/magazine-21151350.

"Ecofeminism Critique on the Green Fuse." *Ecofeminism Critique on the Green Fuse*. N.p., n.d. Web. 17 Feb. 2015. http://www.thegreenfuse.org/ecofemcrit.htm#root.

"History of Women in the Outdoors - HowStuffWorks." *HowStuffWorks*. N.p., n.d. Web. 17 Feb. 2015. http://adventure.howstuffworks.com/outdoor-activities/hunting/clubs-and-organizations/women-in-the-outdoors1.htm/.

"Artemis." *Artemis*. N.p., n.d. Web. 11 Feb. 2015. http://www.pantheon.org/articles/a/artemis.html/.

"Find Your Goddess Archetype - Artemis, Goddess-power.com." *Find Your Goddess Archetype - Artemis, Goddess-*

power.com. N.p., n.d. Web. 16 Feb. 2015. http://goddess-power.com/artemis.htm/.

Hammond, N. G. L., and H. H. Scullard. *The Oxford Classical Dictionary*. Oxford: Clarendon, 1970. Print.

McDowell, Dimity, and Sarah Bowen Shea. *Run like a Mother: How to Get Moving, and Not Lose Your Family, Job, or Sanity*. Kansas City, MO: Andrews McMeel Pub. 2010. Print.

Daniels, Dayna B. "Polygendered and Ponytailed: The Dilemma of Femininity and the Female Athlete." *Women's Press* (2009): 444-46. Web. 6 Mar. 2015.

Steinfeldt, Jesse A., Rebecca Zakrajsek, Hailee Carter, and Matthew Clint Steinfeldt. "Conformity to Gender Norms among Female Student-athletes: Implications for Body Image." *Psychology of Men & Masculinity* 12.4 (2011): 401-16. Web. 6 Mar. 2015.

Krane, Vikki, Precilla Y. L. Choi, Shannon M. Baird, Christine M. Aimar, and Kerrie J. Kauer. "Living the Paradox: Female Athletes Negotiate Femininity and Muscularity." *Sex Roles* 50.5/6 (2004): 315-29. Web. 6 Mar. 2015.

George, Molly. "Making Sense of Muscle: The Body Experiences of Collegiate Women Athletes*." *Sociological Inquiry* 75.3 (2005): 317-45. Web. 6 Mar. 2015.

Chapter 2: There's No Crying in Baseball!

Tamati, Lisa. *Running Hot*. Auckland, N.Z.: Allen & Unwin, 2009. Print.

Brody, Jane E. "Biological Role of Emotional Tears Emerges Through Recent Studies." The New York Times. The New York Times, 30 Aug. 1982. Web. 17 Feb. 2015.

http://www.nytimes.com/1982/08/31/science/biological-role-of-emotional-tears-emerges-through-recent-studies.html.

Brooks, David. "The Heart Grows Smarter." *The New York Times*. The New York Times, 05 Nov. 2012. Web. 17 Feb. 2015. http://www.nytimes.com/2012/11/06/opinion/brooks-the-heart-grows-smarter.html?_r=0/.

"Darkness: How Ultrarunning Can Strip Away Our Emotional Barriers." *Wildplans*. N.p., n.d. Web. 17 Feb. 2015. http://wildplans.com/darkness-how-ultrarunning-can-strip-away-our-emotional-barriers/.

"Doing What She Most Wants To Do: Heather Anderson's Pacific Crest Trail FKT." *iRunFar.com*. N.p., n.d. Web. 17 Feb. 2015. http://www.irunfar.com/2013/09/doing-what-she-most-wants-to-do-heather-andersons-pacific-crest-trail-fkt.html/.

Chapter 3: Race Like a Girl

"Chicking for Beginners - Women's Adventure Magazine." *Women's Adventure Magazine*. N.p., 03 Mar. 2011. Web. 17 Feb. 2015. http://www.womensadventuremagazine.com/blog/chicking-for-beginners/.

Hess, Amanda. "You Can Only Hope To Contain Them." *ESPN*. ESPN Internet Ventures, 16 July 2013. Web. 17 Feb. 2015. http://espn.go.com/espnw/news-commentary/article/9451835/female-athletes-biggest-opponents-their-own-breasts-espn-magazine/.

Bertine, Kathryn. *As Good as Gold: 1 Woman, 9 Sports, 10 Countries, and a 2-year Quest to Make the Summer Olympics*. New

York: ESPN, 2010. Print.

Lankford, Andrea. *Ranger Confidential: Living, Working, and Dying in the National Parks.* Guilford, CT: FalconGuides, 2010. Print.

Nelson, Bryan. "No, Menstruating Women Do Not Attract Bear Attacks." *Mother Jones.* N.p., 15 Aug. 2012. Web. 17 Feb. 2015. http://www.motherjones.com/blue-marble/2012/08/menstruating-women-do-not-attract-bear-attacks/.

"Parks and Menstruation: Sexism, Bears, and the National Park Service." *BitchMagazine.org.* N.p., 08 Aug. 2012. Web. 17 Feb. 2015. http://bitchmagazine.org/post/parks-and-menstruation-sexism-bears-and-the-national-park-service/.

Byl, Christine. *Dirt Work: An Education in the Woods.* Boston, MA: Beacon Press, 2013. Print.

"No Boys Allowed: One Woman's Thoughts on Women Only Races." *Salty Running.* N.p., 24 July 2013. Web. 19 Feb. 2015. http://www.saltyrunning.com/2013/07/24/no-boys-allowed-thoughts-on-women-only-races/.

Miner, Tim. "Wilderness Douchebag Identification System - Trail Sherpa." *Trail Sherpa.* N.p., 10 Oct. 2013. Web. 05 Mar. 2015. http://www.trailsherpa.com/blog/2013/10/10/douchebag-identification-system/.

Dunlap, Scott. "Yiannis Kouros - Ultrarunning's Penultimate Elite/Elitist(?)." *A Trail Runner's Blog.* N.p., 14 Mar. 2008. Web. 19 Feb. 2015. http://www.atrailrunnersblog.com/2008/03/yiannis-kouros-ultrarunnings.html/.

Vanessa Runs

Clews, Charlotte. "Running with Tarahumara Women." *National Running Center*. 26 Nov. 2013. Web. 19 Feb. 2015. http://naturalrunningcenter.com/2013/11/26/running-tarahumara-women/.

McGregor, Jena. "How Women's Tennis Fought for Equal Pay." *Washington Post*. The Washington Post, 5 Sept. 2014. Web. 19 Feb. 2015. http://www.washingtonpost.com/blogs/on-leadership/wp/2014/09/05/how-womens-tennis-fought-for-equal-pay/.

"Pay Inequality in Athletes." *Women's Sports Foundation*. N.p., n.d. Web. 19 Feb. 2015. http://www.womenssportsfoundation.org/en/home/research/articles-and-reports/equity-issues/pay-inequity/.

Clemitson, Suze. "The Long, Hard Road to Equal Pay for Women's Cycling and Sport as a Whole." *The Guardian*. N.p., 6 Mar. 2014. Web. 19 Feb. 2015. http://www.theguardian.com/sport/100-tours-100-tales/2014/mar/06/equal-pay-womens-sport-cycling-koppenbergcross/.

Half the Road: The Passion, Pitfalls & Power of Women's Professional Cycling. Dir. Kathryn Bertine. First Run Features, 2014. Web. 19 Feb. 2015.

"Women in Sports: How Level Is the Playing Field?" *PLANET WORK Women in Sports: How Level Is the Playing Field?* International Labour Organization, 01 Apr. 2006. Web. 19 Feb. 2015. http://www.ilo.org/global/publications/magazines-and-journals/world-of-work-

318

magazine/articles/WCMS_081377/lang--en/index.htm

"Equal Pay For Women Athletes: Elite Prize Purses." *Salty Running*. N.p., 6 Nov. 2012. Web. 19 Feb. 2015. http://www.saltyrunning.com/2012/11/06/equal-pay-for-women-athletes-elite-prize-purses/.

Macur, Juliet. "Women as Athletes, Not Accessories, at Least for a Day." *The New York Times*. The New York Times, 26 July 2014. Web. 19 Feb. 2015. http://www.nytimes.com/2014/07/27/sports/cycling/tour-de-france-2014-women-push-to-compete-in-cyclings-top-event.html?_r=1/.

McDonagh, Eileen L., and Laura Pappano. *Playing with the Boys: Why Separate Is Not Equal in Sports*. Oxford: Oxford UP, 2008. Print.

Eileen McDonagh; Laura Pappano (July 2009). *Playing with the Boys: Why Separate Is Not Equal in Sports*. Oxford University Press US. ISBN 978-0-19-538677-6. Retrieved 29 May 2011.

Reed, Pam. *The Extra Mile: One Woman's Personal Journey to Ultra-running Greatness*. Emmaus, PA: Rodale, 2006. Print.

"We Need To Talk About Getting More Women Into Ultra Running." *Ultra168.com*. N.p., 04 Aug. 2014. Web. 5 Mar. 2015. http://ultra168.com/2014/04/08/we-need-to-talk-about-getting-more-women-into-ultra-running/.

Clemitson, Suze. "The Long, Hard Road to Equal Pay for Women's Cycling and Sport as a Whole." *The Guardian*. N.p., 6 Mar. 2014. Web. 19 Feb. 2015. http://www.theguardian.com/sport/100-tours-100-tales/2014/mar/06/equal-pay-womens-sport-cycling-koppenbergcross/.

"Wife Carrying in North America." *Wife-Carrying.org.* N.p., n.d. Web. 19 Feb. 2015. http://www.wife-carrying.org/.

"History of Big Man." *BA Events.* N.p., n.d. Web. 19 Feb. 2015. http://www.baevents.com/bigmanrun/history.html/.

"Welcome | Walk a Mile in Her Shoes." *Walk a Mile in Her Shoes.* N.p., n.d. Web. 18 Feb. 2015. http://www.walkamileinhershoes.org/.

"Man On The Run 5K - A Charity Run for Men and Boys: Man On The Run." *Man On The Run RSS.* N.p., n.d. Web. 19 Feb. 2015. http://www.manontherun.org/.

Angelini, James, Paul MacArthur, and Andrew Billings. "What's The Gendered Story? Vancouver's Prime Time Olympic Glory on NBC." *Journal of Broadcasting & Electronic Media* 52.2 (2012): 261-79. Web. 6 Mar. 2015.

Davis, Jennifer Pharr. *Called Again: A Story of Love and Triumph.* New York, NY: Beaufort, 2013. Print.

Bertine, Kathryn. "Women's Cycling Prize Money Is For The Birds." *ESPN.* ESPN Internet Ventures, 12 Apr. 2011. Web. 20 Feb. 2015. http://espn.go.com/espnw/blogs/training/article/6327829/women-cycling-prize- money-birds.

Grieve, Frederick, Ryan Zapalac, Julie Partridge, and Paula Parker. "An Examination of Predictors of Watching Televised Sport Programming." *North American Journal of Psychology* 15.1 (2013): 190-94. Web. 6 Mar. 2015.

Wann, Daniel, Paula Waddill, and Mardis Dunham. "Using Sex and Gender Role Orientation to Predict Level of Sport Fandom." *Journal of Sport Behavior* 27.4 (2000): 367-77.

Web. 6 Mar. 2015.

Chapter 4: Putting on the Big Girl Panties

"Lessons in Grit: Jennifer Vogel ~ UltraChixUnite.com." *Lessons in Grit: Jennifer Vogel ~ UltraChixUnite.com.* Ultra Chix Unite, Nov. 2011. Web. 20 Feb. 2015. http://www.ultrachixunite.com/2011/11/jennifer-vogel-lessons-in-grit.html.

Sandberg, Sheryl, and Nell Scovell. *Lean In: Women, Work, and the Will to Lead.* New York, NY: Alfred A. Knopf, 2013. Print.

Brooks, David. "Expressive Attraction." *David Brooks Expressive Attraction Comments.* NY Times, 31 May 2011. Web. 20 Feb. 2015. http://brooks.blogs.nytimes.com/2011/05/31/expressive-attraction/.

Brooks, David. "The Confidence Questions." *The New York Times.* The New York Times, 22 Apr. 2013. Web. 20 Feb. 2015. http://www.nytimes.com/2013/04/23/opinion/brooks-the-confidence-questions.html.

Tate, Allison. "The Mom Stays in the Picture." *The Huffington Post.* TheHuffingtonPost.com, 10 Feb. 2012. Web. 20 Feb. 2015. http://www.huffingtonpost.com/allison-tate/mom-pictures-with-kids_b_1926073.html.

Armstrong, Kristin. *Mile Markers: The 26.2 Most Important Reasons Why Women Run.* Emmaus, Pa: Rodale, 2011. Print.

Samuels, Mina. *Run like a Girl: How Strong Women Make Happy Lives.* Berkeley, CA: Seal, 2011. Print.

Tamati, Lisa, and Nicola McCloy. *Running to Extremes.*

Auckland, N.Z.: Allen & Unwin, 2012. Print.

Beecham, Stan. *Elite Minds: Creating the Competitive Advantage*. Alpharetta, GA: N.p., 2013. Print.

Graham, Jennifer. *Honey, Do You Need a Ride?: Confessions of a Fat Runner*. Halcottsville, NY: Breakaway, 2012. Print.

Friedman, Sally. *Swimming the Channel*. New York: Farrar, Straus and Giroux, 1996. Print.

Cavendar, Krista. "100 Miles. Kill The Bitch." *Running Naked on Sharp Pointy Stuff*. N.p., 10 Sept. 2013. Web. 20 Feb. 2015. http://www.nakedonsharppointystuff.blogspot.com/2013/09/100-miles-kill-bitch.html.

David, Gary, and Nick Lehecka. "The Spirit of the Trail: Culture, Popularity and Prize Money in Ultramarathoning." *The Spirit of the Trail*. UTA.edu, 1 Oct. 2013. Web. 20 Feb. 2015. http://www.uta.edu/huma/agger/fastcapitalism/10_1/david_lehecka10_1.html.

"Voted Best Tour in Southeast Alaska!" *Kroschel Films*. N.p., n.d. Web. 20 Feb. 2015. http://www.kroschelfilms.com/home.

"Why I Can Change The Way You Feel About Your Body Forever." *Body Love Wellness RSS*. N.p., 11 Dec. 2009. Web. 20 Feb. 2015. http://www.bodylovewellness.com/about-golda/.

Sosienski, Shanti. *Women Who Run*. Emeryville, CA: Seal, 2006. Print.

Hays, Kate, Owen Thomas, Ian Maynard, and Mark Bawden. "The Role of Confidence in World-class Sport Performance." *Journal of Sports Sciences* 27.11 (2009): 1185-199. Web. 6 Mar. 2015.

Boudreau, Alison L., and Barbro Giorgi. "The Experience of Self-Discovery and Mental Change in Female Novice Athletes in Connection to Marathon Running." *Journal of Phenomenological Psychology* 41.2 (2010): 234-67. Web. 6 Mar. 2015.

Gaston, Anca, Anita Cramp, and Harry Prapavessis. "Pregnancy—Should Women Put Up Their Feet or Lace Up Their Running Shoes?: Self-Presentation and the Exercise Stereotype Phenomenon During Pregnancy." *Journal of Sport & Exercise Psychology* 34 (2012): 223-37. Web. 6 Mar. 2015.

Chapter 5: That's What (S)He Said
Schaefer, Rebecca. "Tips for Having a Non-Runner Partner." *Trail And Ultra Running*. N.p., 06 May 2014. Web. 20 Feb. 2015. http://trailandultrarunning.com/tips-for-having-a-non-runner-partner/.

Bravo, Lauren. "Chivalry Is Dead! Good Manners Shouldn't Be Gender-Specific." *The Huffington Post UK*. N.p., 16 Jan. 2013. Web. 20 Feb. 2015. http://www.huffingtonpost.co.uk/lauren-bravo/chivalry-is-dead-good-man_b_2479355.html.

"I'M CONFESSIN'." *Ultra Spouse*. N.p., 17 May 2013. Web. 20 Feb. 2015. http://ultraspouse.wordpress.com/2013/05/17/internet-im-disappointed-in-you-youre-supposed/.

Belzberg, Jade. "Married to Ultrarunning." *Married to Ultrarunning*. Trail Runner Magazine, 19 Mar. 2014. Web. 20 Feb. 2015. http://trailrunnermag.com/training/ultrarunning/article/12

35-married-to-ultrarunning/.

Lankford, Andrea. *Ranger Confidential: Living, Working, and Dying in the National Parks*. Guilford, CT: FalconGuides, 2010. Print.

Sandberg, Sheryl, and Nell Scovell. *Lean In: Women, Work, and the Will to Lead*. New York, NY: Alfred A. Knopf, 2013. Print.

McDowell, Dimity, and Sarah Bowen. Shea. *Run like a Mother: How to Get Moving, and Not Lose Your Family, Job, or Sanity*. Kansas City, MO: Andrews McMeel Pub., 2010. Print.

Graham, Jennifer. *Honey, Do You Need a Ride?: Confessions of a Fat Runner*. Halcottsville, NY: Breakaway, 2012. Print

Samuels, Mina. *Run like a Girl: How Strong Women Make Happy Lives*. Berkeley, CA: Seal, 2011. Print.

Reed, Pam. *The Extra Mile: One Woman's Personal Journey to Ultra-running Greatness*. Emmaus, PA: Rodale, 2006. Print.

King, Olga. "A Trail Runner's Love Story." *Trail Runner Magazine*. N.p., 10 Feb. 2014. Web. 20 Feb. 2015. http://www.trailrunnermag.com/people/profiles/1186-a-trail-runners-love-story.

Chapter 6: Mommy, Don't Go!

Dell'antonia, KJ. "Talking About Why Women Can't Have It All." *Motherlode Blog*. NY Times, 21 June 2012. Web. 24 Feb. 2015. http://parenting.blogs.nytimes.com/2012/06/21/talking-about-why-women-cant-have-it-all/.

Rafter, Michelle. "10 Things J.K. Rowling Taught Me about Writing." *WordCount*. MichelleRafter.com, 27 Sept. 2012.

Web. 24 Feb. 2015. http://michellerafter.com/2012/09/27/10-things-j-k-rowling-taught-me-about-writing/#sthash.WT1npG4i.dpuf/.

"Interview With J. K. Rowling | Scholastic.com." *Scholastic Teachers*. N.p., n.d. Web. 24 Feb. 2015. http://www.scholastic.com/teachers/article/interview-j-k-rowling.

Robillard, Jason. "The Martyr Complex: The Poison That Kills Relationships." *The Sexpressionists*. N.p., 05 Dec. 2012. Web. 24 Feb. 2015. http://sexpressionists.blogspot.ca/2012/12/the-martyr-complex-poison-that-kills.html/.

Parker-pope, Tara. "Now, Dad Feels as Stressed as Mom." *The New York Times*. The New York Times, 19 June 2010. Web. 24 Feb. 2015. http://www.nytimes.com/2010/06/20/weekinreview/20parkerpope.html.

Galinsky, Ellen, Kerstin Aumann, and James Bond. "Times Are Changing: Gender and Generation at Work and at Home." *National Study of the Changing Workforce* (2011): 1-24. *Families And Work*. Aug. 2011. Web. 24 Feb. 2015. http://familiesandwork.org/site/research/reports/Times_Are_Changing.pdf/.

"There's Always Someone with a Bigger Boat." *Better Than A Stick In The Eye*. N.p., 29 Oct. 2011. Web. 24 Feb. 2015. http://thesethingshappentootherpeople.blogspot.com/2013/10/theres-always-someone-with-bigger-boat.html/.

Jones-Wilkins, Andy. "Running And The Small Stuff." *iRunFar.com*. N.p., 10 Jan. 2014. Web. 24 Feb. 2015.

http://www.irunfar.com/2014/01/running-and-the-small-stuff.html/.

Alert, Robert. "Re: Hi R/NBA, My Name Is Robert and I'm an Athletic Trainer. This Is My Kobe Bryant Work Ethic Story." Web log comment. *Reddit.com*. N.p., n.d. Web. 24 Feb. 2015. http://www.reddit.com/r/nba/comments/19o38z/h/.

Roes, Geoff. "Is Running Selfish?" *iRunFar.com*. N.p., 20 Nov. 2013. Web. 24 Feb. 2015. http://www.irunfar.com/2013/11/is-running-selfish.html/.

Estés, Clarissa Pinkola. *Women Who Run with the Wolves: Myths and Stories of the Wild Woman Archetype*. New York: Ballantine, 1992. Print.

Tamati, Lisa, and Nicola McCloy. *Running to Extremes*. Auckland, N.Z.: Allen & Unwin, 2012. Print.

Samuels, Mina. *Run like a Girl: How Strong Women Make Happy Lives*. Berkeley, CA: Seal, 2011. Print.

McDowell, Dimity, and Sarah Bowen Shea. *Run like a Mother: How to Get Moving, and Not Lose Your Family, Job, or Sanity*. Kansas City, MO: Andrews McMeel Pub., 2010. Print.

O'Sullivan, Moire. *Mud, Sweat and Tears: An Irish Woman's Journey of Self-Discovery*. N.p: n.d., 2011. Print.

Reed, Pam. *The Extra Mile: One Woman's Personal Journey to Ultra-running Greatness*. Emmaus, PA: Rodale, 2006. Print.

Greenwood, Ellie. "Racing To Work." *Ultrarunning Magazine*. N.p., 14 Jan. 2014. Web. 02 Mar. 2015. http://www.ultrarunning.com/featured/racing-to-work/.

Strayed, Cheryl. *Tiny Beautiful Things: Advice on Love and Life from Dear Sugar*. New York: Vintage, 2012. Print.

Sandberg, Sheryl, and Nell Scovell. *Lean In: Women, Work,*

and the Will to Lead. New York, NY: Alfred A. Knopf, 2013. Print.

Wintsch, Katherine. "Lies Moms Tell Each Other (and Ourselves)." *The Huffington Post.* N.p., 5 Oct. 2013. Web. 02 Mar. 2015. http://www.huffingtonpost.com/katherine-wintsch/lies-moms-tell-each-other_b_3245968.html/.

Brown, Brené. *Daring Greatly: How the Courage to Be Vulnerable Transforms the Way We Live, Love, Parent, and Lead.* New York, NY: Gotham, 2012. Print.

Roster, Catherine A. "Girl Power" and Participation in Macho Recreation: The Case of Female Harley Riders." *Leisure Sciences* 29.5 (2007): 443-61. Web. 6 Mar. 2015.

Hicks, Meghan. "Doing What She Most Wants To Do: Heather Anderson's Pacific Crest Trail FKT." *iRunFar.com.* N.p., 17 Sept. 2013. Web. 02 Mar. 2015. http://www.irunfar.com/2013/09/doing-what-she-most-wants-to-do-heather-andersons-pacific-crest-trail-fkt.html/.

Lutz, Leon. "Why Do You Have to Run So Much?" *iRunFar.com.* N.p., 21 Apr. 2013. Web. 02 Mar. 2015. http://www.irunfar.com/2013/08/why-do-you-have-to-run-so-much.html/.

Chapter 7: Ally or Adversary?

Powell, Bryan. "Nikki Kimball Post-2013 Western States 100 Interview." *iRunFar.com.* N.p., 2 July 2013. Web. 03 Mar. 2015. http://www.irunfar.com/2013/07/nikki-kimball-post-2013-western-states-100-interview.html/.

Mock, Justin. "Meltzer, Hawker Champion Inaugural Run Rabbit Run." *Runner's World.* N.p., 17 Sept. 2012. Web. 03 Mar.

2015. http://m.runnersworld.com/trail-racing/meltzer-hawker-champion-inaugural-run-rabbit-run/.

Samuels, Mina. *Run like a Girl: How Strong Women Make Happy Lives.* Berkeley, CA: Seal, 2011. Print.

Vincent, Norah. *Self-made Man: One Woman's Journey into Manhood and Back Again.* New York: Viking, 2006. Print.

Gay, Roxane. *Bad Feminist: Essays.* New York, NY: Harper Perennial, 2014. Print.

Tamati, Lisa. *Running Hot.* Auckland, N.Z.: Allen & Unwin, 2009. Print.

Reed, Pam. *The Extra Mile: One Woman's Personal Journey to Ultra-running Greatness.* Emmaus, PA: Rodale, 2006. Print.

O'Neil, Devon. "Blood Sport." *Blood Sport.* Trail Runner Magazine, 6 May 2013. Web. 11 Mar. 2015. http://www.trailrunnermag.com/people/profiles/634-blood-sport.

Margolies, Lynn. "Competition Among Women: Myth and Reality." *Psych Central.com.* Psych Central, 03 Mar. 2013. Web. 03 Mar. 2015. http://psychcentral.com/lib/competition-among-women-myth-and-reality/0007562.

"Women's Running Bracket: The Final Showdown." *Salty Running.* N.p., 11 Apr. 2013. Web. 3 Mar. 2015. http://www.saltyrunning.com/2013/04/11/womens-running-bracket-the-final-showdown/.

Tierney, John. "A Cold War Fought by Women." *The New York Times.* The New York Times, 18 Nov. 2013. Web. 03 Mar. 2015. http://www.nytimes.com/2013/11/19/science/a-cold-war-fought-by-women.html?_r=2&.

Friedman, Ann. "Shine Theory: Why Powerful Women

Make the Greatest Friends." *NYMag.com*. N.p., 31 May 2013. Web. 05 Mar. 2015. http://nymag.com/thecut/2013/05/shine-theory-how-to-stop-female-competition.html.

Wolf, Naomi. *The Beauty Myth: How Images of Beauty Are Used Against Women*. New York: W. Morrow, 1991. Print.

Armstrong, Kristin. *Mile Markers: The 26.2 Most Important Reasons Why Women Run*. Emmaus, PA: Rodale, 2011. Print.

Brown, Brené. *Daring Greatly: How the Courage to Be Vulnerable Transforms the Way We Live, Love, Parent, and Lead*. New York, NY: Gotham, 2012. Print.

Angier, Natalie. *Woman: An Intimate Geography*. Boston, MA: Houghton Mifflin, 1999. Print.

Belzberg, Jade. "5 Questions with Dave Mackey and Magdalena Boulet." *Trail Runner Magazine*. N.p., 06 May 2014. Web. 05 Mar. 2015. http://trailrunnermag.com/people/q-and-a/1310-5-questions-with-dave-mackey-and-magdalena-boulet.

O'Neil, Devon. "Blood Sport." *Trail Runner Magazine*. N.p., 16 May 2013. Web. 05 Mar. 2015. http://www.trailrunnermag.com/people/profiles/article/634-blood-sport.

Marano, Hara Estroff. "What Is Solitude? Loneliness Is Marked by a Sense of Isolation. Solitude, on the Other Hand, Is a State of Being Alone without Being Lonely and Can Lead to Self-awareness." *Psychology Today*. N.p., 1 July 2003. Web. 05 Mar. 2015. http://www.psychologytoday.com/articles/200308/what-is-solitude.

Johnston, Mark W. *Edward Abbey's "Desert Solitaire": Its Relationship to the Bible*. Portland, OR: TREN, 1990. Print.

Roberts, Suzanne. *Almost Somewhere: Twenty-eight Days on the John Muir Trail*. Lincoln, NE: U of Nebraska, 2012. Print.

Garratt, Rodney J., Catherine Weinberger, and Nick Johnson. "The State Street Mile: Age And Gender Differences In Competition Aversion In The Field." *Economic Inquiry* 51.1 (2013): 806-15. Web. 6 Mar. 2015.

Niederle, Muriel, and Lise Vesterlund. "Gender Differences in Competition." *Negotiation Journal* 24.4 (2008): 447-63. Web. 6 Mar. 2015.

Gupta, Nabanita Datta, Anders Poulsen, and Marie Claire Villeval. "Gender Matching And Competitiveness: Experimental Evidence." *Economic Inquiry* 51.1 (2013): 816-35. Web. 6 Mar. 2015.

Martin, Jeffrey, Jennifer Waldron, Andria McCabe, and Yun Seok Choi. "The Impact of Girls on the Run on Self-Concept and Fat Attitudes." *Journal of Clinical Sports Psychology* 3 (2009): 127-38. Web. 6 Mar. 2015.

Chapter 8: Rapists and Other Creepers

Lankford, Andrea. *Ranger Confidential: Living, Working, and Dying in the National Parks*. Guilford, CT: FalconGuides, 2010. Print.

Greenwood, Ellie. "Twenty-Seven Percent: Why Aren't More Women Running Ultras?" *iRunFar.com*. N.p., 8 Oct. 2012. Web. 05 Mar. 2015. http://www.irunfar.com/2012/10/twenty-seven-percent-why-arent-more-women-running-ultras.html.

Roberts, Suzanne. *Almost Somewhere: Twenty-eight Days on the John Muir Trail*. Lincoln, NE: U of Nebraska, 2012. Print.

Robillard, Jason. *Never Wipe Your Ass with a Squirrel: A Trail Running, Ultramarathon, and Wilderness Survival Guide for Weird Folks*. New York: CreateSpace Independent Platform, 2013. Print.

Robillard, Jason. "Runners: How to Avoid Being Robbed, Beaten, and Raped." *Barefoot Running University*. N.p., 2 July 2013. Web. 05 Mar. 2015. http://barefootrunninguniversity.com/2013/07/02/runners-how-to-avoid-being-robbed-beaten-and-raped/.

Homer, Jill. "Is There Enough?" *Jill Outside*. N.p., 9 Apr. 2013. Web. 05 Mar. 2015. http://arcticglass.blogspot.com/2013/04/is-there-enough.html.

Strayed, Cheryl. *Wild: From Lost to Found on the Pacific Crest Trail*. New York: Alfred A. Knopf, 2012. Print.

"We Need To Talk About Getting More Women Into Ultra Running." *Ultra168.com*. N.p., 04 Aug. 2014. Web. 5 Mar. 2015. http://ultra168.com/2014/04/08/we-need-to-talk-about-getting-more-women-into-ultra-running/.

"IOC Adopts Consensus Statement on Sexual Harassment and Abuse in Sport." *Olympic.org*. N.p., 02 Aug. 2007. Web. 05 Mar. 2015. http://www.olympic.org/content/news/media-resources/manual-news/1999-2009/2007/02/08/ioc-adopts-consensus-statement-on-sexual-harassment-and-abuse-in-sport/.

Pfister, Gertrud, and Mari Kristin. Sisjord. *Gender and Sport: Changes and Challenges*. Germany: Waxmann Verlag

Vanessa Runs

GmbH, 2013. Print.

"Top Women-Only Races Around the World." *The Active Times*. N.p., n.d. Web. 05 Mar. 2015. http://www.theactivetimes.com/top-women-only-races-around-world.

Fortmann, Gretel, and Jo Brischetto. "Summit Sisters - Women's Trail Running, Personal Training, Wellness and Fitness Retreats." *Summit Sisters*. N.p., n.d. Web. 05 Mar. 2015. http://www.summitsisters.com.au/.

Vincent, Norah. *Self-made Man: One Woman's Journey into Manhood and Back Again*. New York, NY: Viking, 2006. Print.

Wolfe, Nathaniel. "A Tale of Two Titties." *Shifting Strands*. N.p., 20 July 2013. Web. 05 Mar. 2015. http://shiftingstrands.blogspot.com/2013/07/a-tale-of-two-titties.html.

Solnit, Rebecc. "Tomgram: Rebecca Solnit, #YesAllWomen Changes the Story." *TomDispatch.com*. N.p., 4 June 2014. Web. 05 Mar. 2015. http://www.tomdispatch.com/post/175850/tomgram%3A_rebecca_solnit%2C_%23yes%20%3Eallwomen_changes_the_story/.

Chapter 9: Ew, My Thighs are Touching!

Wolf, Naomi. *The Beauty Myth: How Images of Beauty Are Used against Women*. New York, NY: W. Morrow, 1991. Print.

Rodriguez, Vanessa. "Overcoming Anorexia Through Running: A Story of Courage." *ACTIVE.com*. N.p., n.d. Web. 05 Mar. 2015. http://www.active.com/nutrition/articles/overcoming-anorexia-through-running-a-story-of-courage?page=1.

Reed, Pam. *The Extra Mile: One Woman's Personal Journey to Ultra-running Greatness*. Emmaus, PA: Rodale, 2006. Print.

Anderson, Mimi. "The Only Way of Finding the Limits of the Possible Is by Going Beyond Them into the Impossible." *Marvellous Mimi*. N.p., n.d. Web. 05 Mar. 2015. http://marvellousmimi.com/v2/about-mimi/.

Arnold, Carrie. "A Good Thing Gone Wrong?" *ED Bites*. N.p., 14 July 2008. Web. 05 Mar. 2015. http://ed-bites.blogspot.com/2008/07/good-thing-gone-wrong.html/.

Davis, Jennifer Pharr. *Called Again: A Story of Love and Triumph*. New York, NY: Beaufort, 2013. Print.

Reed, Pam. *The Extra Mile: One Woman's Personal Journey to Ultra-running Greatness*. Emmaus, PA: Rodale, 2006. Print.

Leedy, M. Gail. "Commitment to Distance Running: Coping Mechanism or Addiction?" - *Free Online Library*. Journal of Sport Behavior, 1 Sept. 2000. Web. 05 Mar. 2015. http://www.thefreelibrary.com/Commitment+to+Distance+Running%3a+Coping+Mechanism+or+Addiction%3f-a065306581/.

Diagnostic and Statistical Manual of Mental Disorders: DSM-5. Washington, D.C.: American Psychiatric Association, 2013. Print.

Cogan, Karen D. *Eating Disorders* 9 (n.d.): 183-201. Web. 6 Mar. 2015.

Blackmer, Victoria, H. Russell Searight, and Susan Ratwik. "The Relationship Between Eating Attitudes, Body Image and Perceived Family-of-Origin Climate Among College Athletes." *North American Journal of Psychology* 12.3 (2011): 435-46. Web. 6

Mar. 2015.

Reinking, Mark, and Laura Alexander. "Prevalence of Disordered-Eating Behaviors in Undergraduate Female Collegiate Athletes and Nonathletes." *Journal of Athletic Training* 40.1 (2005): 47-51. Web. 6 Mar. 2015.

Holm-Denoma, Jill M., Vanessa Scaringi, Kathryn H. Gordon, Kimberly A. Van Orden, and Thomas E. Joiner. "Eating Disorder Symptoms among Undergraduate Varsity Athletes, Club Athletes, Independent Exercisers, and Nonexercisers." *International Journal of Eating Disorders* 42.1 (2009): 47-53. Web. 6 Mar. 2015.

Papathomas, Anthony, and David Lalallee. "Narrative Constructions of Anorexia and Abuse: An Athlete's Search for Meaning in Trauma." *Journal of Loss and Trauma* 17 (2012): 293-318. Web. 6 Mar. 2015.

Bruin, A. P. Karin De, Raôul R. D. Oudejans, Frank C. Bakker, and Liesbeth Woertman. "Contextual Body Image and Athletes' Disordered Eating: The Contribution of Athletic Body Image to Disordered Eating in High Performance Women Athletes." *European Eating Disorders Review* 19.3 (2011): 201-15. Web. 6 Mar. 2015

Chapter 10: Boobs, Babies and Other Bumps in the Road

Stein, Elissa, and Susan Kim. *Flow: The Cultural Story of Menstruation*. New York: St. Martin's Griffin, 2009. Print.

Ostman, Cami. *Second Wind: One Woman's Midlife Quest to Run Seven Marathons on Seven Continents*. Berkeley, CA: Seal, 2010. Print.

Reed, Pam. *The Extra Mile: One Woman's Personal Journey*

to *Ultra-running Greatness*. Emmaus, PA: Rodale, 2006. Print.

Rastogi, Nina. "What's the Environmental Impact of My Period?" *Slate.com*. N.p., 03 Mar. 2010. Web. 02 Mar. 2015. http://www.slate.com/articles/health_and_science/the_green_lantern/2010/03/greening_the_crimson_tide.html/.

Nelson, Bryan. "No, Menstruating Women Do Not Attract Bear Attacks." *Mother Jones*. N.p., 15 Aug. 2012. Web. 17 Feb. 2015.

http://www.motherjones.com/blue-marble/2012/08/menstruating-women-do-not-attract-bear-attacks/.

Butler, Kiera. "Do Menstruating Women Attract Sharks?" *Mother Jones*. N.p., 16 Aug. 2012. Web. 05 Mar. 2015. http://www.motherjones.com/blue-marble/2012/08/do-menstruating-women-attract-shark-attacks/.

"Walt Disney The Story Of Menstruation." *YouTube*. 23 March 2009. Web. 05 Mar. 2015. http://www.youtube.com/watch?v=eLhld_PI2zg&feature=youtu.be/.

Benna, Jennifer. "Pregnancy, Birth and Running 100 Miles, A Ramble." *A Girls Guide to Trail Running*. N.p., 29 Jan. 2014. Web. 05 Mar. 2015.

http://www.jenbenna.com/?p=811/.

Jhung, Lisa. "Come Back Strong." *Runner's World*. N.p., 31 Aug. 2010. Web. 05 Mar. 2015. http://www.runnersworld.com/workouts/come-back-strong/.

"The Mother - Salomon Running TV S03 E04." *YouTube*. N.p., 15 Jan. 2014. Web. 05 Mar. 2015.

https://www.youtube.com/watch?v=oauocB3p9lM&feature=youtu.be/.

Associated Press. "Alysia Montano Runs 800 at Nationals." *ESPN*. N.p., 27 June 2014. Web. 05 Mar. 2015. http://espn.go.com/olympics/trackandfield/story/_/id/11142115/pregnant-runner-alysia-montano-runs-800-meters-us-track-field-championships/.

Stevenson-Gargiulo, Elizabeth. *Running Through Pregnancy*. N.p., n.d. Web. 05 Mar. 2015. http://www.runningthroughpregnancy.com/.

McDowell, Dimity, and Sarah Bowen. Shea. *Run like a Mother: How to Get Moving – and Not Lose Your Job, Family, or Sanity*. Kansas City, MO: Andrews McMeel, 2010. Print.

Lawless, Robbie. "Emma Roca: A Force Of Nature." *iRunFar.com*. N.p., 2 June 2014. Web. 05 Mar. 2015. http://www.irunfar.com/2014/06/emma-roca-a-force-of-nature.html/.

McDougall, Christopher. *Born to Run: A Hidden Tribe, Superathletes, and the Greatest Race the World Has Never Seen*. New York, NY: Alfred A. Knopf, 2009. Print.

Samakow, Jessica. "Nirvana Jennette, Mom Forced Out Of Church For Breastfeeding, Aims To Change Georgia Law [UPDATED]." *The Huffington Post*. N.p., 03 Aug. 2012. Web. 05 Mar. 2015. http://www.huffingtonpost.com/2012/02/24/nirvana-jennette-georgia-nurse-in_n_1297667.html/.

Samakow, Jessica. "Hollister Nurse-In: Breastfeeding Advocates Feud With Shopping Mall Following Protest (VIDEO)." *The Huffington Post*. N.p., 01 Aug. 2013. Web. 05

Mar. 2015.
http://www.huffingtonpost.com/2013/01/07/hollister-nurse-in_n_2425541.html/.

Schranz, Eric. "Liza Howard Interview."
UltraRunnerPodcast.com. N.p., 16 Apr. 2014. Web. 05 Mar. 2015.
http://ultrarunnerpodcast.com/liza-howard-interview/.

Sager, Jeanne. "Breastfeeding Mom Shamed for Nursing
9-Week-Old ... in Private." *Cafe Mom*. The Stir, 23 Apr. 2014.
Web. 05 Mar. 2015.
http://thestir.cafemom.com/baby/171510/breastfeeding_mo
m_shamed_for_nursing/.

Chalmers, Sarah. "Here's to Jo Pavey and the Mothers of
Sporting Re-invention." *The Telegraph*. Telegraph Media
Group, 14 Aug. 2014. Web. 05 Mar. 2015.
http://www.telegraph.co.uk/women/womens-
life/11031262/Heres-to-Jo-Pavey-and-the-mothers-of-
sporting-re-invention.html/.

Olmer, Barbara. "Returning to Ultras After Pregnancy -
Page 2." *Trail Runner Magazine*. N.p., 10 June 2013. Web. 05
Mar. 2015.
http://www.trailrunnermag.com/people/adventure/article/
732-returning-to-ultras-after-pregnancy/page-2/.

Hess, Amanda. "You Can Only Hope To Contain Them."
ESPN. N.p., 16 July 2013. Web. 05 Mar. 2015.
http://espn.go.com/espnw/news-
commentary/article/9451835/female-athletes-biggest-
opponents-their-own-breasts-espn-magazine/.

Chapter 11: Respect Your Masters

Hooper, Joseph. "The Man Who Would Stop Time." *Popular Science*. N.p., 2 Aug. 2011. Web. 05 Mar. 2015. http://www.popsci.com/science/article/2011-07/man-who-would-stop-time?nopaging=1/.

Winter, Katy. "Meet the 77-year-old Supergran Who Runs 100km Ultra-marathons for Fun." *Mail Online*. Associated Newspapers, 15 Nov. 2013. Web. 05 Mar. 2015. http://www.dailymail.co.uk/femail/article-2507771/Meet-77-year-old-Supergran-runs-100km-ultra-marathons-fun-51-year-old-hot-heels-250km-race.html/.

Harris, Lisa. "Joan Joesting-Mahoney, 76, Life Well Lived." *Perimeter Bicycling*. N.p., 5 May 2014. Web. 05 Mar. 2015. http://www.perimeterbicycling.com/blog/2014/05/05/joan-joesting-mahoney-76-life-well-lived/.

Davis, John. "Do You Get Better at the Ultra Marathon Distance as You Get Older?" *Runners Connect*. N.p., 28 Apr. 2014. Web. 05 Mar. 2015. http://runnersconnect.net/running-training-articles/does-age-matter-in-ultramarathon/.

Tamati, Lisa. *Running Hot*. Auckland, N.Z.: Allen & Unwin, 2009. Print.

Angier, Natalie. *Woman: An Intimate Geography*. Boston, MA: Houghton Mifflin, 1999. Print.

Peter, Laura, Christoph Rust, Beat Knechtle, and Romauld Lepers. "Result Filters." *National Center for Biotechnology Information*. U.S. National Library of Medicine, Jan. 2014. Web. 05 Mar. 2015. http://www.ncbi.nlm.nih.gov/pubmed/?term=24473558/.

Samuels, Mina. *Run like a Girl: How Strong Women Make*

Happy Lives. Berkeley, CA: Seal, 2011. Print.

Wolf, Naomi. "A Wrinkle in Time: Twenty Years after 'The Beauty Myth,' Naomi Wolf Addresses The Aging Myth." *Washington Post*. N.p., 27 May 2011. Web. 05 Mar. 2015. http://www.washingtonpost.com/lifestyle/magazine/a-wrinkle-in-time-twenty-years-after-the-beauty-myth-naomi-wolf-addresses-the-aging-myth/2011/05/11/AGiEhvCH_story.html/.

"The Shrinkage Factor: Aging And Ultrarunning." *iRunFar.com*. N.p., 22 Jan. 2014. Web. 05 Mar. 2015. http://www.irunfar.com/2014/01/the-shrinkage-factor-aging-and-ultrarunning.html/.

Chalmers, Sarah. "Here's to Jo Pavey and the Mothers of Sporting Re-invention." *The Telegraph*. Telegraph Media Group, 14 Aug. 2014. Web. 05 Mar. 2015. http://www.telegraph.co.uk/women/womens-life/11031262/Heres-to-Jo-Pavey-and-the-mothers-of-sporting-re-invention.html.

Barker, Sarah. "Running 100 Miles Is Easier Now: A Talk With The Father of Ultra Trailrunning." *Fittish*. Deadspin.com, 26 June 2014. Web. 05 Mar. 2015. http://fittish.deadspin.com/running-100-miles-is-easier-now-a-talk-with-gordy-ains-1596410639/.

Wroblewski, Andrew, Francesca Amati, Mark Smiley, and Bret Goodpaster. "Chronic Exercise Preserves Lean Muscle Mass in Masters Athletes." *The Physician and Sports Medicine*. N.p., Sept. 2011. Web. 5 Mar. 2015. https://physsportsmed.org/doi/10.3810/psm.2011.09.1933/.

Brown, Nancy Marie. "A Natural History of Menopause |

Penn State University." *Penn State News*. N.p., 1 May 1998. Web. 05 Mar. 2015. http://news.psu.edu/story/141542/1998/05/01/research/natural-history-menopause/.

Foxcroft, Louise. *Hot Flushes, Cold Science: The History of the Modern Menopause*. London: Granta, 2009. Print.

Miller, Magnolia. "35 Symptoms of Perimenopause." *Healthline*. N.p., 23 Feb. 2012. Web. 05 Mar. 2015. http://www.healthline.com/health-blogs/hold-that-pause/35-symptoms-perimenopause/.

Harpaz, Mickey. "Menopause Myths On Weight Gain And Age Dispelled." *The Huffington Post*. TheHuffingtonPost.com, 14 May 2012. Web. 05 Mar. 2015. http://www.huffingtonpost.com/mickey-harpaz/menopause-myths_b_1260596.html/.

ARA Staff. "THE CLINIC: Is Menopause to Blame for Compromised Running Performance?" The American Running Association, 13 Sept. 2012. Web. 05 Mar. 2015. http://www.americanrunning.org/w/article/the-clinic-is-menopause-to-blame-for-compromised-running-performance/.

Mishra, Nalini, V. N. Mishra, and Devanshi. "Exercise beyond Menopause: Dos and Don'ts." *Journal of Mid-Life Health*. Medknow Publications & Media Pvt Ltd, Dec. 2011. Web. 05 Mar. 2015. http://www.ncbi.nlm.nih.gov/pmc/articles/PMC3296386/.

Vaughan, Kathy. "Running Through Perimenopause." *UltraPedestrian*. N.p., 25 Sept. 2014. Web. 05 Mar. 2015. http://ultrapedestrian.blogspot.com/2014/09/running-through-perimenopause.html/.

Dupont, Doug. "The Best Ultra-Marathon Runners Are 35+ Years Old." *Breaking Muscle*. N.p., n.d. Web. 05 Mar. 2015. http://breakingmuscle.com/running/running-does-age-make-champions/.

Vertinsky, Patricia. "Eternally Wounded Women? Feminist Perspectives on Physical Activity and Aging or A Woman's P(l)ace in the Marathon of Life." *Journal of Aging and Physical Activity* 8 (2000): 386-406. Web. 6 Mar. 2015.

Chapter 12: Final Words

Payne, Shannon. "I'm No Femi-nazi But..." *Wanderings Ponderings and Runderings*. N.p., 14 Dec. 2014. Web. 05 Mar. 2015. http://wanderingsponderingsandrunderings.wordpress.com /2014/12/14/im-no-femi-nazi-but/.

Sheehan, George. *Running & Being: The Total Experience*. New York, NY: Rodale, 2013. Print.

"Outdoor Participation: Numbers Up, but the Bucket's Leaking and Adolescent Girls Are Opting out." *S News Outdoor*. N.p., 2012. Web. 05 Mar. 2015. http://www.snewsnet.com/news/outdoor-participation-numbers-up-but-the-buckets-leaking-and-adolescent-girls-opt-out/?utm_source=newsletter&utm_medium=outdoor&utm_c ampaign=link/.

Wellington, Chrissie, and Michael Aylwin. *A Life without Limits: A World Champion's Journey*. New York, NY: Hachette Book Group, 2012. Print.

"We Need To Talk About Getting More Women Into Ultra

Running." *Ultra168.com*. N.p., 04 Aug. 2014. Web. 5 Mar. 2015. http://ultra168.com/2014/04/08/we-need-to-talk-about-getting-more-women-into-ultra-running/.

Collazo, Abigail. "Chivalry Must Die: On Women's Expectations and Men's Obligations." *Everyday Feminism*. N.p., 28 Sept. 2012. Web. 05 Mar. 2015. http://everydayfeminism.com/2012/09/chivalry-must-die/?1&utm_content=buffer5da72&utm_medium=social&utm_source=facebook.com&utm_campaign=buffer.

Wolf, Naomi. *The Beauty Myth: How Images of Beauty Are Used against Women*. New York: W. Morrow, 1991. Print.

24603490R00193

Made in the USA
San Bernardino, CA
02 October 2015